HOTEL MODERNITY

Edinburgh Critical Studies in Modernist Culture
Series Editors: Tim Armstrong and Rebecca Beasley

Available

Modernism and Magic: Experiments with Spiritualism, Theosophy and the Occult
Leigh Wilson

Sonic Modernity: Representing Sound in Literature, Culture and the Arts
Sam Halliday

Modernism and the Frankfurt School
Tyrus Miller

Lesbian Modernism: Censorship, Sexuality and Genre Fiction
Elizabeth English

Modern Print Artefacts: Textual Materiality and Literary Value in British Print Culture, 1890–1930s
Patrick Collier

Cheap Modernism: Expanding Markets, Publishers' Series and the Avant-Garde
Lise Jaillant

Portable Modernisms: The Art of Travelling Light
Emily Ridge

Hieroglyphic Modernisms: Writing and New Media in the Twentieth Century
Jesse Schotter

Modernism, Fiction and Mathematics
Nina Engelhardt

Modernist Life Histories: Biological Theory and the Experimental Bildungsroman
Daniel Aureliano Newman

Modernism, Space and the City: Outsiders and Affect in Paris, Vienna, Berlin, and London
Andrew Thacker

Modernism Edited: Marianne Moore and the Dial *Magazine*
Victoria Bazin

Modernism and Time Machines
Charles Tung

Primordial Modernism: Animals, Ideas, transition (1927–1938)
Cathryn Setz

Modernism and Still Life: Artists, Writers, Dancers
Claudia Tobin

The Modernist Exoskeleton: Insects, War, Literary Form
Rachel Murray

Novel Sensations: Modernist Fiction and the Problem of Qualia
Jon Day

Hotel Modernity: Corporate Space in Literature and Film
Robbie Moore

Forthcoming

Modernism and the Idea of Everyday Life
Leena Kore-Schröder

Modernism and Religion: Poetry and the Rise of Mysticism
Jamie Callison

Abstraction in Modernism and Modernity: Human and Inhuman
Jeff Wallace

The Modernist Anthropocene: Nonhuman Life and Planetary Change in James Joyce, Virginia Woolf and Djuna Barnes
Peter Adkins

Visionary Company: Hart Crane and Modernist Periodicals
Francesca Bratton

Asbestos: The Last Modernist Object
Arthur Rose

www.edinburghuniversitypress.com/series/ecsmc

HOTEL MODERNITY

Corporate Space in Literature and Film

Robbie Moore

EDINBURGH
University Press

Edinburgh University Press is one of the leading university presses in the UK. We publish academic books and journals in our selected subject areas across the humanities and social sciences, combining cutting-edge scholarship with high editorial and production values to produce academic works of lasting importance. For more information visit our website: edinburghuniversitypress.com

© Robbie Moore, 2021, 2023

Edinburgh University Press Ltd
The Tun – Holyrood Road
12(2f) Jackson's Entry
Edinburgh EH8 8PJ

First published in hardback by Edinburgh University Press 2021

Typeset in 10/12.5 Adobe Sabon by
IDSUK (DataConnection) Ltd

A CIP record for this book is available from the British Library

ISBN 978 1 4744 5665 4 (hardback)
ISBN 978 1 4744 5666 1 (paperback)
ISBN 978 1 4744 5667 8 (webready PDF)
ISBN 978 1 4744 5668 5 (epub)

The right of Robbie Moore to be identified as the author of this work has been asserted in accordance with the Copyright, Designs and Patents Act 1988 and the Copyright and Related Rights Regulations 2003 (SI No. 2498).

CONTENTS

List of Figures	vi
Acknowledgments	viii
Series Editors' Preface	x
Introduction	1
1 Lounging Bodies: The Lobby and Piazza	27
2 Stain Resistance: The Parlour and Reading-Room	59
3 'Ritz': The Roof Garden	92
4 Hotel Angst: The Corridor and Elevator	122
5 The Hotel Auteur: The Manager's Office	151
Bibliography	193
Index	214

FIGURES

1.1	Astor House, Broadway, New York, date unknown (Source: Library of Congress)	28
1.2	Rear piazza, Grand Union Hotel, Saratoga, New York, c.1870–80 (Source: Library of Congress)	36
1.3	Group on the porch, Saratoga Springs, New York, c.1860–70 (Source: Library of Congress)	37
1.4	Piazza of the Royal Poinciana, Palm Beach, Florida, c.1904 (Source: Library of Congress)	39
1.5	Piazza, Hotel Cape May, Cape May, New Jersey, c.1909 (Source: Library of Congress)	40
1.6	United States Hotel dining-room, Saratoga, New York, c.1870–80 (Source: Library of Congress)	41
2.1	Grand Union parlour, Saratoga Springs, New York, c.1870–80 (Source: Library of Congress)	60
2.2	Main parlour, US Hotel, Saratoga Springs, New York, 1895 (Source: Library of Congress)	60
2.3	Dining-room, Hotel Royal Poinciana, Palm Beach, Florida, 1894 (Source: Library of Congress)	69

FIGURES

3.1	Hotel Ritz-Carlton, New York, c.1915 (Credit: Byron Company, New York, NY, Museum of the City of New York, 93.1.1.5390)	104
3.2	Drawing of the Hotel Astor roof garden and environs, 1905 (Credit: Byron Company, New York, NY, Museum of the City of New York, 93.1.1.5390)	112
4.1	Postcard from the Hotel Angst, Bordighera, Italy, c.1910	126
4.2	The first-floor corridor in the Midland Adelphi Hotel, Liverpool, 1912 (Source: Historic England Archive)	141
4.3	Still from *Variety*, directed by Ewald André Dupont, Ufa, 1925	142
4.4	Corridor trouble. Still from *Caught in the Rain*, directed by Charlie Chaplin, Keystone, 1914	143
4.5	Corridor trouble. Still from *Caught in the Rain*, directed by Charlie Chaplin, Keystone, 1914	144
5.1	Dancing bellhops. Still from *The Cocoanuts*, directed by Robert Florey and Joseph Santley, Paramount, 1929	170
5.2	Dancing bellhops. Still from *The Cocoanuts*, directed by Robert Florey and Joseph Santley, Paramount, 1929	171
5.3	Hovering above the lobby. Still from *Grand Hotel*, directed by Edmund Goulding, Metro-Goldwyn-Mayer, 1932	174
5.4	Guests at the registration desk. Still from *Grand Hotel*, directed by Edmund Goulding, Metro-Goldwyn-Mayer, 1932	175
5.5	Interior view looking along a corridor at the Grosvenor Hotel, 1900 (Source: Historic England Archive)	182
5.6	A seated ghost in a long exposure photograph, in the lobby of the Hotel Richmond, Virginia, c.1900–20 (Source: Library of Congress)	184

ACKNOWLEDGMENTS

An earlier version of Chapter 1 first appeared as 'Monster Hotels, Elastic Men, and the Bourgeois Age', in *The Henry James Review*, Volume 34, Issue 2, Summer 2013, pages 113–129. Copyright © 2013 The Johns Hopkins University Press. An earlier version of Chapter 2 was first published as 'Henry James, Hotels, and the Invention of Disposable Space' in *Modernist Cultures*, Volume 7, Issue 2, 2012, pages 254–278. Copyright © 2012 Edinburgh University Press.

This project has travelled with me for over ten years. As an antipodean student in the UK, I was fortunate in my helpers, guides and fellow-travellers. I remain indebted to my PhD supervisor David Trotter for his generosity and wisdom; to Bridget Vincent for her advice and assistance with the dissertation; to my examiners, Rod Mengham and Philip Horne, for their valuable critiques and suggestions; to friends who became extended family; to the Poynton Bequest and Cambridge Australia Scholarships for their financial support to undertake my dissertation; and to Henry the hotel cat, who kept me company as I typed.

Returning to Australia, I found myself newly at home in Hobart, where the community has embraced and supported me and my family through challenging times. At the University of Tasmania – which stands on *lutruwita* Aboriginal land, whose sovereignty was never ceded – my friends and colleagues including Danielle Wood, Elle Leane, Hannah Stark, Lisa Fletcher, Naomi Milthorpe, Ralph Crane, Robert Clarke and Rose Gaby read my work and provided me with endless support and mentorship.

Many thanks of course to the series editors Rebecca Beasley and Tim Armstrong, copyeditor Peter Williams, the two anonymous reviewers, and the editorial team at Edinburgh University Press: Jackie Jones, Ersev Ersoy, Caitlin Murphy, and Fiona Conn, for their encouragement, care, attention and patience as this manuscript has come into being.

Finally, for their immeasurable support, and for teaching me to write stories on a typewriter, my thanks to my parents, Carla and Wal, and to my sister Saskia; to my extensive and wonderful in-law family; and to our beloved friends around the world, to whom I do not write often enough. Thank you to Iris and Rosa for being bright stars. And thank you to Jenny, who has been there throughout, who has contributed her insights and her fearsome puns and quips to this project, whose love and support makes everything possible and to whom this book is dedicated.

SERIES EDITORS' PREFACE

This series of monographs on selected topics in modernism is designed to reflect and extend the range of new work in modernist studies. The studies in the series aim for a breadth of scope and for an expanded sense of the canon of modernism, rather than focusing on individual authors. Literary texts will be considered in terms of contexts including recent cultural histories (modernism and magic; sonic modernity; media studies) and topics of theoretical interest (the everyday; postmodernism; the Frankfurt School); but the series will also re-consider more familiar routes into modernism (modernism and gender; sexuality; politics). The works published will be attentive to the various cultural, intellectual and historical contexts of British, American and European modernisms, and to inter-disciplinary possibilities within modernism, including performance and the visual and plastic arts.

Tim Armstrong and Rebecca Beasley

INTRODUCTION

Looking for a place to stay in Hastings in the winter of 1879, Henry James was confronted with a basic choice: inn or hotel, the old or the new. The Swan Inn was an old posting house on a side-street, and was recommended by a friend who described it as 'mellow' (James interpreted that to mean 'musty'). The Royal Marine Hotel was a much larger and more modern operation on the Parade by the sea. James, claiming 'a certain acquaintance with "royal" hotels', foresaw what he might be in for: 'Large hotels here are almost always owned and carried on by companies, and the company is represented by a well-shaped female figure belonging to the class whose members are more particularly known as "persons".' James pictured this figure as a 'superior young woman sitting at a ledger, in a kind of glass cage, at the bottom of the stairs, and expressing by refined intonations her contempt for a gentleman who should decline to "require" a sitting-room'. She was a hybrid, occupying, as James writes, a 'shadowy position in the social scale'. Part housekeeper, part white-collar worker, she was at once the head servant of a great house and an early prototype of the late-century female typist or the caged telegraphist of James's 'In the Cage' (1896). How to speak with her? Chivalric deference was defunct; a 'person' rather than a madam or a miss, she refused to be sentimentalised or patronised.[1] James's apprehension was shared by many: 'Anxieties about [hotel] clerks and chambermaids', argue A. K. Sandoval-Strausz and Daniel Levinson Wilk,

> arose precisely because longstanding traditions of household hospitality were being replaced [. . .]. In place of a tavern that was kept by a proprietor, comprised members of the family, and offered personalized

attendance, the new hospitality was characterized by a hotel that was operated by a professional manager, employed a large number of wage workers, and provided systematized service.[2]

The guest was no longer welcomed by a proprietor-host but by a functionary of the managerial apparatus. John Ruskin, after a confounding experience in a London hotel, wrote a series of surly letters to the *Morning Post* under his favourite pseudonym, Jonathan Oldbuck, complaining about this new mode of corporate hospitality: 'I long again for the luxury of a road-side inn, of moderate dimensions, with a smiling damsel to wait and a landlady to inquire what fare you prefer. If I go to a joint-stock hotel I can only secure attendance by informing the servants that I pay them if satisfied.'[3] The mythic smiling damsels of a domestic and patriarchal model of hospitality were being supplanted by an institutional model of hospitality with a demystified service provider-customer relationship. (Though that did not prevent the ongoing regulation of service workers' affective performances: 'The value of a personal smile', writes Arlie Russell Hochschild in her classic study of the Delta Airlines Stewardess Training Center, 'is groomed to reflect the company's disposition – its confidence that its planes will not crash, its reassurance that departures and arrivals will be on time, its welcome and its invitation to return.'[4]) This new model of hospitality was made necessary by the sheer scale and capital-intensity of the modern hotel. On his outing to Hastings, James chose to avoid an awkward interaction with institutional hospitality and stayed at the Swan Inn instead, where the host-guest paradigm remained, to his mind, intact. The dinginess of old English inns might have been 'culpably glossed over' in poetry and fiction, James admitted, but at least one could expect to be addressed with due deference. 'It is a satisfaction in moving about the world to be treated as a gentleman,' James wrote, 'and this gratification appears to be more than, in the light of modern science, a Company can profitably undertake to bestow.'[5]

This book is about the kinds of spaces, things, and social relations that hotel companies profitably undertake to bestow. It is about leaving behind the dingy certainties of the Swann Inn, and stepping into the gleaming uncertainties of a modern institution; about the joint-stock hotel as a physical and social milieu for a new kind of urban experience. *Hotel Modernity* charts the growth of corporate hotels from 1870 to 1939 in trans-Atlantic literature and culture. The focus of the book is corporate-financed grand hotels, rather than the *pensioni*, inns, boarding houses, flophouses, and one-night cheap hotels that also proliferate in modern literature. *Hotel Modernity* is not simply about living with strangers, or living beyond the domestic and the familial – experiences common to all of those settings. It is more specifically about the new forms of association and subjectivity generated within corporate space. The book defines corporate space as the new spatial logic and building typologies brought about by incorporated joint stock companies during the nineteenth century. Corporate spaces were urban, capital-intensive, large-scale spaces, financed by an anonymous body of investors. Only in hotels, however, did the individual *live* within corporate space: sleeping in its beds, being fed and tidied by its functionaries, borrowing its books, lounging in its parlours. The hotel structured intimate encounters with the impersonal and the anonymous, representing a radically new mode of experience. *Hotel Modernity* examines the effects of this mode of experience on modern culture, and on the construction and the texture of the novel as a literary form.

The authors selected for special attention in this study – Henry James, F. Scott Fitzgerald, Elizabeth Bowen, Arnold Bennett, Henry Green – are all finely attuned to the intersections of the spatial and the subjective. In their work, milieu defines and constitutes the individual in various ways. Their fiction therefore takes seriously the hotel's disruptive effects, offering richly suggestive analyses of the relationship between new kinds of spatial organisation and new forms of subjective and intersubjective life. These authors grapple with the newness and strangeness of the hotel on the level of form as well as plot. Above all, hotels provoked these writers to rethink the conventions and functions of fictional characters. The broad narrative of the book charts the warping and decentring of the category of 'character' within the corporate, architectural, informatic and technological networks which come to define hotel space in this period. As Maud Ellmann writes in her study of modern 'networked' subjectivity, these networks threaten to 'reduce the human subject to a knot or intersection, rather than an independent agent, in the webs of communication, commodities and capital,' while opening up the potential of 'interpsychic networks of exchange'.[6]

Henry James is vital to this narrative for several reasons. Against traditional readings, *Hotel Modernity* argues that James was an early and uniquely sensitive reader of corporate space, alert to its ambivalent social potential. James allows us to trace the genealogy of hotel modernity back to the 1870s. He provides the historical foundation upon which the rest of the book is built. In the transition from early to late James, we also see a complexifying sense of the individual character's agency within its milieu. James's early fiction and travel writing explores tensions between the individual and the amassed bodies and objects of the hotel lobby, while his coruscating late works locate the hotel guest within a more disorienting milieu of information systems, scientific management and mechanical reproduction. James ushers us in to what he calls a 'hotel-world' of corporate impersonality.[7]

The Affordances of Hotel Space

To elucidate what makes the corporate hotel and 'corporate space' distinct objects of study, I need to make a detour into Pratt's Hotel in James's *The Portrait of a Lady* (1881) – a so-called 'private hotel' which is clearly *not* run on the corporate model (it is described as a 'quiet inn' off Piccadilly).[8] In some ways, Pratt's is indeed a new kind of space with latent potential. It offers a glimpse of the social and narrative forms opened up by hotels beyond the realm of the domestic – forms which represent the central concern of this book. But Pratt's is also a conservative institution. It counters and contains the unsettling nature of its own spatial arrangements. It guards against public exposure even as it seems to facilitate it. The hotel's intimate scale and personal service ('Mr. Pratt in person, in a large bulging white waistcoat, [. . .] remove[d] their dish-covers') reinscribes the old patriarchal paradigm of hospitality.[9] The possibilities of this space, therefore, are delimited by its mode of ownership and management. In Caroline Levine's terms, repurposed from design theory, the forms of the corporate hotel, the private hotel and the private home each have certain 'affordances' – that is, they each have 'particular constrains and possibilities', or 'potential uses or actions latent' in their very shape and substance. Just as 'Glass affords transparency and brittleness' and 'Rhyme affords repetition, anticipation and memorization', so we can think about the latent social and narrative potentialities which make the corporate hotel distinctive in relation to smaller, more privatised spaces.[10]

What *is* quietly radical about Pratt's is the way it compresses and distorts the Victorian middle-class domestic interior, allowing the public corridor and the *boudoir* to be scandalously proximate. In Gardencourt, the Touchett's country estate in *The Portrait of a Lady*, the relationship between the public and private rooms of the house is carefully delineated, as seen when Ralph Touchett points Isabel toward her bedroom:

> They passed out of the smaller drawing-room, into which they had returned from the gallery, and paused in the hall, at the foot of the staircase. Here Ralph presented his companion with her bedroom candle, which he had taken from a niche. [. . .] She looked at him a little; she had taken her candle and placed her foot on the oaken stair. [. . .] She turned away, and he watched her as she slowly ascended. Then, with his hands always in his pockets, he went back to the empty drawing-room.[11]

Gardencourt is the model of high-Victorian architectural discretion, using stairs and vestibules to remove the bedroom from public circulation. The estate is a product of the Victorian imperative to create 'material defences against exposure and to design the interior of the household as a series of safe boxes'.[12] In comparison, Isabel's hotel suite, comprising a private sitting-room opening onto a bedchamber, experiences steady traffic. A waiter enters the sitting-room – 'Suddenly', 'presently' – to announce the arrival of her suitor Caspar Goodwood; after Goodwood departs, the door opens without a forewarning knock, and it is her companion Henrietta Stackpole.[13] Isabel seems, nonetheless, to be amenable to the permeability of this space. While Ralph sees Stackpole's habit of 'walk[ing] in without knocking at the door' as a metaphor for her snooping, journalistic sensibility, Isabel defends her friend and, by extension, the value of the open door:

> 'Yes,' Isabel admitted, 'she doesn't sufficiently recognise the existence of knockers; and indeed I am not sure that she doesn't think them rather a pretentious ornament. She thinks one's door should stand ajar. But I persist in liking her.'[14]

The doorway ajar is a figure of possibility and positively charged ambiguity in much of James's *oeuvre*. Kate Thomas writes of James's allegiance to the queer state of being 'in-between' or 'across' rather than in or out. James's fiction, Thomas argues, is interested in the figural and literal 'swinging door between public and private. James relishes that swing and wants little to do with efforts to pin the door either open or shut.'[15] In *The Portrait of a Lady*, Ralph uses a swinging door metaphor to describe, admiringly, the way Isabel tests her suitors while never submitting to any of them: 'She would keep the gate ajar and open a parley.'[16] Isabel, he adds, 'has started on an exploring expedition, and I don't think she will change her course.'[17]

The possibilities represented by the swinging door between public and private, however, are limited by patriarchal relations of power, clearly seen when Goodwood slips through the threshold of Isabel's suite to argue his case for marriage. He grasps Isabel's hand immediately in a handshake: 'Caspar Goodwood came in and shook hands with her. He said nothing till the servant had left the room again.'[18] It would almost be an opening gesture of reciprocity and compromise (the kind of temporary balance of power achieved by Verena and Basil's handshake in *The Bostonians*) if it weren't so unexpected and aggressively one-sided. James pays further attention to Goodwood's physicality, this time with an unmistakable edge of violence:

> To attempt to spare his sensibility or to escape from him edgewise, as one might do from a man who had barred the way less sturdily – this, in dealing with Caspar Goodwood, who would take [the New York Edition changes this to 'grasp'[19]] every sort that one might give him, was wasted agility.[20]

The suffocating picture of the sitting-room contained within Goodwood's hands – barred by his outstretched limbs – is reminiscent of the Dario Sanchez hotel rape case, which went to court in March 1880 as James was writing the novel. Sanchez, 31, was charged with 'having unlawfully taken Mary Langley, an unmarried girl under the age of 16, out of the possession and against the will of her father'. Sanchez entrapped and raped Langley, 14, in a hotel bedroom. The incident occurred at the luxury Langham Hotel, near Oxford Circus, and was reported in *The Times*:

> He told her that he would show her inside the hotel, and that was all she expected him to do. She was surprised at his showing her over a bedroom. She did not go downstairs again because the door was shut. She made no alarm. She asked him to let her out when she found the room was a bedroom. The door was locked. She asked him to let her out, as she wanted to get home, but he replied that it was not late, and he then asked her to take her cloak off.[21]

To the contemporary public, such a case would have given form to a substratum of fear about women's vulnerability in hotels.

Isabel, however, transfigures the scene and wrests it back from Goodwood; she takes his hand, and ends the conversation as if it had been a negotiation all along. 'They stood so for a moment, looking at each other, united by a handclasp which was not merely passive on her side'.[22] Goodwood mutters his parting words, and without telling us they have let go of each other's hands – without any transition – James continues: 'She had laid her hand on the knob of the door that led into her room, and she waited a moment to see whether her visitor would not take his departure.'[23] His hand has become her bedroom doorknob in one of *The Portrait*'s perfectly poised images, an image that demonstrates how much James invested, aesthetically and conceptually, in thresholds between modes of being. The image is echoed multiple times in *The Portrait*, but it invites immediate comparison to the tableau in Gardencourt with Isabel poised, mid-step, on the way to her private chamber ('She looked at him a little; she had taken her candle and placed her foot on the oaken stair').[24] In Pratt's the interstitial space is gone, and Isabel looks at Goodwood from the actual threshold of her bedroom. She is, as it were, taking her own hand and turning away from Goodwood, the doorknob acting as a tactile metonym for the domain of the self that lies within the bedroom. At the same time, she is taking Goodwood by the hand, offering her suitor the ultimately impossible glimpse of that private core. Fleetingly provocative, Isabel dismisses Goodwood just as she holds ajar her sexuality. She triumphs over the threat of sexual violence by grasping back her own agency. Isabel's agency at this moment is not based on her ownership of the space and the inviolability of her monadic self. Rather, it is a compromise between the locked and the unlocked, something she achieves by manipulating the thresholds and connective spaces of a hotel suite.

The relative compression and permeability of the public and the private in Pratt's is tangible and consequential in terms of this scene's narrative and symbolic valency. Nonetheless, the organisation of Pratt's spaces does not fundamentally break with traditional domestic architecture. After all, private hotels like Pratt's in London's West End were merely town houses or mansions converted for lodgers.[25] 'The almost universal defect of the older class of hotels in London is', according to an 1875 London guidebook, 'that they are too often private dwellings extemporized for purposes of public accommodation – not buildings erected with the distinct object for which they are used. Hence the London hotels, generally, are confined and awkward in their arrangements.'[26] Another guidebook has a positive spin: 'The reader will bear in mind that these "private hotels" so-called have nothing in common with the huge joint-stock company concerns. Having more of a residential character, these hotels are quiet, and less frequented by the busy class of travellers.'[27] For that reason, another guidebook suggests, the 'old-fashioned high-class private hotels' around Piccadilly, 'where a bedroom and sitting room [. . .] may be had as in a private house', offer a seemlier experience than large hotels – 'especially for ladies'.[28] For those concerned with propriety and shy of publicity, their exposure to fellow guests and the general travelling public could be kept to a minimum in such establishments. The provision of private sitting-rooms, like Isabel's, allowed guests to entertain friends in seclusion and removed the need for public parlours.[29] Some private hotels had common sitting and smoking rooms which could be used for a fee, but others lacked even a common dining room, with meals instead being served individually in the guests' suites.[30] With its premium on individual service and privacy, it is not surprising that the scenes in Pratt's are all concerned with the spatial politics of the private *boudoir*, and not the negotiation of hotel public space or hotel crowds. Isabel must contend with frequent interruptions from her acquaintances, but never needs to concern herself with strangers. In fact, we never see Isabel leave her room during her stay at Pratt's. Isabel's withdrawal from public space, despite her room's apparent permeability, makes the scenes in her private suite begin to feel claustrophobic. During her interview with Goodwood, Isabel looks through the hotel window like a prisoner contemplating her solitary confinement: she 'stood a moment looking into the dusky vacancy of the street, where a turbid gaslight alone represented social animation'.[31] She tells Goodwood that '"The world strikes me as small"', a stark revision of her sentiments earlier in the novel.[32] With Goodwood's departure, Isabel retreats into the gloomy hotel bedroom; in the revised New York Edition, she suddenly expresses a desire to become as impassive as the bedroom furniture: 'She only asked, however, to put on the cover, to case herself again in brown holland'.[33] With this revision, the claustrophobic contraction of this space is complete, even as she thrills with her triumph over Goodwood.

Pratt's is therefore a site of profound ambivalence. Several critics have argued that *The Portrait of a Lady* is animated by the conflict between Isabel's vision of 'the world as a place of brightness, of free expansion', and the various imprisoning structures that she encounters: the structures of marriage and domesticity, and the structures of the Touchett, Warburton and Osmond estates, which vie to entrap her.[34] It is tempting, then, to read Pratt's as a momentary escape from these prison-houses. Here she has, for a brief moment, a room of her own. This reading would enhance the significance of an abandoned idea jotted down in James's notebooks: an alternative ending in which Isabel returns to Pratt's before setting off on her final destination, thereby quietly unsettling the binary choice between Gardencourt and Osmond's villa.[35] Pratt's could further be read as an afterimage of the author's own feelings of independence in London. In its location and its form, Pratt's appears to be modelled on the small and respectable Story's Hotel, a private hotel where James stayed for two weeks in 1875 on his way to the Continent.[36] (He would later settle in the area from 1876, and returned there throughout his life.) For James, just after completing the heroic labours of *Roderick Hudson*, Story's Hotel represented a staging-post in his initiation into Europe. He felt flushed with fantasies of mastery as he sat in his private hotel sitting-room to compose a letter to his parents, which began: 'I take possession of the old world – I inhale it – I appropriate it!'[37] Isabel follows the same pathway as James in her initiation, so that her independence is double-coded with James's discovery of authorial power. Yet Isabel, as we've seen, experiences this space (located amid Piccadilly's clubland, within a geography of male commercial and social exchange) very differently as a woman. With its patriarchal mode of hospitality and its isolating and individuating architecture, Pratt's might equally be considered another of the novel's many domestic prisons, guarded over by an attentive turnkey.

Joint-Stock Concerns

Family firms, small partnerships and privately-run businesses like Pratt's remained prevalent in the American and British economies throughout the nineteenth century. But a competitor – the incorporated joint-stock company, ancestor of the modern corporation – was rapidly becoming the preferred vehicle for complex businesses. Joint-stock companies were associations composed of 'a relatively large number of members', with 'a separation of management and ownership and more or less freely transferable shares'.[38] With incorporation, joint-stock companies could act as a single entity, able to 'hold property, sue and be sued, enter contracts, and continue in existence beyond the lifetime or membership of any of its participants'.[39] The corporate entity provided a kind of 'persona' for 'disparate capitals or investors to act as a unity on the juridical stage'.[40]

The corporate form had two key benefits for those in business. Firstly, it was an efficient way of pooling capital from a large number of investors. For this reason, the corporation in the first half of the nineteenth-century was mainly associated with capital-intensive sectors in the American and British economies, like banking, insurance and transport – particularly railways. Secondly, the corporation was a more impersonal business form. Before incorporation, business was largely undertaken within kinship networks. Without bureaucratic means of managing risk, and with all partners financially liable for the firm's debts, decisions were grounded on personal contact and (inevitably imperfect) assessments of personal character, or what Stefan Collini calls 'moral collateral'.[41] The corporation was, conversely, an abstract association capable of transacting business beyond the boundaries of a knowable community. The ownership of a corporation was dispersed among an amorphous body of shareholders, who could buy in or sell out at any time. These shareholders no longer took part in the daily operation of the company: that function was delegated to a centralised management. Shareholders also enjoyed limited liability (thanks to a wave of state-based legislation in the United States commencing in the 1810s and the 1855 Limited Liability Act in Britain), meaning each investor bore only limited personal responsibility for the company's debts, only up to the value of their personal shareholdings. Capital was therefore decoupled from personal relations of trust and obligation. The impersonal corporate form was, in James Beniger's terms, a 'control technology': an infrastructural or informational system needed to coordinate an increasingly specialised industrial economy. Corporate structures facilitated the shift 'from local segmented markets to higher levels of organization – what might be seen as the growing "systemness" of society.'[42]

Corporations came to possess metaphoric corporeality, yet (in Edgar Allan Poe's phrase) had 'neither bodies to be kicked, nor souls to be damned'.[43] As John O'Brien argues, they are an 'offense to representation, a legal fiction whose abstraction seems to mystify as much as it defines the relationship between individuals and larger social entities'.[44] Mark McGurl has written on the corporation's own solution to this ontological problem: its assumption of a visible identity through corporate artefacts and particularly architecture. 'Self-representation was a way for the corporation to lay visible claim to a privileged, indeed dominating, place on the landscape of American market culture,' as well as 'a way to quell the corporation's anxieties about its odd identic status as a legal fiction'. Architecture provided a means for 'the abstract body of business, corporeal but invisible, to convince itself of the "reality" and sturdiness of its own existence'.[45] James Taylor similarly points to the monumental structures of British joint-stock banks, insurance companies and railway companies as attempts to 'evoke feelings of solidity and permanence, to try to dispel fears that companies were transitory, unstable and untrustworthy'. Whereas older forms of business partnerships tended to be financially conservative, for joint-stock companies, 'show and display were necessary [. . .] because it was by these means that it won the confidence of the public'.[46]

The corporation introduced a fundamentally new way of organising space, and not just a new way of doing business. In early nineteenth-century retail, for instance, standardisation of prices and goods was rare, which meant that purchasing involved personally dealing with the owner of a shop, discussing the quality of the item and haggling over the price. With goods generally kept in a storeroom and collected by the owner on request, the cramped shopfront was 'little more than a backdrop for the drama of the personal encounter and act of purchase'.[47] In America, one venerable and persistent retail model, the general or country store, was a 'Characteristically dark, odorous plac[e] lined with shelving and cluttered with piles of merchandise', presided over by a storekeeper on a platform overlooking the scene.[48] There are continuities between the scope and social functions of the general store and the new retail forms that would emerge, and both these retail forms coexisted historically. Yet the rise of the department store in American cities in the mid-nineteenth century, a process 'thoroughly embedded in the growth of corporate capitalism', represented a substantial divergence from old models.[49] According to Vicki Howard, the key innovations of the American department store model were the one-price system, large sales volumes and rapid stock turnover, departmentalised organisation, centralisation of non-selling functions, and customer services and amenities. Crucially, department stores organised and displayed goods for customers, allowing them to browse and assess for themselves. This necessitated a dramatic expansion of floor space, as in A. T. Stewart's Manhattan department stores which were centrally located, purpose-built, multi-floored palaces.[50] Recalled by James as 'vast, marmorean, plate-glassy', they were flooded with light through hundreds of plate glass windows and glass domes.[51] With stores on this scale, direct dealings with an owner were no longer possible or necessary; customers dealt with sales clerks who were the human face of the firm.[52]

A similar process of architectural expansion, systemisation and de-personalisation was underway in British banking. London's private banks before the 1830s resembled discreet Georgian town houses, with business taking place in private parlours modelled on domestic drawing rooms. But as Iain S. Black writes, that business model came under attack by joint-stock banking:

> Private banking predominantly relied upon face-to-face contact between client and banker, within the intimacy of small and personalized office spaces. This emphasis on interpersonal relationships helped forge the bonds of trust so important to validate money transactions. The growth of joint-stock banking saw dramatic changes in these internal spaces, as the banking hall was transformed to accommodate a larger, more impersonal, and more socially diverse customer base. The attention devoted to ever more imposing banking halls reflected this bureaucratization of banking. For the new clientele, trust in the fidelity of the joint-stock

banker relied more on the scale and richness of the bank's architecture to compensate for the loss of personal contact.[53]

These shifts in retail and banking make instructive parallels with developments in the hospitality industry. Hotels, like department stores and banking halls, displaced small and familial spaces of business, not merely with a bigger, grander form of the same, but with a new and architecturally distinct typology. In the late-eighteenth century in Britain and the United States, the terms 'inn' and 'tavern' were used interchangeably with 'hotel', a word imported from the French to signify class and distinction. By the 1820s, however, American hotels were a demonstratively new species, 'functionally and symbolically distinct from inns and taverns', according to A. K. Sandoval-Strausz.[54] The City Hotel in Baltimore, for instance, which opened in 1826, contained two hundred guest rooms, huge ballrooms and dining rooms, bathing rooms, a barber shop, a post office, a reading room and a bar, all lit with industrial gaslights. It was financed as a speculative venture through a limited stock offering. For Sandoval-Strausz, what was revolutionary about the City Hotel and the hotels that followed it was its mode of service and public culture, as well as its 'distinctly American vision of mobility, civil society, democracy, and, ultimately, space'.[55] The hotel was a 'social technology': a 'new way of organising people'.[56] For Molly Berger, the hotel was distinctive through its 'adoption of commercial architecture, the movement towards financing projects through modern corporate structures, the separation of management from ownership, and the integration of technological systems into the building design'. Berger locates the hotel within an accelerated lifecycle of mobile capital: from speculation, technological innovation, novelty and consumption to obsolescence and ruin.[57] Underlying all of these revolutionary features was scale. The civic ambition and scale of the City Hotel was really its determinative feature, which reached its apotheosis in the skyscraper hotels of the 1920s.

The department store, the banking hall and the hotel are all examples of what could collectively be termed corporate space.[58] Analysed together, the shared features of these spaces become visible. Corporate spaces were capital-intensive; they therefore required modern corporate financing structures, aggregating capital from a large body of investors. Corporate organisation meant that ownership of the company was separated from day-to-day management. Built on a large scale, corporate spaces sold goods and services en masse. To make this possible, corporate spaces utilised 'subdivision, individuation, and exploitation', or the creation of a rationalised labour force within a rationalised architectural plan.[59] Corporate spaces were designed to assert their presence in the civic landscape, positioned on main boulevards or near critical urban hubs. And finally, corporate spaces deployed architecture as advertising and spectacle, to reassure the public about the solidity of the enterprise or to dazzle customers with the theatre of consumption. Despite their rational, departmentalised and cellular design, corporate spaces were invested with libidinal energies.

From America to Britain

While the familial and the corporate modes of hospitality still stood side by side, the hotel's presence in literature started to be felt. When Miles Coverdale returns to the city and the 'entangled life of many men together' in Hawthorne's *The Blithedale Romance* (1852), he sets himself up on the third floor of a large hotel. The space entangles and disentangles Coverdale from the knotted crowd. From his high vantage he can look out over the city, and he spends the following chapters spying on the activities inside a neighbouring boarding house. Yet even as he sits in perfect privacy, Coverdale's room reverberates with the sound of other people: 'Beneath and around me, I heard the stir of the hotel; [. . .] steps echoing on the stair-case; the ringing of a bell [. . .]; the porter lumbering past my door with baggage, which he thumped down upon the floors of neighboring chambers.' The hotel sounds blend with 'the tumult of the pavements', the 'foot-tramp and the clangor' of soldiers and a military band, the jangle of city bells calling out 'the engine-men and their machines', and the noise of a nearby mechanical diorama with its wind-up 'imitative cannon and musketry'.[60] Hawthorne's hotel is a mechanism in a mechanical landscape, in which many isolated units perform their separate roles. In the new cellular logic of hotel space, the individuation of Coverdale in his chamber is the precondition for his incorporation into an institutional communality.

The British, who had not yet imported this foreign technology, had to experience corporate hotels vicariously, as when Dickens rerouted *The Life and Adventures of Martin Chuzzlewit* (1844) to America. Journeying to the Eden Settlement operated by the Eden Land Corporation, Chuzzlewit visits the 'National Hotel', a metaphor for the big, slapdash American Republic. The National is an exoskeletal organism, composed almost entirely of encircling public passageways which guide the narrator, with a bathetic thud, to the void at the hotel's centre. Nothing here is interior, nothing is private:

> There were interminable whitewashed staircases, long whitewashed galleries up stairs and down stairs, scores of little whitewashed bedrooms, and a four-sided verandah to every story in the house, which formed a large brick square with an uncomfortable court-yard in the centre: where some clothes were drying.[61]

Dickens himself had mixed reviews of American hotels in his *American Notes*: 'we [. . .] straightaway repaired to an extremely comfortable hotel: except, as usual, in the article of bedrooms, which, in almost every place we visited, were very conductive to early rising.' He seems to have been particularly content, however, in the more familiar environment of a little inn in the town of Lebanon, Illinois, which 'In point of cleanliness and comfort [. . .] would have suffered by no comparison with any English alehouse, of a homely kind, in England.'[62]

Ten years later, while editor of the journal *Household Words*, Dickens found himself in the middle of a debate about the state of England's hotels. Alfred Smith had published a pamphlet titled *The English Hotel Nuisance* (1855), in which he contended that America and Europe had turned large-scale hospitality into a 'perfect science', while England suffered with 'bow-windowed, old-chamber-maided, stone-passaged, tobacco-odoured' inns and hopelessly unambitious commercial hotels.[63] Dickens sent out his apprentice journalist, George Augustus Sala, to write a contradictory article for *Household Words* on the subject. According to Sala, writing in retrospect in *London Up To Date* (1894), 'Dickens, although a Radical in politics, was curiously Conservative in many social matters, and he was rather opposed than favourable to Grand Hotels.'[64] Sala disappointed Dickens and backed Smith's call for the importation of American-style hotels.[65] Believing that the 'vast majority of English hotels [. . .] were of the kind described in the *Pickwick Papers*' – and not in a good way – Sala became an advocate for what he called the 'Hotel Brobdingnag', or the monstrous international grand hotel, to the extent, in fact, that he claims to have drawn up a prospectus for a Grand Hotel Company, which he tried to hawk, unsuccessfully, around the City of London in 1856.[66]

It was not Sala, however, but joint-stock railway companies that finally brought the American-style corporate hotel to London. The railways wielded hefty capital and were well connected – hundreds of Members of Parliament and landed gentlemen were railway company directors by the 1840s. Parliament authorised the creation of more than 800 railway companies with limited liability privileges between 1833 and 1850, making rail networks 'the most visible embodiment of joint-stock power'.[67] Inter-city travel and the demand for temporary accommodation surged with the reticulation of the railway system. In 1833, around three and a half million journeys in Britain were undertaken by post-horse, canal-boat or the coach-and-mail service. Thirty years later, over 204 million journeys were taken annually by rail. This 'increase in inter-city traffic', writes John Kellert, 'was quite beyond the capacity of the traditional inns and lodgings to accommodate, and entirely new and greatly enlarged premises had to be built to cater for it.'[68] The railways themselves established hotel corporations to finance and manage large-scale hotels, including the Great Western Royal Hotel at Paddington Station in 1854 – a hundred-bedroom, £86,000 giant, which was also 'highly successful as a commercial speculation'[69] – followed by the 300-bedroom Grosvenor at Victoria Station in 1860, which was 'almost a little town under one roof'.[70] Railway hotels were the first corporate hotels in London, and together with the railway's displacement of the old coaching houses, the alliance of rail and corporate capital dramatically altered the British hospitality industry.

The old routes of long-distance carrying had been largely bypassed, and many inns that were once 'handsomely, often extravagantly equipped' were becoming 'little more than glorified alehouses'.[71] By 1863, a commentator could already remark that:

> [It is] to the railways, which immolated the old order of hotels, we owe the new growth of those palatial structures which are reared by joint-stock companies, and managed with methodical regularity. The antique inns had been toppling, even before the iron avalanche overwhelmed them, and they sank at once before the triumphant march of the steam-horse.[72]

Some mourned the inn's decline. A correspondent in the *Standard* in 1878 lamented the loss of personal service at British inns, while deriding the 'over-populated joint-stock company barracks' where staff 'feel no more personal interest in [the guest] than the clerks at Somerset House in the gentleman who calls to stamp a document'.[73] Here, as in Ruskin's pseudonymous letter, we see the hotel's corporate underpinning being evoked pejoratively as a metonym for the institution's impersonality.

In the English novel, the hotel became inextricably linked with the culture of the railways. This can be seen in the rise of sensation fiction and the blockbuster success of Mary Elizabeth Braddon's *Lady Audley's Secret* (1862). Braddon's novel, as Nicholas Daly notes, is both extraordinarily mobile – searching for the truth, amateur detective Robert Audley darts between London, Southampton, Portsmouth, Liverpool, Dorset, Yorkshire and Audley Court – and extraordinarily brisk, with a new kind of time consciousness and a new sense of nervous energy. The sensation novel must be considered a railway novel, Daly argues, not only for its temporal armature and thematic obsessions, but because it was sold at railway stations and read in railway carriages.[74] As a railway novel, *Lady Audley's Secret* is also a hotel novel. It provides an epitaph for the old ('the benighted stranger [. . .] might have easily [. . .] mistaken the hospitable mansion for a good, old-fashioned inn, such as have faded from this earth since the last mail coach and prancing tits took their last melancholy journey to the knacker's yard'), while pulling back the curtain on the new – as when Robert steps off a train at the seaside resort of 'Wildernsea':[75]

> The porter opened a wooden door in the station wall, and Robert Audley found himself upon a wide bowling-green of smooth grass, which surrounded a huge square building that loomed darkly on him through the winter's night, its black solidity only relieved by two lighted windows, far apart from each other, and glimmering redly like beacons on the darkness.
>
> 'This is the Victoria Hotel, sir,' said the porter.[76]

The 'Yorkshire watering-place' of Wildernsea is a barely disguised fictionalisation of Withernsea, Yorkshire. The real town of Withernsea was a confection of the incorporated Hull and Holderness Railway Company. In 1854, seven years before *Lady Audley's Secret* was serialised, the company had chosen a barren village of 109 souls (which was constantly losing buildings to the encroachment of the sea) in which to construct a rail terminus and the forty-bedroom Queen's Hotel – according to one reviewer, 'one of the most commodious hotels on the east coast, spacious to a fault'.[77] The Company hoped to transform the village into a seaside resort and dormitory town for Hull.[78] A small new township was staked out; later, in the 1870s, the Railway Company established the Withernsea Pier, Promenade, Gas and General Improvement Co. Ltd to construct homes and public works. Hull and Holderness claimed that 70,000 visited the resort during its opening seasons in 1854 and 1855.[79] What Robert Audley sees, then, as the porter opens the gate to the Victoria Hotel, is joint-stock capital staking its claim on new territory. Braddon's language transforms this place into a colony: from the dreamscape of Robert's rail journey to Wildernsea ('The shrieking engine bore him [. . .], whirling him over desert wastes [. . .]. This northern road was strange and unfamiliar'), to his first thought upon arrival at the station ('I wonder whether settlers in the backwoods of America feel as solitary and strange as I feel to-night?').[80] The description of Robert landing in the Wildernsea backwoods echoes the 'wilds of the new world' and the 'diggings or the backwoods' of the Australian gold fields, where George Talboys makes his instant fortune in the opening of the novel.[81] The most advanced iteration of the corporate form, therefore, has metaphorically returned to its roots in the chartered corporations of colonialism.

When the American narrator of Henry James's story 'A Passionate Pilgrim' (1871) arrives in London with his 'resolute preference for old inns', and finds 'a certain antique hostelry far to the east of Temple Bar, deep in what I used to denominate the Johnsonian city',[82] it is clear that inns were already becoming a curiosity for the tourist circuit, and a place for the demotic traveller to display their connoisseurship and cultural capital. 'The privileged traveller would seek out old inns', writes Kevin J. James, 'as an affirmation of social solidarity with others who shared a particular appreciation of England's national history, as well as the class-informed aesthetic appeal of the picturesque represented by the regionally distinctive, apparently ramshackle visual appearance of the country inn.'[83] In the coffee-room of the inn he meets the pilgrim of the title, Clement Searle, another American traveller who has come to England to reclaim his bedevilled ancestry. The narrator follows Searle to his supposed ancestral seat in the Malvern Hills, deep in the west of England, where they lodge in a second inn to stage a confrontation with Searle's family. Divided between two points of view, the tone and the genre of 'A Passionate Pilgrim' vacillate erratically. The narrator is the curious though detached observer performing the role of the modern tourist, with many of his descriptive passages of local colour lifted word-for-word from travel accounts James himself recorded in his letters during his own tour of England; and with him Searle, the romantic adventurer driven mad by a quest, whose plot is awkwardly grafted onto the narrator's travelogue. The result is Ann Radcliffe in the covers of a Baedeker. By day, over 'burnished pewters of rustic ale', the narrator admires the thatched roof and 'homely' porch of the Malvern Hills inn; by night it is *unheimlich*, producing a genuine apparition: the ghost of a curate's daughter.[84] Yet the ghost is presented at several degrees remove, appearing first before Searle, who then recounts the words of the apparition to the narrator. Here and elsewhere, as T. J. Lustig writes, 'James countered the explosive threat of the ghostly by containing it within the experience of a particular individual and by an increasing emphasis on formal framing.'[85] Structurally detached, the stable rationality of the narrator remains undisturbed. Hence he can push on the next morning and take a sightseeing tour of Oxford, even as his sickly, morphine-addled companion begins to rave and hallucinate before the walls of a college. This odd couple, and their divergent, compulsive interest in inns, are indices of the inn's slow economic decline. Disconnected from the circulation of coach travellers and rendered outmoded in the rail era, the inn was experienced simultaneously as otherworldly and quaint: as a site for phantasms and postcards.

Daniel Maudlin cautions against exaggerating the distinctions between hotels and inns, particularly the large-scale 'principal inns' of the late-eighteenth and early-nineteenth centuries in both Britain and America, and thereby misrepresenting the birth of the hotel as a revolutionary moment. Maudlin points to the scale, grandeur and social function of principal inns, and the instability and arbitrariness of the signifier 'hotel' in this period: 'the change in name from inn to hotel denotes fashionable terminology more than a specific correlation to any immediate changes in form or function'.[86] Yet in the American context, Sandoval-Strausz argues that it was precisely the success of the hotel's distinctive form that lead to inns and taverns rebadging themselves, misleadingly, as hotels.[87] Beyond this transitional moment, the distinctiveness of the hotel as an architectural typology and social technology only strengthened. As we've seen, the arrival of the joint-stock railway hotel in Britain in the 1850s registers in many contemporaneous accounts as new and distinctive in structural, aesthetic, economic, social and symbolic terms. Nonetheless, Maudlin's claim that the 'obscuring lens of post-Romantic rural nostalgia' has situated the hotel in an artificially stark, binary relation with the inn is an important one.[88] James's 'A Passionate Pilgrim' demonstrates precisely this point: indicating the ongoing symbolic function of the inn, burnished in the glow of nostalgia, in discourses of modern sociability and space. The inn, Kevin J. James writes, became 'naturalized into the English countryside – and into interpretations of the country's pre-industrial past – as a signifier of the pastoral and the picturesque.'[89] The imagined binary opposition of inn and hotel (alongside the opposition of home and hotel, as discussed in Chapter 2) provided a means for writers on both sides of the Atlantic to dramatise, debate, rhapsodise, mourn and mystify the development of urban modernity.

Hotel Modernity

The readings in *Hotel Modernity* begin with details: with close readings of novelistic and cinematic descriptions of space, as well as travel writing, business documents, interior decoration books, architecture periodicals, hotel trade journals, hotel management guidebooks and advertisements. Incorporating the multidisciplinary insights of recent hotel research, the book pays close attention to the interactions of the human body with space; to furniture, materials and surfaces, layout and management; taking the hotel not as a singular space but as a compound of functional zones serving different social purposes, and creating different narrative possibilities. Amassed, these details tell a story about corporate capitalism and modernity. As Berger and Sandoval-Strausz both contend in their hotel histories, the development of the hotel provides a way of mapping the progress of capitalist modernity.

Proceeding chronologically, this book is limited to the critical years of 1870 to 1939. Not only was this a period of social, economic, political and literary revolution, it was also a period when hotels were at the forefront of those developments, when hotel space was most charged with meaning and most charged with social possibility. Hotels were, in those years, exemplary spaces of the modern. With their plate glass windows and internal shopping avenues, they encouraged consumerism in the manner of arcades and department stores. They contained large public spaces for gazing, lounging, publicity, flirtation and pecuniary emulation. Their managerial structure was part of a revolution in labour organisation and information control. They were an early adopter of chain and franchise structures, of branded and standardised spaces. They were political headquarters, meeting places of business clubs and associations, and outposts for banks, brokerages and the new age of finance capitalism. They were a testing ground for a transformation in gender relations, in the mobility and independence of women, in the political organisation of suffrage campaigns, and the loosening of the institutions of marriage and the family. They were a spur to cosmopolitanism and the circulation of global capital. They supported the growth of the railway networks. Their innovative structural template helped drag residential architecture from closeted Victorianism to rationalised modernism. They pioneered industrial building materials, modern plumbing, lighting, electrification and air-conditioning. They incorporated huge telephone banks, elevators and other technological conveniences before they were common. They were hubs for the newspaper business and for the sale of paperback books. They owned and broadcast their own jazz bands and dance bands, and presided over the birth of radio. And they were meeting points and living quarters for transatlantic novelists, poets, actors and directors, and occupied a central place in their imaginations. This network of economic and cultural influence had been established by 1870 and was withering away by 1939.

Hotel Modernity begins in the oversized American hotel lobbies found in James's early travel journalism, 'Daisy Miller' and *The American*. For James, the lobby produced a new kind of body: the stretched-out, elastic body of leisured bourgeois men. James's fiction contains a hidden genealogy of long-legged men, many of whom were drawn to big hotel spaces: from Christopher Newman to Ralph Touchett, Basil Ransom, Hyacinth Robinson, Tony Bream, Mr Waymarsh and Merton Densher, and an array of nameless loiterers. If the genteel ideal of the well-mannered body was self-control and self-possession, James's long-legged men breach the genteel code. They stretch, slouch and lounge beyond permissible boundaries: primed, like Christopher Newman, to 'stretch out and haul in', to possess and aggressively occupy space.[90] Their elasticity confounds the margin between self and other, and by melding into hotel divans and architectural structures, they also confound the margin between human and stuff. Hotel lobbies and hotel bodies are shown to be disruptive agents in Victorian culture with ambivalent social potential.

Chapter 2, centred on James's early short fiction and his overlooked comic novel *The Reverberator*, examines late nineteenth-century hotel parlours and reading-rooms. The chapter examines the materiality of these spaces, like their wipeable encaustic tiles and stain-resistant vitreous dinnerware. These surfaces resisted the stains and accretions of inhabitation. Their history was perpetually wiped clean. The chapter connects the stain resistance of hotel public spaces with the amnesiac practices of consumption and disposal that were carried out here. Reading-rooms rarely contained permanent book collections; instead, they fostered a trade in abandoned Tauchnitz editions and odd volumes of serial fiction. In *The Reverberator*, these amnesiac spaces are set against the suffocating permanence and curatorial obsessions of old Parisian families. In this minor novel, James explores the emancipatory potential of the hotel's disposable culture – and the pleasures of minor, interstitial experience.

The Ritz, analysed in Chapter 3, was a fiction of global finance: a licensing apparatus for a loose, decentralised and self-propagating franchise, which attached the Ritz name to dozens of hotels, along with apartment blocks, golfing communities, cruise ships, furniture and cigars. The value of the Ritz was not in bricks and mortar but in its name and its brand. The Ritz aesthetic was an anticipation of corporate minimalism: white walls and white curtains with minimal decorative ornaments, culminating in the evaporated surfaces of its rooftop gardens. Its whiteness and transparency were fitting architectural expressions of the Ritz as a deterritorialised brand. Like the Ritz, F. Scott Fitzgerald (or 'Fitz') was a branded entity. For Fitzgerald, the pleasure of the Ritz and its roof garden was in its nothingness: a desirable nowhere into which the moneyed elite could escape. Chapter 3 reads 'The Diamond as Big as the Ritz' as an allegory for capital's struggle to escape the physicality of bricks and mortar. It then considers the divergent fates of the fashionable and the penniless in Fitzgerald's major fiction, where those with means strive toward the mobility and immateriality of 'Ritz' and of capital itself.

Chapter 4 reads Elizabeth Bowen's first novel, *The Hotel* (1927), in light of the hotel schtick of Chaplin's early comedies and the mobile framing of hotel space in F. W. Murnau's *Der Letze Mann* (1924). Bowen understood the blankness of corporate hotel space as analogous to a studio set: looking around an empty drawing-room, one of Bowen's characters begins to find 'the mise en scène queerly important'.[91] The cast of Bowen's cinematic hotel are out of date for the 1920s: country vicars, London doctors, officers, old administrators of the Indian empire. Their power – as a class and as narrative agents – is expressed spatially, whether that be through the occupation of bigger rooms on better floors of the hotel, or through the occupation of the narrative foreground. Their power therefore relies on a static, pre-cinematic visual language: contemplative distance, stable perspectives and stable relations between foreground and background. Bowen's cinematic hotel, however, with its roaming camera-eye, dizzying focal effects, comic doubles and slapstick routines, unsettles that static visual order, collapsing these characters' careful demarcations of territory. Bowen's novel finds the spatialised class relations of the hotel to be a brittle construct, ripe for collapse.

Chapter 5 follows the rise of hotel managerialism from the turn of the twentieth century to the 1930s. The chapter starts with the observation that the newly professionalised role of hotel manager gained cultural authority through the rhetoric of scientific management and rationalisation, even as the hotel manager in this period was repeatedly figured as a kind of artist and the hotel as a work of art. Moving from Henry James's figuration of the Waldorf-Astoria's management as a shadowy rival author, preprocessing and abbreviating the social world, to Arnold Bennett's and Sinclair Lewis's manager-poets of the 1930s, and the managerial eye of MGM's *Grand Hotel*, the chapter considers the hotel manager as a classed and gendered fantasy figure of authorial power and omniscience. Henry Green's resistance to managerial and narratorial authority in *Party Going* (1939), set in the near-bankrupt, funereal Grosvenor Hotel in Victoria Station at the end of the grand hotel era, brings the historical narrative of the book to a close.

Hotel Postmodernity

This book doesn't venture into hotel postmodernity, though there are abundant possibilities for a potential guest list. The period from 1870 to 1939 is a discrete era in hotel and urban history; the war marks an absolute break, after which quite different architectural, technological and cultural forms can be found. A brief sketch of post-war developments in America will indicate the paradigm shift that took place after 1939.

During the 1920s, the American hotel industry had experienced a period of massive over-investment and corporate consolidation, as I document in Chapter 3. In Manhattan, for instance, the number of hotels abruptly doubled in the last years of the 1920s, while the number of hotel rooms more than doubled as hotels became larger and larger corporate concerns.[92] The popularity of American hotels peaked in 1929, with 75 per cent of travellers lodging in hotels rather than other forms of accommodation. But the Depression crushed the industry: by 1939, only 32 per cent of lodgers were staying in hotels, with the rest preferring cheaper motels; a wave of hotel bankruptcies followed.[93] Eighty per cent of American hotels went into receivership.[94] The Second World War marked a very real hinge-point in the history of the hotel. The investment decisions made after the war – investment that had been suppressed for two decades – favoured a new hotel paradigm. Just as the railway boom and company law reform fostered a new generation of English hotels in the 1850s, so the automobile boom, the 1956 Federal Aid Highway Act and a 1954 tax code provision for accelerated depreciation – allowing companies to write-off construction costs on non-urban greenfield sites – spurred a motel-building boom in America.[95] In general, the motel was recognisable for its extra-urban location, its accessibility by car rather than public transit, its smaller scale (often confined to a single-storey), its elimination of elaborate front of house arrangements (the formal lobbies, the dress codes, the hierarchies of tippable doormen, bellhops and clerks) and abandonment of the hotel's pretentions of civic centrality (the ballrooms, dining halls, public meeting spaces and offices). It was a lightweight model that suited the times. There were around three thousand motels in America in 1928, and 13,500 in 1939. By 1950, there were more motels in America than hotels; by 1960, motels numbered 60,000.[96] Their dominance was a direct threat to a suddenly very tired-looking pre-war generation of urban hotels. The occupancy rates of the hotels that remained afloat fell back from 85 per cent in 1948 to 67 per cent in 1958.[97] Changes needed to be made to the hundred-year-old hotel typology. To compete, hotels became more like motels. The compromise model, which rapidly became the dominant model of the 1960s, was the corporate motel-hotel hybrid, or the 'motor hotel'. Travelodge (founded 1939, incorporated 1946) and Holiday Inn (founded 1952, incorporated 1954) were the lynchpins, redefining hotel space as accessible, informal, predictable and 'family friendly', with air-conditioning, swimming pools and television sets as standard.[98] These were very different kinds of structures from the pre-war hotel: allied more with the suburban than the urban, their public and communal spaces were to a large degree eviscerated. Civic amenity – so crucial in separating hotels from inns in the nineteenth century – was gone. Hotel culture, if not the culture at large, had braced itself for the publication of Nabokov's *Lolita* (1955).

If the Grand Hotel paradigm persisted in the luxury chain hotels of the post-war era – Sheraton, InterContinental, Hyatt, Hilton – it persisted only as a simulacrum. These hotels, too, were structurally distinct from their predecessors. Their association with Marshall Plan funds and Cold War geopolitics, with airline corporations and airports, with office parks and International Style, and with global branding and the developing world situates them firmly in the era of late capitalism rather than the industrial capitalism of the corporate grand hotel. As Annabel Wharton describes the historical leap in her study of Hilton Hotels and the Cold War, the luxury hotel shifted from 'Fordist space to the space of McDonaldization'.[99] Rather than occupying the centre of city life, these hotels connected together a diffuse global network for an airborne business and political elite. While these post-war developments are fertile ground for further study, there is no room in this book to cover the very different questions the era poses. I look instead at the foundations of the contemporary age, tracing the origins of corporate space back to the social world of the 1870s.

Notes

1. Henry James, 'An English Winter Watering-place', *Collected Travel Writings: Great Britain and America*, ed. Richard Howard (New York: Library of America, 1993), pp. 226–8.
2. A. K. Sandoval-Strausz and Daniel Levinson Wilk, 'Princes and Maids of the City Hotel: The Cultural Politics of Commercial Hospitality in America', 25 *Journal of Decorative and Propaganda Arts* (2005), pp. 168–9.
3. Jonathan Oldbuck, 'Attendance Included in the Bill', *Morning Post*, 2 July 1863, p. 3; Timothy Hilton, *John Ruskin* (New Haven, CT and London: Yale University Press, 2002), pp. 306–7.
4. Arlie Russell Hochschild, *The Managed Heart: Commercialization of Human Feeling* (Berkeley, CA: University of California Press, 2012), p. 4.
5. James, 'An English Winter Watering-place', 226–8.
6. Maud Ellmann, *The Nets of Modernism: Henry James, Virginia Woolf, James Joyce, and Sigmund Freud* (Cambridge: Cambridge University Press, 2010), p. 2 and p. 39.
7. Henry James, *The American Scene*, in *Collected Travel Writings: Great Britain and America*, ed. Richard Howard (New York: Library of America, 1993), p. 440.
8. Henry James, *The Portrait of a Lady*, in *Novels: 1881–1886*, ed. William T. Stafford (New York: Library of America, 1985), p. 333.
9. Ibid., p. 333.
10. Caroline Levine, *Forms: Whole, Rhythm, Hierarchy, Network* (Princeton, NJ: Princeton University Press, 2015), p. 6.
11. James, *The Portrait of a Lady*, p. 239.

12. Karen Chase and Michael Levenson, *The Spectacle of Intimacy: A Public Life for the Victorian Family* (Princeton, NJ and Oxford: Princeton University Press, 2000), p. 143.
13. Ibid., p. 347.
14. Ibid., p. 285.
15. Kate Thomas, *Postal Pleasures: Sex, Scandal, and Victorian Letters* (Oxford: Oxford University Press, 2012), p. 220.
16. James, *The Portrait of a Lady*, p. 473.
17. Ibid., p. 474.
18. Ibid., p. 347.
19. Henry James, *The Portrait of a Lady*, vol. 1 (New York: Charles Scribner's Sons, 1908), p. 219.
20. James, *The Portrait of a Lady*, in *Novels: 1881–1886*, ed. William T. Stafford (New York: Library of America, 1985), p. 350.
21. 'Police', *The Times*, 18 March 1880, p. 2.
22. James, *The Portrait of a Lady*, p. 357.
23. Ibid., p. 358.
24. Ibid., p. 239.
25. 'Cork Street and Savile Row Area: Introduction', in *Survey of London: Volumes 31 and 32, St James Westminster, Part 2*, ed. F. H. W. Sheppard (London: London County Council, 1963), pp. 442–55; Edward Walford, *Old and New London: Volume 4* (London: Cassell, Petter & Galpin, 1878), pp. 291–314.
26. *Illustrated Guide to London and Neighbourhood* (London: William Collins, 1875), p. 118.
27. Charles Eyre Pascoe, *London of To-day: An Illustrated Handbook for the Season* (Boston: Roberts Brothers, 1888), p. 36.
28. *Collins' Guide to London and Neighbourhood* (London: William Collins, 1880), pp. 150–1.
29. Molly Berger, *Hotel Dreams: Luxury, Technology, and Urban Ambition in America, 1829–1929* (Baltimore, MD: Johns Hopkins University Press, 2011), p. 126.
30. Stephen Mennell, *All Manners of Food: Eating and Taste in England and France from the Middle Ages to the Present* (Champaign: Illini Books, 1996), p. 155.
31. James, *The Portrait of a Lady*, p. 354.
32. Ibid., p. 355.
33. James, *The Portrait of a Lady*, vol. 1 (New York: Charles Scribner's Sons, 1908), p. 232.
34. Ibid., p. 241; Victoria Coulson, 'Prisons, Palaces, and the Architecture of the Imagination', in *Palgrave Advances in Henry James Studies*, ed. Peter Rawlings (London: Palgrave Macmillan, 2007), pp. 169–91.
35. Henry James, *The Complete Notebooks of Henry James*, eds Leon Edel and Lyall H. Powers (Oxford and New York: Oxford University Press, 1987), p. 16.
36. Pratt's is said to be 'in a street that ran at right angles to Piccadilly', which corresponds to Dover Street where Story's Hotel was located. James, *The Portrait of a Lady*, p. 333.
37. Henry James, *Letters: Volume 1, 1843–1875*, ed. Leon Edel (Cambridge, MA: Harvard University Press, 1974–84), p. 484 (1 November 1875).

38. Paddy Ireland, 'Capitalism without the Capitalist: The Joint Stock Company Share and the Emergence of the Modern Doctrine of Separate Corporate Personality', 17 (1) *Journal of Legal History* (1996), p. 42.
39. Alan Trachtenberg, *The Incorporation of America: Culture and Society in the Gilded Age*, 2nd edn (New York: Hill & Wang, 2007), p. 83.
40. Mark Neocleous, *Imagining the State* (Maidenhead: Open University Press, 2003), pp. 80–2.
41. Stefan Collini, *Public Moralists: Political Thought and Intellectual Life in Britain, 1850–1930* (Oxford: Clarendon Press, 1991), p. 106.
42. James R. Beniger, *The Control Revolution: Technological and Economic Origins of the Information Society* (Cambridge, MA and London: Harvard University Press, 1986), p. 11.
43. Edgar Allan Poe, 'The Business Man', in *Poetry and Tales*, ed. Patrick Quinn (New York: Library of America, 1984), p. 379.
44. John O'Brien, *Literature Incorporated: The Cultural Unconscious of the Business Corporation, 1650–1850* (Chicago: University of Chicago Press, 2016), p. 4.
45. Mark McGurl, 'Making It Big: Picturing the Radio Age in *King Kong*', 22 (3) *Critical Inquiry* (Spring, 1996), p. 417.
46. James Taylor, *Creating Capitalism: Joint-Stock Enterprise in British Politics and Culture, 1800–1870* (London: Royal Historical Society, 2006), pp. 35–6.
47. Mona Domosh, *Invented Cities: The Creation of Landscape in Nineteenth-Century New York and Boston* (New Haven, CT: Yale University Press, 1996), pp. 37–8.
48. Vicki Howard, *From Main Street to Mall: The Rise and Fall of the American Department Store* (Philadelphia: University of Pennsylvania Press, 2015), p. 27.
49. Louisa Iarocci, *The Urban Department Store in America, 1850–1930* (Farnham: Ashgate, 2014), p. 102.
50. Vicki Howard, *From Main Street to Mall: The Rise and Fall of the American Department Store* (Philadelphia: University of Pennsylvania Press, 2015), pp. 11–13.
51. Henry James, *A Small Boy and Others* (New York: Charles Scribner's Sons, 1913), p. 66.
52. Domosh, *Invented Cities*, p. 38.
53. Iain S. Black, 'Spaces of Capital: Bank Office Building in the City of London, 1830–1870', 26 (3) *Journal of Historical Geography* (2000), p. 371.
54. A. K. Sandoval-Strausz, *Hotel: An American History* (New Haven, CT: Yale University Press, 2007), p. 20.
55. Ibid., p. 9.
56. Ibid., p. 43.
57. Molly Berger, *Hotel Dreams: Luxury, Technology, and Urban Ambition in America, 1829–1929* (Baltimore, MD: Johns Hopkins University Press, 2011), p. 25. See also Daniel M. Abramson, *Obsolescence: An Architectural History* (Chicago and London: Chicago University Press, 2016), p. 106.
58. Robbie Moore, 'Corporate Space', in *The Routledge Companion to Literature and Economics*, eds Matt Seybold and Michelle Chihara (New York: Routledge, 2019), pp. 210–18.
59. Sandoval-Strausz, *Hotel*, 184.

60. Nathaniel Hawthorne, *The Blithedale Romance* (Boston: Ticknor, Reed, & Fields, 1852), pp. 173–4.
61. Charles Dickens, *Martin Chuzzlewit*, ed. Margaret Cardwell (Oxford and New York: Oxford University Press, 1984), p. 301.
62. Charles Dickens, *American Notes for General Circulation*, eds John S. Whitley and Arnold Goldman (Penguin: Harmondsworth, 1972), p. 121 and p. 226.
63. Albert Smith, *The English Hotel Nuisance* (London: David Bryce, 1855), p. 11 and p. 10.
64. George Augustus Sala, *London Up To Date* (London: Adam & Charles Black, 1895), 147.
65. See also Peter Blake, 'Charles Dickens, George Augustus Sala and *Household Words*', *Dickens Quarterly* 26 (March 2009), pp. 34–5, which claims that Dickens was simply disappointed with the laxity and flippancy of Sala's research methods.
66. Sala, *London Up To Date*, p. 147.
67. Taylor, *Creating Capitalism*, pp. 166–70 and p. 7.
68. John R. Kellett, *The Impact of Railways on Victorian Cities* (London: Routledge & Kegan Paul, 1969), p. 319.
69. *London and Its Environs: A Practical Guide to the Metropolis and Its Vicinity* (Edinburgh: Adam & Charles Black, 1862), p. 23.
70. 'The Grosvenor Hotel', *The Builder*, 1 June 1861, p. 375.
71. Peter Clark, *The English Alehouse: A Social History, 1200–1830* (London: Longman, 1983), p. 10.
72. 'Hotels', *Chambers's Journal of Popular Literature, Science and Art*, 30 May 1863, p. 347.
73. 'English Hotels,' *The Standard*, 24 August 1878, p. 2.
74. Nicholas Daly, 'Railway Novels: Sensation Fiction and the Modernization of the Senses', 66 (2) *ELH* (Summer 1999), pp. 461–87.
75. Mary Elizabeth Braddon, *Lady Audley's Secret*, ed. Lyn Pykett (Oxford: Oxford University Press, 2012), p. 101.
76. Ibid., pp. 206–7.
77. *Seaside Watering Places: Being a Guide to Strangers in Search of a Suitable Place in Which to Spend Their Holidays* (London: The Bazaar, 1876), p. 69.
78. Jack Simmons, *The Railway in Town and Country 1830–1914* (London: David & Charles, 1986), p. 114.
79. 'Hull and Holderness Railway', *Herapath's Journal*, 12 January 1856, p. 48.
80. Braddon, *Lady Audley's Secret*, p. 206.
81. Ibid., p. 24 and p. 44.
82. Henry James, 'A Passionate Pilgrim', in *Complete Stories: 1864–1874*, ed. Jean Strouse (New York: Library of America, 1999), p. 543.
83. Kevin J. James, 'Afterword', in *Anglo-American Travelers and the Hotel Experience in Nineteenth-Century Literature*, eds Monika M. Elbert and Susanne Schmid (New York and London: Routledge, 2018), p. 271.
84. James, 'A Passionate Pilgrim', p. 562.
85. T. J. Lustig, *Henry James and the Ghostly* (Cambridge: Cambridge University Press, 1994), p. 3.

86. Kevin J. James, A. K. Sandoval-Strausz, Daniel Maudlin, Maurizio Peleggi, Cédric Humair and Molly W. Berger, 'The Hotel in History: Evolving Perspectives', 9 (1) *Journal of Tourism History* (2017), p. 98.
87. Sandoval-Strausz, *Hotel*, p. 43.
88. James et al., 'The Hotel in History', p. 96.
89. James, 'Afterword', p. 270.
90. Henry James, *The American*, in *Novels: 1871–1880*, ed. William T. Stafford (New York: Library of America, 1983), p. 545.
91. Elizabeth Bowen, *The Hotel* (London: Vintage, 2003), p. 105.
92. Paul Ingram and Joel A. C. Baum, 'Chain Affiliation and the Failure of Manhattan Hotels, 1898–1980', 42 (1) *Administrative Science Quarterly* (March 1997), pp. 79–80.
93. John A. Jakle, Keith A. Schulle and Jefferson S. Rogers, *The Motel in America* (Baltimore, MD: Johns Hopkins University Press, 1996), p. 67.
94. John A. Jakle and Keith A. Schulle, *America's Main Street Hotels: Transiency and Community in the Early Auto Age* (Knoxville, TN: University of Tennessee Press, 2009), p. 66.
95. Bernadette Hanlon, John R. Short and Thomas J. Vicino, *Cities and Suburbs: New Metropolitan Realities in the US* (Oxford and New York: Routledge, 2010), p. 48; Jakle and Schulle, *America's Main Street Hotels*, p. 156.
96. Jakle et al., *The Motel in America*, 20.
97. William Kaszynski, *The American Highway: The History and Culture of Roads in the United States* (Jefferson, NC: McFarland, 2000), p. 158.
98. Ibid., pp. 156–60.
99. Annabel Jane Wharton, *Building the Cold War: Hilton International Hotels and Modern Architecture* (Chicago: Chicago University Press, 2001), p. 171.

I

LOUNGING BODIES: THE LOBBY AND PIAZZA

William James was born in the Astor House, New York, a five-storey hotel occupying an entire block on Broadway. William's brother, Henry James, would recall Astor House as a place of almost prenatal comfort and security. It 'continued to project its massive image', Henry wrote, 'that of a great square block of granite with vast dark warm interiors, across some of the later and more sensitive stages of my infancy' (Figure 1.1).[1] The James family were restless, moving frequently, and spent many of their summers in hotels. In Henry's *A Small Boy and Others* (1913), a spotty textual daguerreotype of his earliest memories of New York City, the author suggests that hotels 'probably cast a stronger spell upon the spirit of our childhood [. . .] than any scene presented to us up to our reaching our teens'.[2] He writes that the kinds of domestic arrangements he observed during his early hotel days provided his 'first vision of the liberal life', where the social shame of unconventional living was easily outweighed by the expansion of one's imagination:

> I find that I draw from the singularly unobliterated memory of the particulars of all that experience the power quite to glory in our shame; of so entrancing an interest did I feel it at the time to *be* an hotel child, and so little would I have exchanged my lot with that of any small person more privately bred. We were private enough in all conscience, I think I must have felt, the rest of the year; and at what age mustn't I quite have succumbed to the charm of the world seen in a larger way? For there,

Figure 1.1 Astor House, Broadway, New York, date unknown (Source: Library of Congress).

> incomparably, was the chance to dawdle and gape; there were human appearances in endless variety and on the exhibition-stage of a piazza that my gape measured almost as by miles; it was even as if I had become positively conscious that the social scene so peopled would pretty well always say more to me than anything else.[3]

The world seen in a larger way: this is James's most wholehearted homage to the hotel and its capacity to shape modern, cosmopolitan subjectivity. James, traditionally considered an artist of private homes and private consciousness, is here surprisingly unequivocal about the good that came from hotel living: not just from the pleasures of hotel dawdling, but from the galvanising effect of hotel culture on a young mind. The sentiment James expresses here echoes his 1888 essay 'London' in which James talks of his pleasure in the city's seasonal lulls, when it is emptied of friends and filled with strangers: when, in James's words, 'the exhilarating sense of the presence of every one he doesn't know becomes by so much the deeper.'[4] Gage McWeeny argues in a reading of this essay that 'In his preference for the many over the few, the impersonal intimacy of strangers over those who are friends and acquaintances, James's pleasure in getting away from those who are closest to him is also hard to distinguish from a social desire that is as vast as London itself.'[5] In both *A Small Boy and Others* and 'London', the experience of 'impersonal intimacy' – being unattached and disinterested and comfortable with strangers – is the basis for James's social vision, and for his work as a writer. The hotel, a paradigmatic space of impersonal intimacy, is positioned in *A Small Boy and Others* as pivotal in James's writerly development. The moment James becomes 'positively conscious' of the value of hotel society reads like an epiphany: a revelation not only of the social organism, but of the social organism as theatre, as raw material, as the artist's great subject. If this is the case, then Henry James the novelist was born on a hotel piazza.

While James's account of his hotel childhood comes late in his career, it is not inconsistent with what came before. Earlier works feature the trope of seeing the world in a larger way from inside a hotel. It is used, for instance, when Maisie Farange arrives at her French hotel in *What Maisie Knew* (1897). Here too is the sense of hotel space as inherently theatrical, a place to perform and to watch performances:

> This emotion [. . .] was speedily quenched in others, above all in *the great ecstasy of a larger impression of life*. She was 'abroad' and she gave herself up to it [. . .]. Her vocation was to see the world and to thrill with enjoyment of the picture; she had grown older in five minutes and had by the time they reached the hotel recognised in the institutions and manners of France a multitude of affinities and messages.[6]

The trope can be traced further backward to *The Portrait of a Lady* (1881), where in a striking anticipation of *A Small Boy and Others* James describes Isabel Archer's own hotel childhood:

> Even when her father had left his daughters for three months at Neufchâtel with a French *bonne*, who eloped with a Russian nobleman, staying at the same hotel – even in this irregular situation (an incident of the girl's eleventh year) she had been neither frightened nor ashamed, but had thought it a picturesque episode in a liberal education. *Her father had a large way of looking at life*, of which his restlessness and even his occasional incoherency of conduct had been only a proof.[7]

James's restatement of this trope in more or less identical terms across thirty-five years, refracted from fiction to autobiography, suggests that his early affection for hotels was deeply embedded. But these passages, narrating the experiences of children, also point to the conditional nature of James's affection. It's simply easier for James to celebrate hotels in the guise of a child than as an adult, before sex comes into the equation. Maisie, Isabel and the young James see only wonder and opportunity in the hotel because they haven't yet been inculcated with the social codes of the adult world, in which the hotel had darker associations (especially from French novels and the newspapers) with adultery and prostitution, irregular and dispossessed families – and 'shame'. As a journalist warned in 1869, 'How many women can trace their first infidelity to the necessarily demoralizing influences of public houses – to loneliness, leisure, need of society, interesting companions, abundance of opportunity, and potent temptation!' Hotels, the journalist concludes, are only 'agreeable and desirable for masculine celibates'.[8] This is the moral baggage piled in the lobbies of James's hotels, baggage that clutters up his vision of cosmopolitan hotel liberalism.

For James, traces of Victorian censoriousness are inescapable. Shame haunts the above passages; the adult writer worries about the shameful underbelly of hotels, even if his young charges do not. His contemporary readership would have worried about it too, even as they were being pushed to acknowledge the romance of a childhood lived in unusual circumstances. If shame is only partially suspended in the accounts of Maisie, Isabel and young James, it is a heavier burden for James's adult characters, especially his women. Even if we don't caricature James in the manner of Max Beerbohm – who in 1904 drew a prurient James squatting, captivated and bewildered, attempting to maintain his dignity, beside the keyhole of a hotel boudoir[9] – sex still remains a complication for James in representing what he describes as hotel 'promiscuity'.[10]

The cosmopolitan ease that James finds in hotels doesn't disappear once his characters mature, but it becomes less rapturous and more guarded. James's counterbalancing suspicion of hotels can be seen throughout his early fiction and non-fiction, from his travel reportage for *The Nation* through the scandalous hotel of *Watch and Ward* (1871), the moral panic of 'Daisy Miller' (1878), the dirty lobbies of *The Bostonians* (1886) and the satire of *The Reverberator* (1888). Betsy Klimasmith argues that hotels in James are symptomatic of larger process of urban upheaval – places that erase history and evaporate any hope of privacy or interiority. Hotels, Klimasmith writes, were part of the publicity machine of the modern metropolis, overwhelming the boundaries between the public and the private. James's fictions enact the disappearance of these boundaries, even as they display some residual 'nostalgia for the home' as a now impossible 'site of containment'.[11] Undoubtedly, James did link hotels into a broader critique of mass culture and 'publicity', most directly in *The Bostonians* and *The Reverberator*. But we must also account for the rapturous hotel experiences in James's fiction, and consider the possibility that James found some enjoyment in, or use for, publicity: that, in Richard Salmon's words, 'James's saturation in the cultural codes of publicity and performance [. . .] seems positively to have enabled his recognition of the liberating mutability of the modern self.'[12] The reason James is central to this study is because of this exploratory engagement with an institution he knew intimately. He uses hotels as a testing ground, as a way of trialling the possibilities, the boundaries and the dangers of the mutable modern self.

James was a perceptive reader of architecture. For Victoria Coulson, 'the place of architecture' in James is 'the possibility of thinking', providing a structure in which to locate and constitute the self.[13] Otten's project in *A Superficial Reading of Henry James* is to 'physicalize James's meanings and imagery, for example, replacing the materially amorphous concept of point of view with a shell of material things that defines consciousness.' The enveloping shell of architecture supplies Jamesian consciousness, he argues, with 'a habitat and a definition'.[14] In this chapter, however, I set aside the question of consciousness entirely: it is the materiality of hotel experience, the shell itself, and its effect on the human body that are my central concerns here.

Hotel Bodies

James's fiction contains a hidden genealogy of male characters with 'long legs': from George Fenton in *Watch and Ward* through to Christopher Newman, Mr Ruck from 'The Pension Beaurepas', Ralph Touchett, Basil Ransom, Hyacinth Robinson, Tony Bream from *The Other House*, Mr Waymarsh, Merton Densher and Newton Winch from 'A Round of Visits' (along with a handful of other examples). Some of these bodies have been analysed individually – notably the amply symbolic body of Christopher Newman.[15] Isolated bodily characteristics in James's fiction – such as corpulence – have also been productively discussed in the context of a single work.[16] Here, however, I begin with the premise that James's long-legged men are a loosely related family, reading across multiple novels and stories to piece together their collective attributes, their habits (lounging, stretching, smoking, spitting) and, most important, their intimate affiliation with architectural haunts, in particular the oversized lobbies of corporate hotels. Assembling a sociological portrait of a Jamesian body type makes visible the way bodies and built environments work in alliance in James's fiction and the way such alliances can alternatively reproduce or transfigure the social order. Concentrating on a constellation of long bodies in James's early fiction also shows James testing out, and then moving to moderate and contain, a threatening form of masculine physicality.

This focus on ordinary habits and haunts is informed by the sociology of everyday life – a much theorised yet slippery object of analysis in recent decades. I locate Jamesian 'everyday life' in the iterative relationships between bodies and spaces, or, following the architectural historian and theorist Dell Upton, in the 'nexus of spaces and times that repeatedly trigger bodily habits and cultural memories'.[17] Upton's model of everyday life provides an alternative way of reading the social practices represented in James's fiction, which are often arranged under the heading of 'manners'. In contrast to manners, a concept with a similarly slippery history, 'everyday life' has no connotations of ossified rules or mores.[18] While it is a domain of routine (of activities 'half-conscious and half-rote'), Upton suggests that everyday patterns can be disrupted and transformed through the contingency of events, or through conflicts between different codes of 'posture, movement, and space-holding'.[19] His model proposes a flexible relationship between individual bodies and the social body that 'allow[s] one to act in a way that is at once habitual *and* improvisatory, rote *and* novel.'[20] I argue that James, too, conceived of the relationship between bodies and spaces as fluid, producing new forms of social manners in competition with the prevailing social regime. This dynamism inoculates the social world of James's fiction from ossification. His social world is fluid not just because of the play of cultures, sexualities and subjectivities within it, but because of the vitality of Jamesian 'everyday life' and the unsettling influence of different architectures and bodily habits from which it is composed.

James could not count himself among the long-legged and lanky, being (like Lambert Strether) 'of middle height' and with the propensity for episodic portliness.[21] 'I am as broad as I am long,' he wrote in a letter in June 1879 during one such episode; 'as fat as a butter-tub & as red as a British materfamilias'.[22] If, as William Veeder diagnoses, James was keeping the world at a distance with his round, androgynous body, the long-legged men of James's fiction represented a more aggressive form of bodily excess.[23] Already in his first novel, *Watch and Ward*, the long male body is a species apart, and an object of fascination and rivalry, desire and disgust. Richard Lawrence, the 'compact and sturdy', soft-featured and overtly feminised hero of the novel, finds a challenger to the hand of Nora Lambert in the 'tall and lean' villain, George Fenton.[24] Fenton, with his 'long legs' (and strangely disproportionate feet) makes Lawrence 'feel like a small boy' in his presence, and 'sapped the roots of the poor fellow's comfortable consciousness of being a man of the world.'[25] The leg is here overtly deployed as a displaced phallic symbol – a displacement with a long pedigree in eighteenth- and nineteenth-century culture.[26] While Lawrence feels ungrounded by the other man, Fenton strides confidently into Lawrence's territory, seemingly able to catch and corner Nora 'with a single shuffle of his long legs'.[27] All of Fenton's looseness and excessiveness, his financial wiles and his abject sexuality, become attached to and symbolised through those ill-disciplined legs. As he attempts to con Nora in his city office, he 'sat on the edge of his desk, swinging his leg'.[28] Earlier, Lawrence watches Fenton through a window as he

> lounge[s] along by Nora's side, with his hands in his pockets, a cigar in his mouth, his shoulders raised to his ears, and a pair of tattered slippers on his absurdly diminutive feet. Not only had Nora forgiven him this last breach of civility, but she had forthwith begun to work him a new pair of slippers.[29]

Fenton's is the prototypical ill-mannered body in James's fiction: a body that can't keep to itself, that lounges even while walking, that extends itself with prosthetic objects and with clouds of smoke and ash, and whose loose, disproportioned limbs are always threatening to stretch out, grasp or otherwise invade the space of others. If the ideal of the well-mannered body was self-control and self-possession, James's lounging men breach that genteel code. Their elasticity confounds the margin between self and other. And by melding into accessories and furniture and architectural structures, their bodies also confound the margin between human and object. These men travesty social as well as novelistic good manners, refusing to be deeply conscious, individuated characters, presenting instead a blank and sometimes threatening physicality.

James uses long-leggedness in his fiction as a way of suggesting a dissonance between the male body and society, with characters who don't realise how much space they take up (or indeed who deliberately take up too much space), who compulsively pace and stretch, or else sprawl themselves over furniture: like the insidious attorney Mr Striker in *Roderick Hudson*, who is found 'on the sofa, half sitting, half lounging, in the attitude of a visitor outstaying ceremony, with one long leg flung over the other and a large foot in a clumsy boot swinging to and fro continually'.[30] When situated inside a drawing-room or arranged on a sofa, long legs threaten traditional decorum. The fustier chambers and halls of private society are too cramped and too uncomfortable for their size. In 'The Pension Beaurepas', Mrs and Miss Ruck rest in the garden of the pension 'side by side, with folded hands, contemplating material objects', but Mr Ruck cannot be contained, sitting 'with a roll of American newspapers in his lap and his high hat pushed back, swinging one of his long legs and reading the New York Herald'.[31] Restless and out of place, these men are on a perpetual search for leg-room.

James's long-legged men prefer airier, modern spaces and modern furniture, such as the simple yet commodious cane chairs that were enjoying a production boom and a new peak of popularity in America.[32] The long-legged Basil Ransom from *The Bostonians*, like Christopher Newman from *The American*, has simple tastes, acquired beyond the metropolitan centres of America's northeast. Having little time for Victorian clutter, his conception of material comfort 'consisted mainly of the vision of plenty of cigars and brandy and water and newspapers, and a cane-bottomed arm-chair of the right inclination, from which he could stretch his legs'.[33] Gilbert Osmond in *The Portrait of a Lady* (not himself described as long-legged) has a living space whose modernity is linked to its accommodation of the new male physiology. In the New York Edition revision, Osmond's Florentine villa mixes tasteful antiques with 'modern furniture in which large allowance had been made for a lounging generation; it was to be noticed that all the chairs were deep and well padded.'[34]

From the distanced perspective of this later revision, James implicitly historicises the lounger. Long legs belong to an emergent generation with new habits, new needs and a new sense of design. What binds James's long-legged men together is class. His 'lounging generation' is simply another name for the new bourgeois leisure class – ranging from those living comfortably on white-collar incomes, to those described by the *New York Times* in 1885 as a growing 'club-lounging class' of '"income" men'.[35] Most, though not all, of James's long-legged men are bourgeois professionals: Mr Striker, Waymarsh and Ransom are lawyers; Densher is a journalist; Mr Ruck, Christopher Newman and Newton Winch have won and lost in business and finance; Tony Bream is a banker; and Ralph Touchett briefly worked in his father's bank (where he was given a stool too short for his legs – he preferred to stand). Fenton, finally, is a bourgeois imposter: a penniless con-artist who nonetheless keeps an office in the city.[36] By figuring the leisured bourgeoisie through their long legs, James is signalling that they possess not only a distinct mindset but a new kind of body and an altered relationship with the spaces they move through. Evoking a kind of social evolutionism, James foregrounds the place of the human body in the historical process. The body is both an expression and an agent of history. The long-legged bourgeois is an adaptation to the capitalist economy: primed, like Christopher Newman, to 'stretch out and haul in'.[37] But long legs also change history: the desire for more stretching-room drives a quiet revolution in manners, furniture and architecture, soon to make redundant the 'agoraphobic Victorian townhouses of the old leisure class'.[38]

'To Inhabit Very Large Rooms'

The social implications of long-leggedness can be seen most clearly in the spaces to which James's long-legged men are habitually drawn: to the lobbies and piazzas of grand hotels. Fenton, in James's *Watch and Ward*, is the first of many long-legged characters who finds comfort in lobbies. Staking out his rival in the public area of a hotel, Fenton 'stretched his long legs awhile on one of the divans in the hall'.[39] The elasticity of Fenton suits the architecture. The defining feature of America's corporate hotels was their monstrous scale. They were a different organism altogether from older, family-run institutions like inns, taverns and *pensioni*, which in architectural terms were mere variations on the domestic vernacular.[40] The commercial hotel's different order of magnitude is what made it, in a very real sense, modern. To build something as big as a hotel necessitated the backing of financiers or joint-stock companies. The management of its multifarious spaces was aided by a cellular architectural plan, optimised for efficiency and control. Its many floors spurred the development of new infrastructure and technologies and the many services offered to guests required a large and hierarchised wage labour force. The corporate hotel's scale, finally, cultivated an impersonal social scene of publicity and pecuniary emulation, especially in the gigantic lobby spaces which epitomised the impersonal intimacy of hotel life.

The first American hotel lobby, in the pioneering Tremont House in Boston (1829), adopted the imposing style of a Greek Revival temple. Entering through sixteen-foot tall folding doors, guests would find themselves in a rotunda finished with ionic columns and stained glass evoking frescos from the Baths of Titus. Receiving rooms, an office and porter's room were arrayed around and opened onto the rotunda.[41] The decorations were testament to the symbolic power of this new architectural form. During a tour of America in 1847, the Argentinean politician Domingo Faustino Sarmiento claimed that America's hotels had displaced cathedrals as sites of communion: 'Where the importance of the individual reaches the heights it has in American democracy, the temple's power diminishes in proportion to the multiplication of sects, and the hotel inherits the dome of the ancient tabernacle and takes on the aspect of the baths of emperors.'[42] Recalling America's other secular shrines, like the political architecture of Washington, DC and the commercial architecture of federal banks, the Tremont's rotunda-lobby was positioned as nation-building infrastructure at the centre of Boston's civic life. Throughout the nineteenth century, lobby spaces were 'strategic sites for the urban bourgeoisie to network, build up its group identity, and enhance its socio-economic power'.[43] Lobbies became sites of exchange: of information, money, services, goods and identities. They were waiting and lounging rooms for the city that were also charged with 'promiscuous energy' and the fizz of narrative possibility.[44] 'It is this combination of movement and stasis, space and events,' writes Douglas Tallack, 'which suggests a reading of the hotel lobby as emblematic of certain aspects of modernity: broadly speaking, its routine yet kaleidoscopic, assembling and disassembling, comic and disturbing character.'[45]

James's defining experience of lounging in gigantic hotel spaces was during his tour of American resorts in 1870, a year before the publication of *Watch and Ward*. James spent the summer writing wry, bemused sketches on travel and hotel life for the *Nation*, and in a piece titled 'Saratoga', he studied the goings-on at Saratoga's 'monster' Grand Union Hotel.[46] The hotel was encircled by a mile of piazzas – covered veranda-like spaces where chairs were freely arranged and entertainments were organised. This was, apparently, the largest such piazza in the world. It was not picturesque, James writes, but it served its purpose: 'that of affording sitting-space in the open air to an immense number of persons'.[47] Between the piazza and the street is a '"stoop" of mighty area, which, at most hours of the day and evening, is a favoured lounging-place of men' (Figure 1.2).[48] With these gigantic interfaces between civic space and the spaces of private commerce, Saratoga adopted a more democratic model of resort architecture than the increasingly privatised sister-resort of Newport, whose hotels were being pulled down and replaced by villas and cottages.

HOTEL MODERNITY

Figure 1.2 Rear piazza, Grand Union Hotel, Saratoga, New York, c.1870–80 (Source: Library of Congress)

'Throughout the late nineteenth century,' writes Jon Sterngass in his study of resort culture, 'Americans viewed Saratoga and Newport as archetypes representing conflicting ideals of social life.'[49] So James could very easily frame Saratogan loungers as the natural products of democratic architecture:

> They suggest to my fancy the swarming vastness – the multifarious possibilities and activities – of our young civilisation. [. . .] As they sit with their white hats tilted forward, and their chairs tilted back, and their feet tilted up, and their cigars and toothpicks forming various angles with these various lines, I seem to see in their faces a tacit reference to the affairs of a continent.[50]

James's miniature Republic of the piazza was governed by a patriarchal vision of the public sphere. As Molly Berger writes, 'at the most fundamental level the hotel, owned by a corporation chartered by the state, derived its existence from the consent of its franchised citizens, specifically its men, who then imbued it with public, masculine ownership.'[51]

American hotels were notorious for their male loungers (Figure 1.3). Touring New York's hotels in 1854, the British travel writer Isabella Bird noted that 'Groups of extraordinary-looking human beings' from 'all nations' were

Figure 1.3 Group on the porch, Saratoga Springs, New York, c.1860–70 (Source: Library of Congress)

'always lounging on the door-steps, smoking, whittling, and reading newspapers'.[52] 'The visitor enters a great hall by the front door, and almost invariably finds it full of men who are idling about,' Trollope wrote of his 1861 American tour, 'sitting round on stationary seats, talking in a listless manner, and getting through their time as though the place were a public lounging-room. And so it is. The chances are that not half the crowd are guests at the hotel.'[53] The American novelist and columnist Fanny Fern had a unique perspective on hotels and hotel piazzas: leaving her abusive second husband, she took her children and moved into a Boston hotel, where she took up a pseudonym and began her career in writing. In her column on 'The Etiquette of Hotel Piazzas', Fern shows women battling for space against the encroachments of men, as when a man drags his chair

> in front of the window, and with his heels on the pillar of the piazza, and his head close to your window, lights an odious pipe, and commences filling your room with its vileness, compelling your immediate retreat, because he prefers the spot opposite to your window to the smoker's end of the piazza.[54]

Fern, addressing her female readership as 'you, the occupant of a piazza-room', suggested that single hotel women invested their security and identity in the private rooms they hire, while men aggressively marked out their territory in the hotel's public areas.[55] The genders met each other across permeable thresholds. Men could look in ('Is it piazza-etiquette for strangers, who have ascertained "that that is *her* room" to lean close to the window-sill, the better to observe the habits of the animal inside?') while women could listen out ('when one's blinds are closed upon the unwary, it is interesting to hear a narrative of oneself from the stranger within the gates') and could gather intelligence on the public hypocrisies of private gentlemen ('It is also edifying to learn that [. . .] "Mr. Smith is a horrible brute, in his own room, to his wife, although always ready to pick up gracefully the handkerchief of any other lady"').[56] The need to strategically engage with and defend against patriarchal occupation of space was intimidating and unsettling for some guests. An editorial in *Harper's Weekly* in 1857 complained of the 'loathsome and contemptible [. . .] creatures' who 'hang about hotel doors and stare at passers-by'.[57] Letters to newspapers complained of men spitting on floors, putting feet on tables and lying across sofas.[58] Some hotels tried to circumvent the threat of lounging men by constructing separate, side 'ladies' entrances' or 'family entrances', effectively displacing women from the scene altogether.[59]

Yet the piazza's sheer size, its liminality between indoor and out, and its lack of fixed furniture offered the piazza-dweller of both genders a sense of social plasticity (Figures 1.4 and 1.5). Because this was such a new type of space, there were few guidelines for prescribed social behaviour compared to the clearly gendered zone of a ladies' parlour, or the old, accreted social codes of the dining room.[60] Fern notes that the question of piazza etiquette was still open: 'I am not aware that any one has treated this momentous subject.'[61] Another writer on manners, M. E. W. Sherwood, offers seemingly contradictory piazza advice. She introduces us to the figure of the female piazza lounger, and deplores her sexual suggestiveness ('to lounge about on the piazza at New London, Long Beach, Saratoga or Richfield in a *negligée* only suited to one's bedroom; [. . .] to be loud, defiant and brazen – has been the plan of too many American women in the great publicity of a watering place [. . .] Flirtation goes on conspicuously at these places'); yet Sherwood also condones shallow piazza acquaintanceships with hotel strangers:

> The gentleman should strive to avoid exhibitions of jealousy if his *fiancée* chooses to dance with another man, and the lady should be equally cool over her lover's behaviour. [. . .] It is quite proper at a watering place to speak without an introduction to those whom you meet every day. Gentlemen should always raise their hats to their fair fellow-boarders, and the acquaintance of ladies on a hotel piazza can hurt no one. The day the party leaves the hotel, that day the acquaintance can cease if the people so choose.[62]

Figure 1.4 Piazza of the Royal Poinciana, Palm Beach, Florida, c.1904
(Source: Library of Congress)

Figure 1.5 Piazza, Hotel Cape May, Cape May, New Jersey, c.1909
(Source: Library of Congress)

That sense of codes being gently loosened (with shifting definitions of what is 'quite proper') also comes through in James's essay on 'Saratoga' in regard to race. During the 1870s, there was a greater proportion of Black citizens in Saratoga (around 5 per cent) than in New York or Chicago, comprising tourists, residents and seasonal hospitality workers. All of the headwaiters and head bellmen in Saratoga's major hotels were Black, including at the Grand Union (Figure 1.6).[63] Members of the Black upper class frequented Saratoga during the 1870s and beyond. Most stayed in Black-owned inns rather than resort hotels, despite the brief window opened up by the Civil Rights Act of 1875 which tried to enforce equal treatment for Black tourists in American public accommodations.[64] Nonetheless, the Black presence in Saratoga is almost invisible to James, except in a brief moment when hotel labour becomes racially marked. James notes that the racially unmarked bourgeois guests are 'lounging with the negro waiters, and the boot-blacks, and the news-vendors' – a diverse assembly of proletariat and businessman, united in leisure rather than work.[65] The fleeting moment of male solidarity suggests how the open, horizontal piazza space might serve in a limited way to dissolve difference and hierarchy.

This kind of lounging and interpersonal mingling is peculiar to men in James. James's men often find pleasure in losing themselves in the company of otherness: in other people, or other objects. Victoria Coulson's analysis of material culture

Figure 1.6 United States Hotel dining-room, Saratoga, New York, c. 1870–80 (Source: Library of Congress)

in late James is enlightening on this point. In James's late prose, Coulson argues, the boundary between 'people, things, and signification' is 'sticky' – that is not only permeable and negotiable but messily entangled.[66] Coulson suggests that James's characters respond to 'stickiness' in a strikingly gendered fashion. 'While women fear and loathe the sticky touch of the abject,' Coulson writes, 'Jamesian men may find it delightful.' Jamesian women 'tend to prefer the material culture of the eighteenth century in general and of *Ancien Regime* France in particular', because it 'encodes ideas of clarity and control. It speaks of order and hierarchy, of secure structures of meaning in which physical objects loyally serve their human masters.'[67] James's men, on the other hand, will often seek out contaminating objects. They flock to furniture that is 'soft, padded, absorbing, a great enfolding substantial form whose materiality is inescapable'. Lounging, then, is the 'archetypal scene of [. . .] abject masculine sensibility' in James, where men wallow in each other's company while sinking into soft upholstery and clouds of smoke.[68]

That sensibility can be found in early James, too. James's Saratogan loungers – 'with their white hats tilted forward, and their chairs tilted back, and their feet tilted up, and their cigars and toothpicks forming various angles with these various lines' – recall the men lounging on the verandah of the National Hotel in Dickens's *Martin Chuzzlewit*, where Martin apprehends 'a great many pairs of boots and shoes, and the smoke of a great many cigars, but no other evidences of human habitation.'[69] In both cases, loungers are extravagant and untidy and perfectly sympathetic with the architecture, dissolving the difference between person and object, as well as between person and person. The angled limbs of male bodies blur with the angles of the stoop and with the things the men wear, sit on, and chew. The men become one with the matter that clutters up the piazza. James built this observation into his fiction. In *The Bostonians*, the 'elbowing loungers' in a Boston hotel lobby sit crammed 'amid the piled-up luggage' and 'the convenient spittoons'.[70] The luggage and spittoons serve as the auxiliary vessels of the loungers' identity. They are objects that contain material signs (precious or abject) of selfhood, in the process of being intermingled – or in the case of luggage, of being piled-up, shuffled and confused – with the selfhood of others. The chewing and spitting male body certainly makes its sticky mark on hotel space, but the body is also marked by the hotel, becoming no more unique than a piece of lobby furniture.

The hotel lounger's relationship to objects and furniture could be described, following Thomas Otten's reading of the Jamesian body, as prosthetic. The lounger's body 'clusters accessories around itself and [. . .] flows into them in a seemingly unbroken continuum of physiology and artifice.'[71] The prosthetic, Otten writes, was an important trope for Henry and William James, not only because of its place in American literature and culture (not least Ahab) but because their father had suffered a childhood accident that had left him with an amputated leg and a wooden replacement. Through the trope of the prosthetic, Otten argues, the James brothers began to think about the intimate relationship between the self and the artefact, about how the body can be remade and remodelled, and about how the periphery of the body, and the objects it presses against, become tingling extensions or expressions of consciousness. Henry's lounging men, by stretching themselves out into the world of matter, are manifestations of this prosthetic thinking. Their legs, at the extremity of the self, are both artefactual and sensual. Their legs are bulky, obvious, awkward, wooden; but they also feel, and in some sense think. One late example is Densher in *The Wings of the Dove*, who is said to appear 'vague without looking weak – idle without looking empty', attributes that are 'the accident, possibly, of his long legs, which were apt to stretch themselves'.[72] These are strange qualities to blame on one's legs, but the oddness of the description captures the contradiction of the Jamesian body – in which body parts can be completely disconnected from consciousness, behaving like automated attachments, as well as being entirely central to one's affective make-up. The long-legged man was not the only body type in James that confounded the line between consciousness, corporeality and the material world. But long legs help to make visible James's conception of the body's entangled relationship with matter by hyperbolising that relationship, by making it oversized and dissonant and comic.

Christopher Newman, the eponymous hero of *The American*, represents James's most thorough deployment of the American bourgeois body he found in Saratoga. Newman is the corporeal centre of *The American* rather than its central consciousness. His body is constantly on display, outstretched: '[L]ong, lean, and muscular'. Newman is first introduced to us 'reclining at his ease on the great circular divan' in the Louvre, 'with his head thrown back and his legs outstretched, [. . .] staring at Murillo's beautiful moon-borne Madonna in profound enjoyment of his posture'.[73] The novel describes, no fewer than ten times, his habit of sticking his hands in his pockets and 'stretch[ing] his long legs'.[74] James frames this habit as a manifestation of interiority: 'He performed the movement which was so frequent with him, and which was always a sort of symbol of his taking mental possession of a scene – he extended his legs.'[75] But in this early novel, it is the body that elaborately speaks and symbolises, while the interior remains quiet and inaccessible.

James sets Newman's malleable body against the solid habits and habitats of a withering French regime. Newman looks incredulously at the houses of Faubourg St Germain with their front elevations 'as impassive and as suggestive of the concentration of privacy within as the blank walls of Eastern seraglios'. He prefers an American 'ideal of grandeur' exemplified by 'a splendid façade diffusing its brilliancy outward too, irradiating hospitality'.[76] Newman's ideal is the corporate hotel. If Newman squirms in drawing-rooms, he is at ease in lobbies. He 'lounged through Belgium and Holland and the Rhineland', and finds himself 'addicted to standing about in the vestibules and porticos of inns'.[77] Once in Paris, Newman takes pleasure sitting '"in the court of the Grand Hotel [. . .] until two o'clock in the morning, watching the coming and going, and the people knocking about"'.[78] Newman's architectural ideal is explained in a section dealing with the purchase of his apartment in Paris:

> He possessed a talent for stretching his legs which quite dispensed with adventitious facilities. His idea of comfort was to inhabit very large rooms, have a great many of them, and be conscious of their possessing a number of patented mechanical devices – half of which he should never have occasion to use. The apartments should be light and brilliant and lofty; he had once said that he liked rooms in which you wanted to keep your hat on.[79]

What he's looking for is an apartment that functions like an American hotel: uncluttered with personal effects and wired up with technological novelties, an event space as well as a living space, as big and indifferent as a lobby. Newman likes these kinds of spaces because they are open and light, but also because they subtly loosen the influence of the conventions he finds so oppressive in Parisian society. In their largeness and emptiness, these spaces lack the familiar signals and structures (vestibules, nooks, internal doors) that served to determine and solidify Victorian manners. In making you feel like 'you wanted to keep your hat on' indoors, they denaturalise the relationship between established codes of behaviour and the built environment.

In a more sophisticated pairing of two body types than the pasteboard hero and villain of *Watch and Ward*, Newman gradually forms a bond with the faded aristocrat M. de Bellegarde, who has, compared to Newman's elongated form, an outdated kind of body: 'He was below the middle height, and robust and agile in figure.'[80] Furthermore, Bellegarde's body seems doomed to be treated badly by the advance of time. He 'had a mortal dread of the robustness overtaking the agility; he was afraid of growing stout; he was too short, as he said, to afford a belly.'[81] When Bellegarde visits Newman's lobby-like apartment on Boulevard Haussmann, he is hesitant and overawed, chortling nervously at his surroundings and uncertain about whether or not he can smoke: '"Surely, I may not smoke here [. . .] It is too large. It is like smoking in a ball-room, or a church"'.[82] It's a scene of the old order encountering the new: an aristocrat inside the bourgeois architecture of Haussmann's Paris. Newman insists that Bellegarde must smoke, and insists that he make as much noise as he likes: '"Laugh as loud as you please; I like to see my visitors cheerful."' He demonstrates the proper way to inhabit a cavernous room in his typical style: '"Well, here I am as large as life," said Newman, extending his legs'.[83] For James, such modern bourgeois interiors may be a little crass (Newman's apartment is 'gilded from floor to ceiling a foot thick') but they are also intriguing: allowing masculinity to uncoil, to fill the void left by tradition and manners with tobacco vapours, long legs and laughter.[84]

If Newman's body suits the new age, how does James imagine, figuratively, that he came to possess it? Is his body manufactured – a by-product of, or adaptation to, American capitalism? Or is it a natural, inherited, instinctual American body (the 'lean, sallow, angular Yankee of tradition'), suggestive of America's natural advantage in commercial affairs?[85] The metaphor of rubber and elasticity that James associates with Newman's stretching body suggests both possibilities. Rubber, writes David Trotter, was a substance 'at once ancient and modern, exotic and mundane', a natural plastic often violently expropriated by colonial regimes from the Brazilian and African tropics which, through chemical alteration and industrial manufacture, 'variously coated, supported, and interlined the miracles of modern engineering' in the nineteenth century.[86] The hybridity of rubber – 'the combination it encodes of the raw and the chemically cooked' – made it, Trotter argues, 'the focus of a compelling techno-primitivism' in Modernist culture.[87] In *The American*'s pre-Modernist moment at the beginning of the second industrial revolution, Newman stands as neither natural nor manufactured but as a techno-primitive hybrid. Newman is said to have emerged from 'the elastic soil of the West', and it is in this mythical American 'West' where the natural and industrial connotations of rubber become confused.[88] Trying to impress the Bellegarde family, assembled to assess his suitability as a marriage prospect, Newman begins an ill-fated story about his sister:

> 'One of them is married to the owner of the largest india-rubber house in the West.'
> 'Ah, you make houses also of india-rubber?' inquired the marquise.
> 'You can stretch them as your family increases,' said young Madame de Bellegarde, who was muffling herself in a long white shawl.
> Newman indulged in a burst of hilarity, and explained that the house in which his brother-in-law lived was a large wooden structure, but that he manufactured and sold india-rubber on a colossal scale.[89]

The Bellegardes, adopting a tone of 'vague urbanity', treat Newman as at once an exotic colonial subject, building strange little houses out of strange little materials, and a hyper-modern American capitalist.[90] Their moment of wilful cultural misprision conjures the image of a high-tech western homestead, encoded simultaneously with the tropics and with the factory, constructed with natural materials yet capable of synthetic transformations. The moment reveals how Newman is doubly dubious for the Bellegardes, both for his primitivism and for his technologies. Yet the marquise's vision of an *unheimlich* rubberised log cabin strangely befits the eponymous American, whose elastic form is so often in conflict with the inelastic House of Bellegarde and the inelastic domestic architecture of Europe. Through the surreal juxtapositions of joke-logic or dream-logic, the Bellegardes find a way to comprehend Newman's hybrid, prostheticised body.

'I AM NOT A COURIER'

The leg-stretching hotel lounger played an equally interesting role at the margins of James's early fiction. In 'An International Episode', the travelling Englishmen at the centre of the tale peer curiously into a hotel lobby and see 'a couple of hundred men sitting on divans along a great marble-paved corridor, with their legs stretched out'.[91] *The Bostonians* is rife with unnamed loungers, including in Ransom's little Cape Cod hotel ('Local worthies, of a vague identity, used to lounge there [. . .]. They tipped back their chairs against the wall, seldom spoke'),[92] and in a large Boston hotel, seen at twilight ('Behind great plates of glass the interior of the hotels became visible, with marble-paved lobbies, white with electric lamps, and columns, and Westerners on divans stretching their legs').[93] But it is the lounger as choric background figure in 'Daisy Miller' that demonstrates why James began to consider this body type to be disruptive to novelistic form, as well as to the social scene. The lounger's very anonymity turns out to be contaminative, threatening to collapse the boundary between the peripheral and the central in his text.

James shifted his emphasis from the masculine toward feminine subjectivity after *Roderick Hudson* and *The American*. Even before his shift, however, James was sketching out a future novel with a heroine at its centre and the lounger as her backdrop. When James considered the lounger in his ethnography of Newport and Saratoga, and 'dream[ed] momentarily of a great American novel', he doubted such an indistinct figure could sustain a narrative on his own.[94] Narrative would emerge instead from the singular and the self-contained. Women, socially and aesthetically dominant in hotel space, assumed that role:

> You are struck, to begin with, at the hotels, by the numerical superiority of the women; then, I think, by their personal superiority. It is incontestably the case that in appearance, in manner, in grace, and completeness of aspect, American women surpass their husbands and brothers; the relation being reversed among some of the nations of Europe.[95]

In their 'superiority' and 'completeness', the women stand detached from the crowd: resplendent, iconographic and alone.[96] In his account, James separates women by consigning them to a separate paragraph of analysis. Once introduced, the magnificent singularity of feminine self-fashioning begins to corrode the masculine performance of collective ease:

> She walks more or less of a queen, however, each uninitiated nobody. She often has, in dress, an admirable instinct of elegance and even of what the French call 'chic'. The instinct occasionally amounts to a sort of passion; the result then is wonderful. You look at the coarse brick walls, the rusty iron posts of the piazza, at the shuffling negro waiters, the great tawdry steamboat-cabin of a drawing-room – you see the tilted ill-dressed loungers on the steps – and you finally regret that a figure so exquisite should have so vulgar a setting.[97]

It's as if storm clouds have shrouded the piazza and everything is seen through murky light: the open spaces have been hemmed with coarse brick walls, the piazza has rusted, the waiters are once again burdened by work, the drawing-room is seasickly, and the loungers have grown more dishevelled. When set in relief against the charismatic presence of hotel women, the lounger abruptly becomes a vulgar presence. Lounging men and striding women here represent two directly opposed modes of being. Where loungers foster interpersonal identities, hotel women, James suggests, are not contaminated by the crowd, despite being comfortable with crowds. Their aspiration, their expression of freedom, is to rise above the mess of the merely common: a 'democratisation of elegance' for those who have enjoyed 'neither the advantages of a careful education nor the privileges of an introduction to society'.[98] They seek to break out of their constrictive class position through the performance of a grander self. A heroine such as this, James decided – 'infinitely realistic and yet neither a schoolmistress nor an outcast' – could galvanise a great social novel, a new kind of social novel:[99]

> You feel the impertinence of your old reminiscences of English and French novels, and of the dreary social order in which privacy was the presiding genius and women arrayed themselves for the appreciation of the few. The crowd, the tavern-loungers, the surrounding ugliness and tumult and license, constitute the social medium of the young lady you are so inconsistent as to admire; she is dressed for publicity.[100]

James sketches out the gendered roots of an archetypal narrative of consumer capitalism that will persist beyond Joan Crawford's star turn in *Grand Hotel* (1932). At its heart is an encounter between figure and setting, individual and crowd, stars and bit players, where the background is defined by masculine tumult and the foreground by feminine staginess in a dialectic of watching and being watched. This dynamic became the basis for 'Daisy Miller', which plays out an unspoken conflict between loungers and singular women in a Swiss hotel.

'Daisy Miller' opens in Vevey, on Lake Geneva. At the time, Vevey was being transformed by a flood of investment capital channelled through public limited companies, beginning with La Société Immobilière de l'Hôtel de Vevey, which constructed the town's Grand Hotel and a public promenade in 1868.[101] The rise of a flashy hotel culture and the decline of the Swiss *pension* are presented in James's story as a kind of American conquest: 'it may be said, indeed, that Vevey assumes at this period some of the characteristics of an American watering place. There are sights and sounds which evoke a vision, an echo, of Newport and Saratoga.'[102] Daisy Miller and Frederick Winterbourne, two Americans staying in the same hotel, have arranged a flirtatious (and, according to the rules of the game in Europe, frankly improper) outing to the Castle of Chillon, a popular tourist spot across the lake. The Castle reverberates in the text as a symbol of democratic rebellion, recalling Byron's 'The Prisoner of Chillon'. Daisy appears to be the embodiment of these democratic energies: she is keen on the public steamer, for instance, while Winterbourne is the kind of man who prefers to travel by private carriage. Before their journey, Winterbourne waits for Daisy in their hotel lobby. This scene is important precisely because it is brief and interstitial. Nothing of narrative consequence happens, leaving room for the interstitial practices or 'distracted vision' of everyday life – waiting, lounging, watching.[103] The scene stages a triangular encounter between Winterbourne, Daisy and the lobby loungers, each with their own forms of 'posture, movement, and space-holding'.[104] The scene defines the central conflict of the tale as a struggle between three forms of everydayness – each inflected with gender and class – played out in shared public space:

> He waited for her in the large hall of the hotel, where the couriers, the servants, the foreign tourists, were lounging about and staring. It was not the place he would have chosen, but she had appointed it. She came tripping downstairs, buttoning her long gloves, squeezing her folded parasol against her pretty figure, dressed in the perfection of a soberly elegant travelling-costume. Winterbourne was a man of imagination and, as our ancestors used to say, of sensibility; as he looked at her dress and, on the great staircase, her little rapid, confiding step, he felt as if there were something romantic going forward. He could have believed he was going to elope with her. He passed out with her among all the idle people that were assembled there; they were all looking at her very hard; she had begun to chatter as soon as she joined him.[105]

For John Carlos Rowe, Daisy's 'openness and social gregariousness have a democratic aura', and her ease among the loungers hints at her 'identification with some sort of populist solidarity, albeit left undeveloped in *Daisy Miller*'. The scene, he argues, unites a bourgeois woman with proletarian servants and bourgeois foreigners, suggesting 'one way James imagined how groups differently marginalized in different eras might take a historically long view that would allow them to build effective coalitions.'[106] The key to Rowe's argument is that Daisy forges an unconscious bond with the easy-going loungers – that she, in effect, 'fraternizes with people from the working class'.[107] Daisy, however, merely performs in front of the gathered crowd, using their anonymity as a mirror for her own star status. While the diverse men have formed an unspoken alliance through their everyday habits, Daisy is not part of it. In a novella dotted with images of encirclement and closed social circles, and culminating in a scene in the Roman Colosseum, Daisy finds herself persistently surrounded by an amorphous network of lounging men, whose voyeurism and fantasising begin to circulate in the form of malicious gossip. By the end of the novella in Daisy's hotel in Rome, 'every one is talking about her',[108] there is an 'exchange of jokes' about her 'between the porter and the cab-driver',[109] and 'a smile goes round among all the servants when a gentleman comes and asks for Miss Miller'.[110] The figure of Daisy activates a caustic misogyny always implicit in the exclusive circle of male loungers.

What actually seems to be happening in the lobby is a conflict between the anonymous and the named. As in 'Saratoga', James's idea of a hotel 'general public' is male. Between their 'lounging' and 'staring' and Daisy's 'tripping' and 'chatter[ing]' stands Winterbourne.[111] Blank and formless, Winterbourne is a mediating figure through which the events are focalised. His eyes scan Daisy with desire ('squeezing her folded parasol against her pretty figure') while glancing with revulsion at the loungers ('they were all looking at her very hard'). The reason the loungers seem so much less exuberant and more threatening than elsewhere in James (their aimless 'lounging about' and blank 'staring' suggesting impassivity, boredom and judgment) is that Winterbourne is actively trying to repel them, to distinguish his own lustful stare from the lustful stare of the loungers, and to elevate himself above the status of *just another man*. This problem of good manners or good form becomes a more general problem of novelistic form. Winterbourne's self-proclaimed innocence regarding his relations with Daisy relies on him playing the part of a major character, and not just one more 'gentleman' who 'comes and asks for Miss Miller'.[112] The presence of the blank loungers – a promiscuous mix of workers and foreigners like Winterbourne – threatens to drag Winterbourne to the bottom of a murky pond of anonymity.

Winterbourne's fear of becoming a minor character is amplified by the significant presence of 'couriers', as well as servants and tourists, in the crowd of loungers in the lobby.[113] These couriers are the unnamed doubles of a more significant courier in the novella: Eugenio, who works for the Miller family. Eugenio, wielding a proper name, 'superb whiskers', 'a velvet morning-coat', 'a brilliant watch-chain' and an attitude, is an unusual kind of servant.[114] More potently for Winterbourne, Eugenio is 'tall' and sizes up Winterbourne 'from head to foot'. Eugenio not only organises the Millers' itinerary and luggage but effectively assumes the role of patriarch over a fatherless family. He uses hotel space to fashion himself as a major character. Mrs Costello, Winterbourne's aunt, rubbishes Eugenio for his presumption:

> They treat the courier like a familiar friend – like a gentleman. I shouldn't wonder if he dines with them. Very likely they have never seen a man with such good manners, such fine clothes, so like a gentleman. He probably corresponds to the young lady's idea of a Count. He sits with them in the garden, in the evening. I think he smokes.[115]

'Eugenio' nonetheless still bears the anonymous designation of 'the courier'. He is both a named character and a reproducible, exchangeable embodiment of a social and narrative function. Etymologically, the courier embodies an architectural function as well, through the word's link to the original Italian *corridore* (a runner) and *corridoio* (a running place). Mark Jarzombek writes in his history of corridors that:

> In the fourteenth century, in both Spanish and Italian contexts, a *corridor* referred not to a space but to a courier, someone who as the word's Latin root suggests could run fast. A *corridor* might have been a scout sent behind enemy lines, a governmental messenger, a carrier of money, or even a negotiator arranging mercantile deals and marriages.[116]

'Taking seriously the historically and linguistically embedded relationship between person, communication, and concrete structure', writes Kate Marshall, 'requires maintaining contact with the corridor's immanent mediality,'[117] This etymological link to the interstitial only redoubles Eugenio's allegiance to the world of the lobby-lounging and corridor-lounging male. Eugenio, as courier, is nobody and anybody. For all his magnificence and handsomeness, there are numerous men in 'Daisy Miller' who look and act like him. There is Giovanelli, Daisy's Roman admirer, who is significant enough to be given a name, yet who also seems, in both senses of the word, like a stereotype: 'He smiled and bowed and showed his white teeth, he curled his moustaches and rolled his eyes, and performed all the proper functions of a handsome Italian at an evening party.'[118] There are several other nameless admirers, such that every time Daisy attends a party she seems to bring along a different 'gentleman with a good deal of manner and a wonderful moustache'. (Winterbourne imagines Daisy permanently 'surrounded by half-a-dozen wonderful moustaches'.)[119] Given the absence of Mr Miller and the removal of any natural claim to patriarchal authority, the men of 'Daisy Miller' are constantly trying out and exchanging roles, performing more or less plausible impersonations of a patriarch. Accordingly, the multitude of suitors begin to blur together with Eugenio, not only because Giovanelli and the courier are financially interlinked (Eugenio introduced Giovanelli to Daisy, and if they marry 'the courier will come in for a magnificent commission'), but also because 'the courier continues to be the most *intime*' of all of Daisy's intimate acquaintances: the moustache she loves best.[120] Mrs Costello is insistent on this point, and her insinuations of scandal go beyond the suggestion that common men should know their place. The subtext of her horror is that at any time any of the bewhiskered men could stand in as Daisy's father, servant or lover.

These men are dangerous for Winterbourne because they embody a flexible, comingled form of male subjectivity through which servants, bourgeois gentlemen or counts, minor characters or major characters, all look the same: an identity that is anonymous and interchangeable yet also charismatic and scene-stealing. Winterbourne, on the other hand, lacks a compelling identity or the ability to replicate one. He has no self-fashioned magnificence, as Eugenio and Giovanelli and Daisy do. He is barely even described, appearing as a blind spot in a text overflowing with ethnographic details. He moves, too, differently than others in the text. Where other men lounge and lean (we first see Giovanelli leaning in a louche manner against a tree: he is said to harbour 'far-stretching intentions'), and Daisy appears in perpetual motion with a rapid, tripping step ('"If I didn't walk I should expire"', she says), Winterbourne is repeatedly accused by Daisy of being 'stiff': '"I noticed you were as stiff as an umbrella the first time I saw you"'.[121] The phallic image (in the New York Edition, Daisy's line is changed to 'I noticed you've no more "give" than a ramrod the first time ever I saw you') represents Winterbourne's masculinity as complete, self-contained, and inelastic.¹²² His is a body stiffened by manners, a body that appears 'formal' and 'quaint', rejecting the untidiness and looseness of human instinct.¹²³ Winterbourne is an aristocratic idler rather than a bourgeois lounger, more aligned with Valentin de Bellegarde than his compatriot Christopher Newman. He 'linger[s]' rather than lounges.¹²⁴ He does not mingle, or sink into deep couches. He does not wish to immerse himself or become contaminated by Europe. His rhetoric of innocence regarding his relations with Daisy is a rejection of the stickiness of social relations.

It is Winterbourne's umbrella-like stiffness or lack of 'give' that puts him at risk of erasure. It reduces him to a flat plane or a black line on a page. Paradoxically, the character with whom we spend the most time is somehow also the most invisible and the most two-dimensional. The stretchable male body of the lounger, meanwhile, is able to stride into the centre of the text – his occupation of space suggesting mass and density and dimensionality, even if his personality doesn't appear properly three-dimensional. Like Bellegarde, Winterbourne risks becoming corporeally outdated and being overtaken by the elastic bourgeois body. Observe, for instance, how passive Winterbourne becomes, how he seems to disappear, while in the company of Daisy and while encircled by loungers:

> As the day was splendid, however, and the concourse of vehicles, walkers, and loungers numerous, the young Americans found their progress much delayed. This fact was highly agreeable to Winterbourne, in spite of his consciousness of his singular situation. The slow-moving, idly-gazing Roman crowd bestowed much attention upon the extremely pretty young foreign lady who was passing through it upon his arm; and he wondered what on earth had been in Daisy's mind when she proposed to expose herself, unattended, to its appreciation.¹²⁵

Winterbourne finds himself in a 'singular situation', which in this context seems like a diminution, a realisation that he is single and apart. Unlike Daisy, he is unwilling and unable to play the role of the splendid grandee for the crowd, while his efforts at playing the splendid suitor to Daisy have failed. He is, in this scene, reduced to being a courier, a minor character: 'His own mission, to her sense, apparently, was to consign her to the hands of Mr. Giovanelli.'¹²⁶ Winterbourne complacently acquiesces. He fades – a mere arm to thread a hand through – while Daisy (the star) and the crowd (her audience) visually expand, filled out with strings of adjectives and adverbs (the 'slow-moving, idly-gazing Roman crowd', and the 'extremely pretty young foreign lady') that delay the forward movement of the sentence, just as the crowd delays their stroll. Even Winterbourne's narrative authority – his control over the movement and tempo of the story – must yield to the tempo created by the abundant physicality of Daisy and the loungers of Rome.

It is Eugenio, the self-made major character, who delivers the strongest attack not only on Winterbourne's presumption of innocence but on his presumption of centrality: 'The courier stood looking at Winterbourne, offensively. The young man, at least, thought his manner of looking an offence to Miss Miller; it conveyed an imputation that she "picked up" acquaintances.'[127] The meaning that Winterbourne chooses to take from the incident is that Eugenio believes him to be another of Daisy's acquaintances – a minor player. This supposed insult informs the later scene in the lobby, where a whole group of lounging couriers stare at Winterbourne and Daisy. The lobby scene becomes an echo chamber of Eugenio's rebuke and Winterbourne's guilt. In the way it mirrors, duplicates and disembodies Eugenio's stare, it is also a reminder of how individuality is created and dissipated among the loungers, of the way couriers can become Eugenios and Winterbournes can become 'acquaintances' in a hotel crowd. 'Daisy Miller' asks us to question the difference between the major and the minor in a world where authority is an effect produced by those with a brilliant mimetic capacity and a few material trinkets. 'I am not a courier', Winterbourne oddly protests to his aunt, yet this is a tale where men, like hotel rooms, are indistinguishable and interchangeable.[128] The monstrous commercial hotel and the elastic male body confound the stable hierarchies upon which Winterbourne relies.

'Daisy Miller' appears to mark a shift in James's work away from the paradigmatic long male body of Christopher Newman toward the feminine. Yet by dislodging the lounger from the centre of his work, James paradoxically reaffirms his interest in this body type. That interest always lay in the long male body's anonymity, in its entangled relations with other bodies and other objects, and in 'Daisy Miller' this anonymity is more pronounced and more dangerous than ever. James introduces the inelastic Winterbourne as an agent of containment, yet his capacity to stand apart and stand firm is strongly called into question as the tale unfolds. Indeed, what 'Daisy Miller' points to is the slow yet inevitable defeat of Winterbourne and his kind: the decline of the rigid aristocratic idler and his rhetoric of innocence, and the irrepressibility of the elastic bourgeois lounger, who – no matter how minor he appears in James's fiction – will nonetheless find a way to reclaim its centre.

As for Daisy Miller herself – a character seemingly entrapped by the narrative logic generated by the interrelation of striding women and lounging men – she too violates the border between major and minor. As Winterbourne notes with indignation, her final act is to become a watcher and a lounger, or a deathly parody of one: 'lounging away the evening in this nest of malaria', enveloped in a 'villanous miasma', alongside Giovanelli in the bowels of the Colosseum.[129] In the novella's ironic late turn, Daisy, sick of performing to unappreciative crowds, seeks to slip into the shadows and become a minor character, a mere lounger, in her own tale. Yet in the process of re-gendering the lounger, the figure is transcoded under the sign of death. The stickiness of masculine impersonal intimacy here becomes miasmic. According to Tina Young Choi, 'miasma theory', as the Victorian medical community and sanitary reformers began to articulate it in the 1830s and 1840s, 'envisioned the body as necessarily incoherent, as something that could disperse and circulate like the contents of a leaky cesspool or a volatile compound'.[130] Miasma traduced the boundaries not only between individual selves, but between classes and between the living and the dead, as smells, respirations and bodily after-effects intermingled promiscuously beyond physical demarcations. Miasma was therefore a means of imagining the involuntary connectedness, both troubling and productive, of bodies in urban modernity. But while the experience of social being that Choi calls 'physiological intersubjectivity'[131] is also the basis of the male lounger's charismatic power, for Daisy, physiological intersubjectivity will lead to her death – a death that bluntly polices the boundaries of social possibility in this story.

Notes

1. Henry James, *A Small Boy and Others* (New York: Charles Scribner's Sons, 1913), pp. 7–8.
2. Ibid., p. 30.
3. Ibid., p. 29.
4. Henry James, 'London', in *Collected Travel Writings: Great Britain and America*, ed. Richard Howard (New York: Library of America, 1993), p. 37.
5. Gage McWeeny, *The Comfort of Strangers: Social Life and Literary Form* (Oxford: Oxford University Press, 2016), p. 1.
6. Henry James, *What Masie Knew*, in *Novels: 1896–1899*, ed. Myra Jehlen (New York: Library of America, 2003), p. 559. My emphasis.
7. Henry James, *The Portrait of a Lady*, in *Novels: 1881–1886*, ed. by William T. Stafford (New York: Library of America, 1985), p. 223–4. My emphasis.
8. Junius Henri Browne, *The Great Metropolis: A Mirror of New York* (Hartford, CT: American Publishing, 1869), p. 398.
9. Max Beerbohm, 'Mr Henry James [c. 1904]', in N. John Hall, *Max Beerbohm Caricatures* (New Haven, CT: Yale University Press, 1997), p. 39.
10. Hotels are repeatedly described as 'promiscuous' by James. For instance, from his description of a Washington hotel in 'An International Episode': 'The ground floor of the hotel seemed to be a huge transparent cage, flinging a wide glare of gaslight into the street, of which it formed a sort of public adjunct, absorbing and emitting the passers-by promiscuously.' In *Complete Stories: 1864–1874*, ed. Jean Strouse (New York: Library of America, 1999), p. 329. James here and elsewhere uses the older sense of 'promiscuity', defined by the OED as 'Consisting of assorted parts or elements grouped or massed together without order; mixed and disorderly in composition or character'. But the word is shaded with a more euphemistic meaning. This is most apparent in his 1902 essay on Gabriele D'Annunzio, which inspired Beerbohm's caricature. James writes that the Italian poet's treatment of 'sexual passion' is vulgar because it is '*only* the act of a moment [. . .]. Shut out from the rest of life, shut out from all fruition and assimilation, it has no more dignity than – to

use a homely image – the boots and shoes that we see, in the corridors of promiscuous hotels, standing, often in double pairs, at the doors of rooms.' 'Gabriele D'Annunzio', in *Literary Criticism: French Writers, Other European Writers, The Prefaces to the New York Edition*, eds Leon Edel and Mark Wilson (New York: Library of America, 1984), p. 942.
11. Betsy Klimasmith, *At Home in the City: Urban Domesticity in American Literature and Culture, 1850–1930* (Durham, NH: University of New Hampshire Press, 2005), p. 54.
12. Richard Salmon, *Henry James and the Culture of Publicity* (Cambridge: Cambridge University Press, 1997), p. 11.
13. Victoria Coulson, 'Prisons, Palaces, and the Architecture of the Imagination', in *Palgrave Advances in Henry James Studies*, ed. Peter Rawlings (Basingstoke and New York: Palgrave Macmillan, 2007), p. 187.
14. Thomas Otten, *A Superficial Reading of Henry James: Preoccupations with the Material World* (Columbus, OH: Ohio State University Press, 2006), p. 135.
15. Jeffory A. Clymer, 'The Market in Male Bodies: Henry James's *The American* and Late-Nineteenth-Century Boxing', 25 (2) *Henry James Review* (Spring 2004), pp. 127–45; and Eric Haralson, 'James's *The American*: A (New)man is Being Beaten', 64 (3) *American Literature* (September 1992), pp. 475–95.
16. Daniel Hannah, '"Massed Ambiguity": Fatness in Henry James's *The Ivory Tower*', 53 (4) *Twentieth Century Literature* (Winter 2007), pp. 460–87.
17. Dell Upton, 'Architecture in Everyday Life', 33 (4) *New Literary History* (Autumn 2002), p. 720.
18. Mary Ann O'Farrell, 'Manners', in *Henry James in Context*, ed. David McWhirter (Cambridge: Cambridge University Press, 2010), pp. 192–202.
19. Upton, 'Architecture in Everyday Life', p. 719.
20. Ibid., p. 720.
21. In *A Small Boy and Others*, James recalls donning an outfit inherited from his older cousin, Johnny, for a fancy-dress party. He is too small for the costume – a silk, beribboned version of a French stevedore's outfit. He stood 'short of my proper form by no less than half a leg' and feels he has 'sadly dishonoured, or at least abbreviated, my model'. It 'would have seemed, I conceive, a less monstrous act to attempt to lengthen my legs than to shorten Johnny's *culotte*'. James, *A Small Boy and Others*, p. 191.
22. Henry James, *Henry James: A Life in Letters*, ed. Philip Horne (London: Allen Lane, 1999), pp. 107–8 (15 June 1879).
23. William Veeder, 'Henry James and the Uses of the Feminine', in *Out of Bounds: Male Writers and Gender(ed) Criticism*, eds Laura Claridge and Elizabeth Langland (Amherst, MA: University of Massachusetts Press, 1990), p. 221.
24. Henry James, *Watch and Ward* in *Novels: 1871–1880*, ed. William T. Stafford (New York: Library of America, 1983), p. 3 and p. 45.
25. James, *Watch and Ward*, p. 45.
26. Lawrence Frank, *Charles Dickens and the Romantic Self* (Lincoln, NB: Nebraska University Press, 1984), pp. 26–8.
27. James, *Watch and Ward*, p. 45.

28. Ibid., p. 133.
29. Ibid., pp. 49–50.
30. Henry James, *Roderick Hudson*, in *Novels: 1871–1880*, ed. William T. Stafford (New York: Library of America, 1983), p. 200.
31. Henry James, 'The Pension Beaurepas', in *Complete Stories: 1874–1884*, ed. William L. Vance (New York: Library of America, 1999), p. 413.
32. Marilyn Johnson, 'Art Furniture: Wedding the Beautiful to the Useful', in *Pursuit of Beauty: Americans and the Aesthetic Movement*, ed. Doreen Bolger Burke (New York: Metropolitan Museum of Art, 1986), p. 159.
33. Henry James, *The Bostonians*, in *Novels: 1881–1886*, ed. William T. Stafford (New York: Library of America, 1985), p. 814.
34. Henry James, *The Portrait of a Lady*, Vol. 1 (New York: Charles Scribner's Sons, 1908), p. 327.
35. 'Club Life in New York', *New York Times*, 8 November 1885, p. 6.
36. Hyacinth is a hybrid – a petit-bourgeois book-binder with aristocratic blood – while the long-legged Owen Wingrave and Owen Gereth are more or less aristocratic.
37. Henry James, *The American*, in *Novels: 1871–1880*, ed. William T. Stafford (New York: Library of America, 1983), p. 545.
38. Sarah Luria, 'The Architecture of Manners: Henry James, Edith Wharton and The Mount', in *Domestic Space: Reading the Nineteenth-Century Interior*, eds Igna Bryden and Janet Floyd (Manchester: Manchester University Press, 1999), p. 188.
39. James, *Watch and Ward*, p. 138.
40. Sandoval-Strausz, *Hotel*, p. 20.
41. *A Description of Tremont House* (Boston: Gray and Bowen, 1830), pp. 8–9.
42. Quoted in Berger, *Hotel Dreams*, p. 80.
43. Maureen E. Montgomery, 'Henry James and "The Testimony of the Hotel" to Transatlantic Encounters', in *Anglo-American Travelers and the Hotel Experience in Nineteenth-Century Literature*, eds Monika M. Elbert and Susanne Schmid (New York and London: Routledge, 2018), p. 160.
44. Katz, 'The Hotel Kracauer', 11 (2) *Differences* (Summer 1999), p. 138.
45. Douglas Tallack, '"Waiting, Waiting": The Hotel Lobby in the Modern City', in *The Hieroglyphics of Space*, ed. Neil Leach (London: Routledge, 2002), p. 141.
46. Henry James, 'Saratoga', in *Collected Travel Writings: Great Britain and America*, ed. Richard Howard (New York: Library of America, 1993), p. 750.
47. Ibid., p. 751.
48. Ibid., p. 752.
49. Jon Sterngass, *First Resorts: Pursuing Pleasure at Saratoga Springs, Newport, and Coney Island* (Baltimore, MD: Johns Hopkins University Press, 2001), p. 182.
50. James, 'Saratoga', p. 752.
51. Molly Berger, 'A House Divided: The Culture of the American Luxury Hotel, 1825–1860', in *His and Hers: Gender, Consumption, and Technology*, ed. Roger Horowitz (Charlottesville, VA: University Press of Virginia, 1998), pp. 42 and 48.
52. Isabella Bird Bishop, *The Englishwoman in America* (London: John Murray, 1856), p. 342.

53. Anthony Trollope, *North America: Volume II* (Philadelphia: Lippincott, 1863), p. 287.
54. Fanny Fern, *Ginger-Snaps* (New York: Carleton, 1870), p. 206.
55. Ibid., p. 208.
56. Ibid., pp. 206–7.
57. Quoted in Carolyn Brucken, 'In the Public Eye: Women and the American Luxury Hotel', 31 (4) *Winterthur Portfolio* (Winter 1996), p. 209.
58. Berger, 'A House Divided', p. 55.
59. Brucken, 'In the Public Eye', p. 211; Sandoval-Strausz, *Hotel*, p. 168.
60. Berger, 'A House Divided', p. 51.
61. Fern, *Ginger-Snaps*, p. 206.
62. M. E. W. Sherwood, *The American Code of Manners: A Study of the Usages, Laws and Observances which Govern Intercourse in the Best Social Circles* (New York: W. R. Andrews, 1880), pp. 159 and 166–7.
63. Myra Beth Young Armstead, *Lord, Please Don't Take Me in August: African Americans in Newport and Saratoga, 1870–1930* (Champaign, IL: University of Illinois Press, 1999), pp. 39 and 97.
64. William B. Gatewood, *Aristocrats of Color: The Black Elite 1880–1920* (Fayetteville, AR: University of Arkansas Press, 2000), p. 206.
65. James, 'Saratoga', p. 753.
66. Victoria Coulson, 'Sticky Realism: Armchair Hermeneutics in Late James', 25 (2) *Henry James Review* (Spring 2004), p. 119.
67. Ibid., pp. 18 and 17.
68. Ibid., pp. 122 and 118.
69. Charles Dickens, *Martin Chuzzlewit*, ed. by Margaret Cardwell (Oxford and New York: Oxford University Press, 1984), pp. 300–1.
70. James, *The Bostonians*, p. 897.
71. Otten, *A Superficial Reading*, p. 24.
72. Henry James, *The Wings of the Dove*, in *Novels: 1901–1902*, ed. Leo Bersani (New York: Library of America, 2006), p. 248.
73. James, *The American*, p. 515.
74. Ibid., p. 575.
75. Ibid., p. 593.
76. Ibid., p. 555.
77. Ibid., p. 575.
78. Ibid., p. 531.
79. Ibid., p. 588.
80. Ibid., p. 602.
81. Ibid., pp. 602–3.
82. Ibid., p. 601.
83. Ibid., p. 602.
84. Ibid., p. 588. James also described the Paris Opéra as 'gilded all over a foot thick'. Newman's apartment is clearly meant to typify Second Empire bourgeois architecture. Henry James, *Parisian Sketches: Letters to the New York Tribune, 1875–1876*, eds Leon Edel and Ilse Dusoir Lind (London: Rupert Hart-Davis, 1958), p. 11.

85. James, 'Saratoga', p. 752.
86. David Trotter, 'Techno-Primitivism: Á Propos of *Lady Chatterley's Lover*', 18 (1) *Modernism/modernity* (January 2011), pp. 150 and 1.
87. Trotter, 'Techno-Primitivism', p. 151.
88. James, *The American*, p. 532.
89. Ibid., p. 646.
90. Ibid.
91. Henry James, 'An International Episode', in *Complete Stories: 1874–1884*, ed. William L Vance (New York: Library of America, 1999), p. 329.
92. Henry James, *The Bostonians, in Novels: 1881–1886*, ed. William T. Stafford (New York: Library of America, 1985), p. 1122.
93. Ibid., p. 1197.
94. Henry James, 'Newport', in *Collected Travel Writings: Great Britain and America*, ed. Richard Howard (New York: Library of America, 1993), pp. 762–3.
95. James, 'Saratoga', p. 752.
96. Women were 'objects within the panorama, framed by the hotel setting', and 'an essential element of the luxury promised by these first-class hotels'. Brucken, 'In the Public Eye', p. 218.
97. James, 'Saratoga', p. 753.
98. Ibid., p. 753.
99. Henry James, 'Newport', p. 763.
100. James, 'Saratoga', pp. 753–4.
101. Julie Lapointe, 'Les Sociétés Anonymes à Vocation Hôtelière de l'Arc Lémanique (1826–1914)', in *Le Client de l'Architecte. Du Notable à la Société Immobilière: Les Mutations du Maître de l'Ouvrage en Suisse au XIXe Siècle*, ed. Dave Lüthi (Lausanne: Études de Lettres, 2010), p. 219.
102. Henry James, 'Daisy Miller: A Study', in *Complete Stories: 1874–1884*, ed. William L. Vance (New York: Library of America, 1999), p. 238.
103. Michael Taussig, 'Tactility and Distraction', in *Beyond the Body Proper: Reading the Anthropology of Material Life*, eds Margaret Lock and Judith Farquhar (Durham, NC: Duke University Press, 2007), pp. 259–61.
104. Upton, 'Architecture in Everyday Life', p. 719.
105. James, 'Daisy Miller', pp. 260–1.
106. John Carlos Rowe, 'Henry James in a New Century', in *A Companion to American Fiction, 1865–1914*, eds Robert Paul Lamb and G. R. Thompson (Malden, MA: Blackwell, 2005), p. 524.
107. Rowe, 'Henry James in a New Century', p. 523.
108. James, 'Daisy Miller', p. 277.
109. Ibid., p. 293.
110. Ibid., p. 277.
111. Ibid., pp. 260–1.
112. Ibid., p. 277.
113. Ibid., p. 260.
114. Ibid., pp. 248–9.
115. Ibid., p. 251.

116. Mark Jarzombek, 'Corridor Spaces', 36 (4) *Critical Inquiry* (Summer 2010), p. 731.
117. Kate Marshall, *Corridor: Media Architectures in American Fiction* (Minneapolis, MN and London: University of Minnesota Press, 2013), p. 19.
118. James, 'Daisy Miller', p. 280.
119. Ibid., p. 265.
120. Ibid., pp. 284 and 264.
121. Ibid., pp. 273, 275 and 289
122. Henry James, 'Daisy Miller', in *Daisy Miller, Pandora, Patagonia, and Other Tales*, ed. Jean Gooder (New York: Charles Scribner's Sons, 1909), p. 83.
123. James, 'Daisy Miller', pp. 259 and 268.
124. Ibid., p. 260.
125. Ibid., p. 270–1.
126. Ibid., p. 271.
127. Ibid., p. 249.
128. Ibid., p. 251.
129. Ibid., pp. 291 and 290.
130. Tina Young Choi, *Anonymous Connections: The Body and Narratives of the Social in Victorian Britain* (Ann Arbor, MI: University of Michigan Press, 2015), p. 34.
131. Ibid., p. 37.

2

STAIN RESISTANCE: THE PARLOUR AND READING-ROOM

If hotel lobbies were sticky and contaminative, the Victorian corporate hotel's vast public parlours were notable for their blankness. In the accounts of many writers, hotel parlours (variously delineated as the drawing-room, the sitting-room or the lounge, and often explicitly designated as a space for 'ladies') were described as moonscapes of social aridity. Back in Saratoga's Grand Union Hotel, Henry James describes an 'immense parlour' which seemed 'scantily furnished in proportion to its size. A few dozen rocking-chairs, an equal number of small tables, tripods to the eternal ice-pitcher, serve chiefly to emphasize the vacuous grandeur of the spot' (Figures 2.1 and 2.2).[1] In a Yorkshire seaside resort in Mary Elizabeth Braddon's *Lady Audley's Secret* (1862), an immense parlour becomes a trackless waste: 'it was the landlord himself who ushered Robert into a dreary wilderness of polished mahogany tables and horsehair cushioned chairs, which he called the coffee-room.'[2] Anthony Trollope, poking his nose into the ladies' drawing-rooms in American hotels, finds 'empty deserts':

> Into these rooms no book is ever brought, no needlework is introduced; from them no clatter of many tongues is ever heard. On a marble table in the middle of the room always stands a large pitcher of iced water, and from this a cold, damp, uninviting air is spread through the atmosphere of the ladies' drawing-room.[3]

Figure 2.1 Grand Union parlour, Saratoga Springs, New York, c.1870–80
(Source: Library of Congress)

Figure 2.2 Main parlour, US Hotel, Saratoga Springs, New York, 1895
(Source: Library of Congress)

In the novella *Tony, The Maid* (1887), by émigré American writer Blanche Willis Howard, the hotel parlour is an unnavigable sea: 'In the ladies' drawing room, [. . .] on the vast expanse of shining floor, small and isolated groups – like a kind of human archipelago – gathered evenings with needlework and looked askance at one another.'[4] And for George Augustus Sala, a ladies' parlour is a tomb: 'Once or twice I have tried the ladies' drawing-room in American caravansaries; but I have speedily grown frightened of that family vault handsomely carpeted, with corpses in crinoline, scattered about like the embalmed monks in the catacombs of Palermo.'[5] Writing at the peak of crinoline's vogueishness and circumference, Sala aligns the dress with the space: both are stiff, oversized, unnatural, carceral. The femaleness of hotel parlours, and their failure to encode the values of privacy and modesty demanded of respectable bourgeois women, contributed to the horror of these spaces. Negative reactions to hotel parlours exceeded the cultural disquiet caused by the lobby, which was coded as male.

Barren hotel parlours were an early iteration of a distinctly contemporary form of public space. They were precursors to service and transit zones like airport lounges, bus interchanges, food courts and highway service stations; places of impermanence, individuation, inactivity, ephemera and disposability; the kind of spaces described by the anthropologist Marc Augé as 'non-places'. In his account of 'supermodernity', Augé traces this experience of placelessness back to nineteenth-century tourism:

> It is among solitary 'travellers' of the [nineteenth] century [. . .] that we are most likely to find prophetic evocations of spaces in which neither identity, nor relations, nor history really make any sense; spaces in which solitude is experienced as an overburdening or emptying of individuality, in which only the movement of the fleeting images enables the observer to hypothesize the existence of a past and glimpse the possibility of a future.[6]

These 'prophetic evocations' of non-places shouldn't, of course, lead us to conflate Victorian travel cultures with supermodernity, or to theorise the Victorian hotel ahistorically. With its urban centrality and civic amenity, the grand hotel functioned (in Augé's terms) as a monument and a crossroads, a place of gathering and encountering as well as disassembling. As Robert A. Davidson writes of the grand hotel:

> The possibility of contact between people was attenuated through one's presence in a space that had accrued identity and cachet as a destination unto itself and that at the same time was connected with its locality while serving as a bridge space to the global. In short, the traditional grand hotel existed as a 'place'.[7]

Nonetheless, Augé's keywords here are provisionally useful, and this chapter explores the extent to which identity, relations and history were attenuated in the grand hotel parlour and to what effect.

The hotel parlour was frequently read in this period against its domestic equivalent. For many Victorian writers, hotel parlours signified the absence of home, or the hollowing out of home, replacing what Marc Katz calls the '"deep space" of bourgeois autonomy' with a depthless copy. As Katz writes, the hotel parlour was 'a semblance of a semblance' of domestic space, 'a recapitulation of a coded set of depth effects'. Analysing the grand hotel of the 1920s via the cultural criticism of Siegfried Kracauer and Walter Benjamin, Katz argues that the hotel embodied 'a complex logic by which the nomadic, smooth space of advanced capital continues to call up nostalgic depth effects through various forms of place-making'. As the grand hotel became increasingly rationalised in its form and operation, it 'strategically employed domestic signs to mask its functionalist apparatus'.[8] These nostalgic depth effects long pre-dated the 1920s, and were deeply rooted in Victorian domestic ideology. Sandoval-Strausz's study of hotel history documents how nineteenth-century American hotels from their earliest incarnation adopted the familiar terminology of the family-run tavern or the household, even as they radically reconfigured the domestic spatial paradigm.[9] By 1861, New York's St Nicholas Hotel, one of the largest and most extravagant of its era, could advertise its 1,000-guest capacity and its dining rooms that could seat hundreds, even as it claimed to provide 'home-like comforts'.[10] Yet hotels like these, containing luxury ground-floor shops as well as grand public event spaces, offered mobile upper-class women an emphatically un-home-like experience of urban commercial life: 'many ladies likely came to the St. Nicholas precisely because it was not like home,' writes Barbara Penner.[11] In monster hotels like the St Nicholas, the domestic nomenclature of 'drawing-rooms' persisted, yet the real inspiration for their divisions of space and labour were commercial and government buildings, from arcades and treasuries to the cellular organisation of alms-houses and prisons.[12] As the improvisation of the hotel manager in *Lady Audley's Secret* indicates ('a dreary wilderness [. . .] which he called the coffee-room'), there is a degree of arbitrariness in the signifiers used to designate these new architectural forms.[13]

Looking closely at the way hotels and homes were counterposed in various genres of Victorian writing, it is fascinating to see writers try to articulate an aesthetic of private possession that marked the home, in their view, as distinct and superior. In the home decoration manual *The House Beautiful* (1878), the American Ruskinian art critic Clarence Cook celebrates the home-like charms of English inns ('there was nothing in the room that suggested it had been furnished "on contract"') while deploring the capitalist principles of duplicability and efficiency that determine American hotel style:

> At this hotel we were shown into a big bare room, containing just what was necessary for decent living – a carpet, a bed, a bureau, a looking-glass, a table and four chairs, with the inevitable furnace-hole in the wall [. . .] – a scientific desolation (your room being exactly like every other in the caravansary) which we Americans have carried to perfection.[14]

Cook repeatedly associates hotels with factories ('a popular metaphor for the depersonalizing regimes of the "grand hotel" in this period', according to Kevin J. James[15]), suggesting that hotels are cavernous mechanical contrivances, governed by the iron laws of the market. For Cook, hotels fail to create an interior that stands apart from the roar of production and consumption. Nevertheless, the private home, in Cook's account, is not untouched by the factory. Though he advocates handcrafted, bespoke and second-hand furniture (sourced, preferably, from local farmhouses), he also spends many pages detailing ways to properly curate and display generic decorative pieces. Trifles and bric-à-brac, 'when they are well chosen, and have some beauty of form or color, or workmanship, to recommend them, have a distinct use and value, as educators of certain senses.'[16] Homes mediate and contain consumer culture, Cook argues, through tasteful curation. As David Ellison writes in his account of Victorian interiors, 'Middle-class women, and the servants under their direction, were asked to arrange, clean, burnish, and augment commodities, creating a physical and temporal space between the coarseness of habitual use and the vulgar sheen of newness.'[17] Curation removed the taint of the factory, a process of taking possession that preserved the illusion of the parlour as an inviolable interior. As Ellison writes:

> This ability to bring coherence to the flux of the mobilized interior, to differentiate possessions within from circulated goods without, and to make, in short, transformative sense of the internal and internalized world of things was crucially important as the flow of goods entering the home became less the uncertain trickle of testamentary [disposition] and more a torrent of new consumer commodities.[18]

That torrent of consumer commodities was, indeed, what separated the domestic parlour from the barren desert of the hotel parlour. Paradoxically, while hotels were reviled by some critics for their unmediated proximity to the marketplace, it was their lack of generic knick-knackery that made them seem less lived-in and authentic. According to William Laird MacGregor's Californian travel narrative, what is missing in hotel spaces is numberless and nameless ornaments:

> Although very handsomely furnished as regards carpets, chairs and upholstery, there is a formality, a want of home life about it. No books,

no flowers, none of those thousand little articles for feminine use which you find in private homes, that add so much, not only to the appearance but also to the comfort of a sitting-room.[19]

For Braddon, writing in 1875 in her capacity as editor of *Belgravia*, it is not just the number and the quality of ornaments that is wanting in hotels, but the mess that they create and the air of contingency that marks the domain of the self: 'To my mind your hotel drawing-room has, at the best, a dismal look. It lacks the home-look of occupation, the friendly familiar untidiness of a room that is lived in.'[20]

The association between crammed interiors and 'life' recalls mid-nineteenth-century theories of literary realism, in which a writer's attention to inconsequential details and the thingness of things was the means by which they accessed the real. It's the language we find, for instance, in George Henry Lewes's review of *Jane Eyre*, which he praises for being 'filled out [. . .] with details [. . .]. We have spoken of the reality stamped upon almost every part; and that reality is not confined to the characters and incidents, but is also striking in the descriptions of the various aspects of Nature, and of the houses, rooms, and furniture.' Brontë's descriptions read, says Lewes, like 'a page out of one's own life'.[21] In reading hotel interiors, Victorian writers like Braddon looked for signs of life in random, redundant, messy detail: in the 'thousand little articles' of bric-a-brac, furniture, clothing and amusement (or the 'cheap common things which are the precious necessaries of life', as George Eliot writes in her defence of realism in *Adam Bede*), which do not symbolise individually, but which, when enumerated en masse, generate a background hum that thickens an illusion of reality.[22] In Roland Barthes's terms, these writers walked into a hotel parlour and found its 'reality effect' lacking.[23] The troubling nature of hotel parlours, then, was about more than a want of comfort, modesty, privacy or feminine charm. Critics were fundamentally disconcerted by the uncanniness of living spaces that failed to register the presence of human occupation and possession.

According to Victorian theories of realism, a readable room tells of life: its stuff, properly arranged, burnished and possessed, tells of the individual or family who lives there. The character of the room is imprinted with the character of the inhabitant. The domestic parlour, as Thad Logan argues, was believed to be both private and social, involving the 'articulation of interiority and the interpellation of the "speaking" subject within a larger system of linguistic and social relations'.[24] The domestic parlour was intended as a space where the character of the self, and in particular the female self, was projected outward to the world, where its distinct being was rendered legible in the form of signs for the visitor to read. We find this idea expressed in Florence Caddy's narrativised home decoration book, *Lares and Penates: or, The Background of Life* (1881). Caddy contrasts the impersonality of hotels with the personality of homes: 'Least of all does Alford House resemble an hotel', because it 'bears the stamp of individuality in every front: inventive, without eccentricity'.[25] The trace of the individual – their 'stamp' – certifies the home's value. For Walter Benjamin, the surfaces of the late-nineteenth-century bourgeois home were so thoroughly stamped with the signs of ownership that they projected a kind of defensive inhospitality:

> If you enter a bourgeois room of the 1880s, for all the coziness it radiates, the strongest impression you receive may well be, 'You've got no business here.' And in fact you have no business in that room, for there is no spot on which the owner has not left his mark – the ornaments on the mantelpiece, the antimacassars on the armchairs, the transparencies in the windows, the screen in front of the fire.[26]

Benjamin argues that the bourgeois home collected and cultivated traces of inhabitation. Designed as a private encasement, it created a domain of selfhood that cushioned the individual from the perceived threats of the exterior. Memories and private habits were encoded in the arrangement of its furniture and in the literal impressions left on its surfaces. The bourgeois home fetishised materials like plush, 'in which traces are left especially easily'.[27] Its interior was so thick with signs that it brought into being the detective story and the figure of the master detective, who 'inquires into these traces and follows these tracks', working effectively like a materialist critic of bourgeois culture.[28]

Hotel interiors were not likewise stamped. The markers of individuality sought by readers trained by the realist novel – contingency, redundant detail, friendly familiar untidiness – were missing. But it was also impossible to imagine a referent – a character, a moral being – that would make these markers appear meaningful. In joint-stock hotel parlours, the putative speaking subject was not the individual or the family, but the corporation itself. And as Paddy Ireland writes, nineteenth-century company law was beginning to define the corporation 'as a depersonalised and reified entity, which, in a certain crucial sense, lack[ed] an inherent nature or character'.[29] The hotel thereby severed the rhetorical connection between character and living space, repelling the desire to read the trace of the self on its ostensibly domestic surfaces. As M. E. James declared in *How to Decorate Our Ceilings, Walls and Floors* (1883), 'A room, however beautifully decorated, that tells nothing of the man or woman who lives in it, must always have a grand-hotel effect, chilling and depressing.'[30] Looking for the reality effect, critics found the grand-hotel effect; looking for individuality, they found a corporation. The uncanniness of corporate decoration provided a material encounter, therefore, with the deterritorialising and defamiliarising powers of capital. When Victorian writers leapt into the figurative ('empty deserts', 'dreary wilderness', 'human archipelago'), they were grasping for a means of apprehending the ungrounded and unhomed quality of hotel space as capitalist phantasmagoria. As Anna Kornbluh writes, 'The reality of capital is poetic, unreal, and fictitious; realist depiction of it must therefore involve feigning and forming.'[31]

The Grand Hotel Effect

If the bourgeois interior resembled a clue-filled crime scene, the hotel parlour's blankness resembled a crime scene's scrubbed aftermath. Hotel interiors endlessly tried to remove the trace of previous guests (whether or not they died in the night). Traces of inhabitation (like Fanny Fern's description of a hotel bed 'with sheets still warm with the print of the last occupant', alongside 'wash-bowls grimy with departed paws') were deeply abject in hotel space and were the mark of a failing institution.[32] Threatened daily by the prints and paws of previous occupants, hotels tried to occlude decay by washing and maintaining, and replacing depleted stocks (towels, stationery, crockery) with ready-to-hand duplicates. The objective of hoteliers was, in essence, to suppress time, to reproduce the comforts of an old family home but without the wear and tear, the patina of history.[33] Henry James was unhappily reminded of hotel surfaces when he observed the restored pavements of St Mark's in Venice. Once 'dark, rich, cracked, uneven, spotted with porphyry and time-blackened malachite, polished by the knees of innumerable worshippers', they now seemed like 'the ocean in dead calm', an aesthetic familiar from 'the floor of a London club-house or [. . .] a New York hotel'.[34]

Hotel materials, like vitreous hotel dinnerware (often marketed under the trade name 'hotel china'), assisted in this suppression of time. Designed specifically for heavy-frequency usage in hospitality, hotel china was a thick, heavy, high-fired ceramic, with a smooth and shiny finish. Widely advertised in the 1870s and 1880s, hotel china was the ponderous and far less delicate counterpart of fine china and antique porcelain, which was in high demand as a collectible during this period. Henry James repeatedly deployed porcelain as a metaphor for human frailty and the wounds of life-experience, as in the comparison of Madame Merle in the *Portrait of a Lady* with 'the delicate specimens of rare porcelain' which stand on her mantlepiece – one of which 'already has a wee bit of a tiny crack', as Osmond cruelly observes.[35] Hotel china, conversely, was resistant to cracks, stains, burns and corrosive chemicals, and did not betray its age like the old floors of St Mark's. As one manufacturer promised, it was 'warranted not to crack, and will not turn black when chipped'.[36] Oscar Wilde, for one, was not a fan of this ponderous material. Lecturing New Yorkers on the state of American interior design in 1882, he complained that Chinese labourers in San Francisco drank 'out of the daintiest of china cups, while in costly hotels he was given his chocolate in cups an inch and a quarter thick.'[37]

Resisting the patina of history was also a public health issue. Notorious disease outbreaks underlined the potentially devastating health risks immanent in transient, densely packed hotel populations: like the 'National Hotel disease' case of 1857 in Washington, DC, in which hundreds of hotel guests were sickened and dozens died from a dysentery-like infection. It was suspected at the time to have been caused by sewer miasmas emanating from beneath the establishment.[38] As the sanitary reform movement gained momentum in the 1870s, terms like 'scientific', 'healthful,' 'sanitary' and 'hygienic' were incorporated into grand hotel marketing arsenals. The opening of New York's Buckingham Hotel in 1877, for example, was celebrated with a barrage of this sanitary reform language: the hotel was said to be 'ventilated under the personal supervision of Professor Hyslop'.[39] Nancy Tomes demonstrates how grand hotels were 'among the first commercial institutions to show the marks of the growing concern about infectious disease', from the implementation of modern plumbing, water filtration and germicide in the 1870s, to the early adoption of vacuum cleaners, sanitary dishwashers and washing machines. At the end of the nineteenth century, grand hotels were already instituting the now-familiar practice of presenting new cakes of soap in their original wrappers for each new guest. 'The demand for roller towels, soap dispensers, and room cleansers,' writes Tomes, 'resulted in whole specialised lines of sanitary goods developed just for hotels and similar establishments.'[40]

The corporate hotel's concern with sanitation extended to interior design. It was becoming apparent, as Eileen Cleere writes of domestic sanitary reform debates, that 'sanitation consisted of more than adequate plumbing and good ventilation; cleanliness was an aesthetic and architectural decision that had converted the ephemera of taste into the science of health.'[41] The practical realities of mass hospitality already necessitated new and unfamiliar surface treatments. The 1859 *British American Guide-Book* notes with some surprise that 'In almost all hotels' in America, 'there are no carpets in the dining-saloons, which rather detracts from the apparent comfort in the minds of those who have always been accustomed to dine in rooms nicely carpeted.'[42] The sanitary reform movement only accelerated the phasing out of impressionable surfaces of all kinds. From the 1870s, correspondents in popular and trade journals worried about dankness and dust in hotel rooms, and advocated for fewer textiles and fewer porous surfaces. It was argued that such materials cultivated traces of inhabitation: writes one correspondent to *The Nation*, heavy drapes 'hold the odor of the possible cigar of the previous occupant.'[43] The solution, according to the essayist Gail Hamilton, was to replace 'velvet pile', 'silken brocade' and 'stuffed and sweltering chairs' with 'little light cane sofa[s]' and 'straw matting', which do not hoard 'uncanny deposits for sensitive lungs, and delicate nerves, and vivid imaginations'.[44] By the 1890s, this vision was widely practised, and was ratified by medical professionals. A meeting of the Société Normande d'Hygiène Pratique, reported on by the American medical press, heard a paper on the transmission of infectious diseases in hotels. The paper argued that 'heavy materials, like plush and velvet, should never be used' in hotel rooms for health reasons, as the infections of transitory guests 'retain their virulence' on impressionable surfaces. Walls should be 'hard finished or coated with an impermeable paint which can be washed'. Carpets, furthermore, 'should be rigorously prohibited' along with unwashable curtains, while furniture should be simple, with easily wipeable varnished or waxed surfaces. Such precautions had already been carried out in some hotels, the paper claimed, with sanitary reforms 'destined to extend rapidly'.[45] The ideal hotel interior was therefore becoming increasingly antiseptic at the end of the century. 'Hotels', writes physician and sanitary reformer George Vivian Poore in 1897, 'are like hospitals in this respect, that guests know nothing of the previous occupants of their room, and it must often be that such ignorance is blissful.'[46]

In public and institutional structures from hotels to banks and railway waiting-rooms, a new generation of industrial materials was responding to this need for impermeability and changing the phenomenological experience of surfaces and spaces. Modern encaustic tiles, though still expensive, became fashionable in British public architecture in the mid-nineteenth century and then in America during the 1870s. Clean, decorative, regular and duplicable, decorative encaustic surfaces, along with marble or tile harlequin floors, rapidly became signature transatlantic hotel materials. A London magazine in 1865 compared what used to pass for hotels – 'the squat, confined, and dingy lobby, the irregular narrow passages' – with the new-generation of 'monster hotels under the Limited Liability Act', financed by joint-stock companies: with their 'lofty and well-proportioned hall[s], with [their] evergreens and encaustic tiled flooring, the wide and airy corridors, and the spacious, well-ventilated rooms'.[47] An 1874 entry in *Chambers's Encyclopedia* notes that encaustic tiles were superseding floor-cloths for high-traffic lobbies and corridors.[48] The American Encaustic Tiling Company, at one time the largest tiling manufacturer in the world, was founded in 1875 and specialised in large institutional orders, including for the original Waldorf-Astoria in New York. 'These tiles', wrote one enthusiastic columnist at the opening of the Astoria in 1897, were 'absolutely impervious to moisture and capable of being kept as clean as porcelain'. The Astoria used tiles for floors and walls, 'wherever it was deemed desirable to have a surface that would retain no possible atom of dirt or disease.'[49] The construction of stain-resistant, 'fresh and luminous' spaces (as James in *The American Scene* describes the Royal Poinciana hotel in Palm Beach, Florida), still seemed new and beguiling in the first years of the twentieth century. 'It is difficult to render,' James writes of the same hotel, 'the intensity with which one felt the great sphere of the hotel close round one, covering one in as with high, shining crystal walls, stretching beneath one's feet an immeasurable polished level' (Figure 2.3).[50] Likewise, Mrs Tailleur in May Sinclair's *The Immortal Moment* (1908) is delighted by the surfaces of a Dorset hotel, with its 'clean walls, white as the Cliff it stood on', its 'wide, polished

Figure 2.3 Dining-room, Hotel Royal Poinciana, Palm Beach, Florida, 1894
(Source: Library of Congress)

spaces and clean, brilliant backgrounds, yards of parquetry for the gliding of her feet, and monstrous mirrors for reflecting her face at unexpected angles'.[51] As opposed to plush and impressionable cocoons, these were hard, shimmering stage-sets that flashed reflections across their surfaces.

Masquerade

As the corporate hotel aesthetic emerged, the hotel's blank surfaces became a means of expressing broader cultural anxieties about identity and fraud in a credit economy. The hotel's long association with narratives of fraudulence (from sensation fiction and dime-novels to detective fiction and *Roman noir*) was more than simply a response to the real-life hotel hustles documented in the newspapers. The association speaks to a perception that hotels were symptoms of a more general breakdown in social trust. Much like the drifting Mississippi steamboat that contains the action of Melville's *The Confidence Man*, hotels were a means of figuring modern social relations 'in which the traditional bonds and obligations of kinship, neighbourhood, and shared political, religious, and cultural commitment have been unmoored.' Just as Melville's novel, according to Peter Knight, 'offers a self-reflexive meditation on the problem of reading in a market society', so hotel settings were places which foregrounded the difficulty of reading: not merely because they were full of strangers performing their identities, more or less convincingly, in a social marketplace, but because the hotel space itself was a difficult text to read.[52] The blankness of hotel living spaces undermined what Karen Halttunen calls the sentimental typology of behaviour, in which surface appearances, like one's mode of dress and one's living spaces, were an expression of one's inner moral qualities: a typology that predominated in the conduct manuals of early industrial America.[53] Hotel parlours presented as untrustworthy to nineteenth-century writers trained to look for moral qualities in the arrangement of interiors.

In Britain, anxieties about reading and urban identity were absorbed into the sensation novel, a genre that repeatedly turned to hotels as emblematic settings. In Wilkie Collins's *Basil* (1852), an early progenitor of sensation tropes, the villain Robert Mannion uses a hotel as the base for his fraudulent operations. Mannion is pitted against Collins's eponymous protagonist, who begins the novel with the belief that 'To study the appearance of a man's dwelling-room, is very often nearly equivalent to studying his own character' – as if the material home is the gold standard upon which one's amorphous 'character' is underwritten and guaranteed.[54] But the horror of *Basil* is that surface appearances no longer underwrite value in this way. This is partly connected (as it is in many novels of the period) to the confounding unreadability of the nouveau riche home. The middle-class suburban residence of the Sherwins, where Basil woos his fiancé, is described as 'oppressively new': with a 'brilliantly-varnished door' which 'cracked with a report like a pistol when it was opened', wallpaper that 'looked hardly dry yet', a table 'in a painfully high state of polish' and books which had 'never been moved or opened since they had been bought'.[55] With its slippery surfaces, the Sherwins' home suppresses the traces of inhabitation and personality in the manner of a hotel. There are clear similarities between the *haut-bourgeois* revulsion of hotel parlours and the revulsion of nouveau riche homes like this one. Yet the nouveau riche home is not unreadable in the manner of a hotel. David Trotter, examining a series of varnished nouveau riche homes in Victorian fiction, argues that 'A certain momentum still agitates faintly within the high state of polish' of such spaces: 'the stickiness which coats [the] new identity' of its inhabitants 'and the smell which hangs about it suggests they have not yet settled fully into position.'[56] In their hasty fabrication of a new class identity, the Sherwins (and others, like the Veneerings in *Our Mutual Friend* and the Brigstocks in *The Spoils of Poynton*) have been stained by the process of repairing and veneering over the cracks in their old identities. The stickiness of their new selves will never fully dry and will always betray their impersonations. The nouveau riche, then, are legible as such in Victorian fiction, more often than not. The impersonation is rarely pulled off. Their representation in Victorian fiction serves, in fact, to reinforce faith in the hermeneutic power of the novel to detect and decipher the reality beyond the surface of things, and to police hierarchies of taste and class.

What *Basil* is more concerned with is a more fundamental decoupling of character and surface appearance, and a more vertiginous form of illegibility brought about by modern capitalism. Eva Badowska argues that the sensation novel, in its content, form and pyrotechnic impact on the book market, was an expression of modernity's restless quest for novelty and its consequent 'tendency toward rapid obsolescence'. Nothing is permanent in the sensation novel. Rather than leaving a sticky residue or an unmistakable imprint, the acts of impersonation and fraud that fill the genre's pages are, at least initially, not manifest on the surface of things. There is no lingering smell of veneer betraying the feigned class identities in Braddon's *Lady Audley's Secret*, for instance. Badowska writes:

> [Braddon's novel] questions the reader's faulty assumption that historical events radically mark their actors and scorch the very ground upon which they take place. [. . .] Instead, the novel challenges the reader's belief in the existence of indelible stains by what amounts to an invitation to life in the modern uncanny. According to Braddon, to live in the modern world is to be deprived of the certainty provided by mandrake and blood stains; it is to live in a state of perpetual suspension [. . .].[57]

In sensation novels, terrible crimes may lurk, unseen, within beautiful families and beautiful homes. The genre therefore 'warns us that signifiers and signifieds may not function according to the principle of resemblance', and teaches us to see 'the peacefulness of the bourgeois dwelling as a masquerade'.[58]

In *Basil*, this breakdown in signification is embodied in the impassive confidential clerk Robert Mannion. Mannion's smooth and ageless face ('There was not a wrinkle or line anywhere') is a 'mask' which 'baffled all inquiry'.[59] And unlike Dickens's Wemmick in *Great Expectations*, Mannion keeps his mask in place inside his private home, which does not function as a display case for his authentic self: 'Almost all men, when they stand on their own hearths, in their own homes, instinctively alter more or less from their out-of-door manner: the stiffest people expand, the coldest thaw a little, by their own firesides. It was not so with Mr. Mannion.'[60] It is not surprising, then, that Mannion's central act of villainy is performed inside a hotel – inside a space that tells nothing. Basil hails a cab and follows Mannion to a freshly minted railway hotel in a 'colony of half-finished streets, and half-inhabited houses, which had grown up in the neighbourhood of a great railway station'[61] – the kind of London district that Dickens described in *Household Words* as 'unsettled, dissipated, wandering'.[62] Basil hears, through the papery walls of an adjacent hotel room, his fiancé Margaret Sherwin carrying out a covert affair with Mannion, an affair 'foully hidden for months on months' beyond Basil's detection.[63] After falling in love with Margaret on the 'perambulatory exhibition-room' of a London omnibus, among the 'glittering trinkets' of the city's commercial and financial core (said to resemble the 'fairy-land architecture of a dream'), Basil begins to apprehend his misprision of Margaret and Mannion as a 'hideous phantasmagoria' produced, in some sense, by the modern city itself.[64] Surface appearances in this novel are not a gold standard, grounding a sentimental typology of behaviour; they are a scrim for a magic lantern show.

The breach opened up in *Basil* and sensation fiction at large, between appearance and character, signifier and signified, was part of a larger 'problematic of representation' that rippled through the culture of the mid-century credit economy: a creeping suspicion of face value. Mary Poovey argues that a problematic of representation emerges periodically in capitalism during moments of crisis, like market panics, when the 'authenticating ground' upon which the economy is built seems to evaporate from below, calling the concept of value radically into question.[65] This mid-century crisis was prompted by a loss of faith in the authenticating ground of 'character', and its ability to morally undergird and stabilise financial speculations. As Andrew H. Miller argues:

> Individual investment was subject to personal accountability at the same time that the social relations on which one formerly would have based those investments were becoming impersonal and opaque. [. . .] Knowledge of 'personal character' fades and little is immediately available to replace it; but the stakes in choosing safely to whom one will entrust money remain high.[66]

The proliferation of financial instruments and the growth of the corporate form meant that one could no longer trust surface appearances to divine a business's character and therefore its creditworthiness. In early joint-stock ventures, for example, the lack of regulation, the anonymity and fluidity of directorship and the proliferation of nominal partners and passive investors with little personal knowledge of the company's organisation meant that the 'character' of such ventures was abstract, diffuse and illegible.[67] In 1844, a British Select Committee on Joint-Stock Companies, responding to a string of high-profile corporate fraud cases, noted:

> [Fraudulent and illegitimate businesses] adopt, as far as possible, the outward characteristics common to those of the best kind. They exhibit an array of Directors and officers, – announce a large capital, – adopt the style and title of a company, – issue plausible statements, intimating excellent purposes, – [. . .] use some conspicuous place of business, in a respectable situation, – and employ throughout the country respectable agents and bankers. But many of these characteristics are fictitious.[68]

Such fictitious ventures were not indelibly stained by their illegitimacy. Rather, they provided an early warning that 'signifiers and signifieds may not function according to the principle of resemblance' in the era of corporate capitalism, something that only became clear upon their collapse.

This problematic of representation is played out in Henry James's early short story 'Guest's Confession', published in two parts in the *Atlantic Monthly* in 1872.[69] James read and reviewed Braddon and Collins in the 1860s, and 'Guest's Confession' is a cousin of sensation, with its interest in documents and identity and its patriarchal romance plot shaded by the threat of blackmail. Set in a hotel in an unnamed New England resort town, the story is presided over by a generic financier figure, Edgar Musgrave, and narrated by his stepbrother, David. Edgar ruthlessly separates business from sensibility. When speaking of his business partner, the eponymous John Guest, Musgrave says that he hasn't 'seen the man more than three or four times; our dealings have generally been by letter.'[70] He participates, then, in a new economy of increasingly impersonal networks of association, mediated by contracts, paper money and litigation rather than bonds of personal trust. The system breaks down, inevitably, due to the problem of reading in a market society. Guest misrepresents an ambiguous telegram from Edgar in order to speculate on the sale of Edgar's bonds and loses twenty thousand of Edgar's dollars. Yet Guest is not legible as a villain: 'The last person you'd suspect,' as Edgar admits. When David meets Guest, he muses:

> This genial gentleman, then, was embodied fraud! this sayer of civil things was a doer of monstrously shabby ones! [. . .] I stood for some time reflecting how guilt is not the vulgar bugaboo we fancy it, – that it has organs, senses, affections, passions, for all the world like those of innocence.[71]

Edgar confronts Guest when they unexpectedly check into the same resort hotel. The hotel, in its flattening out of bourgeois interiority, is the ideal setting for an exploration of the unreadability of character and the diminution of trust as the basis for economic relations. The hotel sitting-room in which the climactic confrontation in 'Guest's Confession' takes place, with its duplicability, permeability and surface blankness, becomes a means of figuring the unmooring of stable and legible identities.

The story's confrontation begins when Edgar spots Guest on the hotel piazza among the late revellers. The piazza at night is a blurry, impressionistic place, where shadowy couples lounge: 'Here and there the warm darkness was relieved by the tip of a cigar in suggestive proximity to a light corsage.'[72] One of those cigar-tips turns out to be Guest. His lover departed, Guest is now alone.

Edgar decides to herd Guest indoors, along with Edgar's stepbrother David, the story's narrator:

> A series of small sitting-rooms opened by long windows upon the piazza. These were for the most part lighted and empty. Edgar selected one of them, and, stopping before the window, beckoned to me to come to him. Guest, as I advanced, bestowed upon me a scowl of concentrated protest. 'Be so good as to walk in,' said Edgar [. . .].[73]

The traversable window is shut, the curtains are drawn, the door to the internal corridor is closed and some of the lights are put out. Suddenly we are contained within a vacant interior, with furnishings starkly etched in their scientific desolation: a sofa, a writing table, a chair, a lamp, a pen, a blotting-book, an inkstand. The room is a duplicate: one of a presumably identical 'series' of sitting-rooms laid out in a grid along the piazza facade, making Edgar's selection of one entirely arbitrary. Like John Guest's name – the perfect 'John Doe' for hotel society – the sitting-room is generic, fungible and anonymous.

Curtained and closed up, the sitting-room initially seems like a controlled environment, carefully separated from the seductions of the piazza. Inside, we appear to have entered a different order of representation as well as a different kind of space. The lurid night-time impressionism of the piazza, with its floating, disembodied forms, settles into a plainer register in the sitting-room, and we can look at Guest 'more distinctly'.[74] As Edgar dictates and Guest copies out his words like a clerk, it seems as though the men have refashioned the sitting-room into a simulacrum of an office chamber. The long windows, however, help to turn the scene inside-out. Out on the piazza, the narrator could make out faces and shapes because of a 'zone of light projected from a window'; now inside one of these lit rooms, the characters keep pacing to the windows, pulling aside the curtains and looking out.[75] The two spaces bleed into each other.[76] The sitting-room is a place of permeable and contingent boundaries: not only in the way its facade peels open with full-length windows but also in its lack of genre markers to demarcate the practices expected of its inhabitants. Soon, the atmosphere becomes unusually clammy for a Jamesian tale. The narrator's heart is 'beating very violently', and Edgar, who has dropped the curtains and slammed the door shut 'with a passionate kick', seems to 'tremble and quiver with inexorable purpose'.[77] Guest's face has 'flushed crimson, and the great sweat-drops trickled from his temples', and he is commanded to strip down to his shirt-sleeves and beg for forgiveness on his knees.[78] Sublimating the language of the boudoir, the scene's psychosexual subtext is barely suppressed. The sitting-room is not only coloured by the luridness of the adjacent piazza, it seems to be a darker iteration of the piazza's libidinal drives. Yet the designation of the room shifts again. This will be, Edgar declares, Guest's confessional space: 'Your shirt-sleeves will serve as a kind of sackcloth and ashes,' he shouts to the man on his knees. 'Fold your hands, so.'[79] The sitting-room transforms into a fraudulent site of worship, like the chapel on the outskirts of the resort town with its 'counterfeit graining scarcely dry on its beams and planks'.[80] As Guest signs the paper, his lover, wearing a shawl, bursts into the room and reclaims it as a space of sentimental domesticity ('What on earth have you been doing here? Business? You've no business with business. You came here to rest'), but she is too late to ward off the atavistic spectres that have emerged out of this blank room.[81]

Like the chapel's 'counterfeit graining', the sitting-room's collapsing boundaries are figuratively criminalised, as when Edgar shouts at Guest, 'If it's not forgery sir, it's next door to it, and a very flimsy partition between.'[82] As the conversation heats up, the crisis of trust in business is again imagined in architectural terms. Guest declares:

> 'I supposed I was dealing with a man of common courtesy. But what are you to say to a gentleman who says, "Sir, I trust you," and then looks through the keyhole?'
> 'Upon my word, when I hear you scuttling through the window,' cried Edgar, 'I think it's time I should break down the door.'[83]

The sitting-room is entangled in the language of fraud because its own identity is ungrounded. Nominally a space for domestic sentiments, it shape-shifts throughout the scene, becoming a site of projection and fantasy. Cut loose from its grounding, this room is a free-floating signifier, an anywhere and a nowhere. It is an offence to Victorian bourgeois manners, which relied on a domestic architecture of vigilant demarcations, padding and concealment, defining the boundaries between inside and outside, the domestic and the commercial, the public and the private. According to Karen Chase and Michael Levenson:

> Victorian domesticity was as much a spatial as an affective obsession. Increasingly, to imagine a flourishing private life was to articulate space, to secure boundaries, and to distribute bodies. [. . .] To create material defences against exposure and to design the interior of the household as a series of safe boxes were architectural imperatives prompted by a cultural longing.[84]

Counterfeiting bourgeois domesticity, the corporate hotel erased these defences and pulled domestic space apart. It confused its demarcations, exposed its surfaces, and flattened out its concealed recesses, demystifying the 'sovereign domain of the bourgeois subject'.[85]

Margin of Nothing

And yet James did not determinedly come down on the side of interiority, the private home and bourgeois identity. James's hotel-filled works of the 1870s and 1880s engage with these spaces in a surprisingly curious, exploratory way. The loss of depth, of place, of tactility and idiosyncrasy in the hotel parlour is also what underpins its ambiguous liberatory potential in James's works. The pleasure to be found in vacant hotel spaces was that nothing of great significance happened there. Positioned between spaces with more immediately practical uses, higher activity and greater symbolic investment (like the lobby and the private bedroom), the hotel parlour was a place for lingering in between. Beyond the descriptions of desolate wilderness and deathliness that opened this chapter, some writers professed tentative feelings of pleasure in these rooms, especially because they offered the possibility of being left alone. Miss Aurelia, the protagonist of *Tony, The Maid*, for instance,

> used to steal into a hotel drawing-room, her book in her hand. She was at liberty to read if she wished, or to watch the people covertly, and indulge in innocent speculations about them. Occasionally some woman, also shy and alone, would speak to her. This had been pleasant, and made a little variety. Her [. . .] condition was, in short, freedom – the dove's conception of freedom, not the eagle's, but freedom all the same.[86]

The 'human archipelago' of this drawing-room provides the buffer that she needs to simply sit and stare. The fiction writer and essayist Vernon Lee, a friend and associate of James, expresses this need for a buffer – for a space that is not stimulating or supremely meaningful – in aesthetic terms. 'There seems, moreover, to be a certain queer virtue in mere emptiness, in mere negation,' writes Lee on the sparseness of her Florentine hotel sitting-room. 'We require a *margin* of *nothing* round everything that is to charm us; round our impressions as well as round the material objects which can supply them; for without it we lose all outline, and begin to feel vaguely choked.'[87]

James's neglected comic novel *The Reverberator* (1888), centred on the Dosson family staying in the fictional Hôtel de l'Univers et de Cheltenham in Paris, is in many ways a novel about inconsequentiality: about waiting, about lingering in a city, sitting in hotel parlours, sitting for portraits, waiting for appointments and killing time, about the sensation and psychology of waiting, and the dignity of doing nothing. James uses the cover of a minor work (it 'may be described', he writes in his later Preface, 'as a *jeu d'esprit*') to investigate the interstitial experiences that occur in the interstitial spaces of the hotel.[88] Michael Sayeau argues that such experiences have been obscured in studies of urban modernity, which often take the nervous overstimulation hypothesised by Georg Simmel and Walter Benjamin as their starting point. Instead of the anxious tempo of the factory, the street or the cinema palace, Sayeau points to the 'restless stillness' of the queue, train platform and waiting room, and the 'frantic immobility' of unemployed labourers, as increasingly common features of urban life.[89] Contrary to the productive dawdling that Ross Posnock finds in James's autobiography (Posnock writes that James gathered useful material 'usually during moments of ease – as when the young Henry lies on a hotel bed in London'), *The Reverberator* instead takes the inconsequentiality and unproductiveness of dawdling seriously.[90] There are no great epiphanies in the waiting rooms of this novel. In the same manner that Louise Hornby describes Virginia Woolf's illness, exhaustion and idleness, James's novel

> rebuffs the terms of production and labor that inflect modern ideologies and temporalities [. . .]. Such still bodies oppose a model of forward-moving instrumentality and instead demarcate forms of wasted, aberrant time by occupying the nonstandard, uncounted hours where nothing happens and productivity is sidelined.[91]

The satiric engine of *The Reverberator* is the entanglement between the Dossons, an American father and his two daughters who are passing through Paris, and the Proberts, a 'Gallomaniac' family of Catholic Americans who have married, reproduced and martyred their way into Parisian society over two generations.[92] The Dossons represent American modernity in many of its forms – an over-eager consumption of newspapers, hotels, bourgeois diversions, credit – while the Proberts, with the 'exaggerated reactionary hauteur of the Gallicized American', are somewhat naive about the way the world changed while they fortified themselves in Paris.[93] One of the Dosson daughters, Francie, meets Gaston Probert while having her portrait painted by a young impressionist. Francie and Gaston's uneasy courtship is nearly torn apart when Francie confides some of the Probert family secrets to a journalist with an American gossip rag called *The Reverberator*, leaving Gaston to choose between Francie and his family's inheritance.

The two families have opposing conceptions of property and living space, as can be seen by comparing the reading-rooms they use. Monsieur Probert, the patriarch of the Probert family, 'read a great deal, and very serious books; works about the origin of things – of man, of institutions, of speech, of religion'. His reading-room is barely described; there is only Probert alone, 'turning his pages softly, contentedly, with the lamp-light shining on his refined old head and embroidered dressing-gown', the still point of a little universe whose limits are mystified in shadow.[94] Time and the material world have retreated, and Probert is deep inside his book, 'according to his custom when he sat at home of an evening'. The tableau is suffocatingly thick with images of identity and lineage: of 'origin' and 'custom', and Probert's illuminated head. Probert reinforces and reproduces his values, his identity, through reading. His consciousness might be commingling with the consciousness of the author, but he is firmly tethered to his sense of self through the cocoon of personal property – through his total ownership of space and his ownership of the book itself (he turns *his* pages softly). Probert is commingling not only with words, but with his property and his decor – sinking into it, but also magnified by it.

The reading-room in the Hôtel de l'Univers et de Cheltenham, conversely, is a space where no actual reading gets done. As the room is introduced we find Delia Dosson, the younger Dosson sister, sitting

> with her back to the window, looking straight before her into the conventional room. She was dressed as for the street; her empty hands rested upon the arms of her chair (she had withdrawn her long gloves, which were lying in her lap), and she seemed to be doing nothing as hard as she could.[95]

The blankness of Delia matches the blankness of her surroundings. The hotel doesn't quite have the opulence of the grandest Parisian establishments. The reading-room is particularly plain. It consists

> principally of a bare, highly-polished floor, on which it was easy for a relaxed elderly American to slip [. . .], of a table with a green velvet cloth, of a fireplace with a great deal of fringe and no fire, of a window with a great deal of curtain and no light, and of the Figaro, which [Mr. Dosson] couldn't read, and the New York Herald, which he had already read.[96]

In honour of the relaxed elderly American, this is what might be described as slippery space. Another slippery hotel space in James – a hotel in *The Ambassadors* with a 'slippery staircase' and a 'small slippery *salle à manger*' – suggests that 'slippery' describes something inherent in the formal properties of hotels.[97] The reading-room is slippery not only because of the quality of its surfaces, but because it is *all* surfaces: the eyes (and the feet) glide easily across it. There is nothing to hang on to. This is a room where surface treatments have been applied to bare objects ('a table with [. . .], a fireplace with [. . .], a window with [. . .]'), with the effect that everything seems temporary and hasty; we can imagine the velvet cloth sliding off the table and the newspapers slipping onto the floor. The way James's Dickensian paragraph itself rolls forward, rhythmically and epigrammatically, suggests a room taken in as a single impression, without any nooks buried in subordinate clauses or unexpected curiosities hidden between brackets. It creates a complete and depthless two-dimensional image.[98]

Mr Dosson, who opens the novel by walking into the reading-room, is slippery space personified. We see him 'wandering further into the room and drawing his feet over the floor without lifting them', gliding frictionlessly across its surface.

His failure to sink into the space precludes deep thought. 'Whatever he did he ever seemed to wander: he had a transitory air, an aspect of weary yet patient non-arrival, even when he sat (as he was capable of sitting for hours) in the court of the inn.'[99] Nothing captures his interest. The restless passivity or 'patient non-arrival' of Dosson is an evolutionary adaptation to the reading-room; a room that invites its guests to sit but not to settle, to stay for hours but never leave an imprint on its stain-resistant surfaces.

Like the sitting-room in 'Guest's Confession', the reading-room is permeable, dispensing with the need for a proper entrance and demarcating its territory with 'a superfluous drapery in the doorway'.[100] It has the sentimental trappings of a domestic space but without the comfort or the intimacy. It has the practicality of a business room but without the utility of a proper newsprint archive. (Its failure to fulfil a business role sends Mr Dosson to a different and more effective reading-room inside the branch office of an American bank.) The actual function of the hotel reading-room is improvised, determined by the whim of its guests. It suits the Dosson daughters in particular as a waiting- or meeting-room. Withdrawn one step from the publicity of the lobby, and one step from the privacy of the Dossons' private hotel drawing-room, it becomes a hinge point, a middle-ground where the Dossons can meet with men at the correct level of remove, according to the new laws of hotel propriety. '"Well, this is a good place to meet"', Mr Dosson notes vaguely, as if improvising a new social law on the spot. That the laws of this room are still fluid is further suggested by what Delia is wearing in it: 'dressed as for the street' but with her gloves off, caught between inside and outside, public and private.[101]

The openness of the semi-public room is confirmed by a strange fictional apparition that lurks there. Neither narrator nor character, this disembodied 'auditor' is evoked by James as a potential rather than an actual presence:

> If an auditor had chanced to be present for the quarter of an hour that elapsed and had had any attention to give to these vulgar young persons he would have wondered perhaps at there being so much mystery on one side and so much curiosity on the other – wondered at least at the elaboration of inscrutable projects on the part of a girl who looked to the casual eye as if she were stolidly passive.[102]

This hovering point of view wanders in and out of the scene as if it were a figuration of the anonymous traffic flowing in and out of the drapery in the doorway. The auditor not only inserts an anonymous presence into the scene, it makes us, the reader, look at the main characters through the eyes of a stranger, rather than through the explicating perspective of the narrator or the consciousness of a fellow character. In a room where anonymous figures mingle, the main characters are made to seem anonymous as well: 'A spectator, looking from Mr. George Flack to Miss Francie Dosson, would have been much at a loss to guess what special relation could exist between them.'[103] Matthew Rubery associates this shadowy third with *The Reverberator*'s concern with journalism. The presence of the journalist George Flack in this and other scenes, he argues, means that the dialogue is suffused with newspaper consciousness. Characters tailor their speech as if they were speaking to a journalist as well as to the strangers that buy the newspapers – to 'an unseen third party in a triangulated relationship with interviewer and interviewee'.[104] Newspaper consciousness in fact works as a useful analogy for hotel parlour consciousness: both encompass the experience of being excerpted from one's milieu, and pasted into a white room, or an inch of column-space, for a stranger to study.

The transformation of characters into unknowable strangers is associated with the illegibility of hotel space. Delia is described with the same language and imagery used to describe the room itself: she is 'empty' and 'blank' and 'always looked the same', a generic mould livened up by discretionary spending at the Bon Marché – by the human equivalent of green velvet and big curtains.[105] (Though as James witheringly declares, 'all the contrivances of Paris could not make her look different'.)[106] In a revision for the New York Edition, James added a wilfully strange metaphor directly linking Delia's blank face with the blank architecture she inhabits:

> It was a plain clean round pattern face, marked for recognition among so many only perhaps by a small figure, the sprig on a china plate, that might have denoted deep obstinacy; and yet, with its settled smoothness, it was neither stupid nor hard. It was as calm as a room kept dusted and aired for candid earnest occasions, the meeting of unanimous committees and the discussion of flourishing businesses.[107]

The metaphor registers only an absence of meaning: the two halves of the metaphor reflecting their emptiness back at each other. Neither architecture nor the human face can tell us anything about the reality behind the appearance.

A Trail of Forgotten Tauchnitzes

Even as hotels erase any trace left by any individual guest, the anonymous, collective trace of the crowd is irrepressible and makes itself felt through a hotel's inevitable decay. From the pioneering Boston Exchange Coffee House to the old Waldorf-Astoria, many notable American hotels were quickly worn out and were frequently pulled down. '[I]n addition to the annual renovations, the amount of necessary repair work to keep three hundred or more rooms in condition of sale is tremendous', writes Lucius M. Boomer, the manager of the old Waldorf-Astoria, which itself contained more than a thousand rooms.

> [I]n a home people live who have more or less property interest in it, and therefore some interest in careful use of it; the opposite is true in hotels. Furthermore, in transient hotels the very nature of the business requires and assumes a degree of wear and tear in proportion to the volume of business, the rapidity with which patrons come and go, and the class of patronage catered to.[108]

Waste and decay provide the key to reading illegible, slippery hotel space. The patterns left by waste and decay, for instance, allow Sherlock Holmes to deduce that a threatening letter to Sir Henry Baskerville originated in a hotel sitting-room. Composed of ink and cut-up newsprint, the letter bears the negative trace of the hotel's overcrowding and overuse:

> 'If you examine it carefully you will see that both the pen and the ink have given the writer trouble. The pen has spluttered twice in a single word, and has run dry three times in a short address, showing that there was very little ink in the bottle. Now, a private pen or ink-bottle is seldom allowed to be in such a state, and the combination of the two must be quite rare. But you know the hotel ink and the hotel pen, where it is rare to get anything else. Yes, I have very little hesitation in saying that could we examine the wastepaper baskets of the hotels round Charing Cross until we found the remains of the mutilated *Times* leader we could lay our hands straight upon the person who sent this singular message.'[109]

The trace reveals little specificity, merely sending one of Holmes's helpers on a fruitless search through twenty-three hotels around Charing Cross. Holmes hasn't hit upon the tell-tale trace of the Savoy, for instance, but the tell-tale trace of hotel decay.

However, there was one form of waste that hotels not only tolerated, but actively cultivated: discarded books, as in the Spraggs' private sitting-room in Edith Wharton's *The Custom of the Country*, where except for a palm tree in a gilt basket and 'a copy of "The Hound of the Baskervilles" which lay beside it, the room showed no traces of human use'.[110] *The Hound of the Baskervilles* is later 'replaced' by 'the "fiction number" of a magazine'.[111] The book's fate is unknown, but one possibility is that it was dumped among other unwanted books in the hotel reading-room. As an object that shows the marks of its age and the traces of its multiple owners, the hotel book offers a way to read the suppressed temporality of hotel space, and to imagine the cycle of consumption that buttresses the hotel system. In *The Custom of the Country*, Wharton uses discarded hotel books to figure the distortions hotels inflict on temporal consciousness. After a string of disappointments and reduced to virtual exile, Undine Spragg looks for something to occupy her time in a seaside hotel:

> [Undine] had never before known a world as colourless and negative as that of the large white hotel where everybody went to bed at nine, and donkey-rides over stony hills were the only alternative to slow drives along dusty roads. Many of the dwellers in this temple of repose found even these exercises too stimulating, and preferred to sit for hours under the palms in the garden, playing Patience, embroidering, or reading odd volumes of Tauchnitz. Undine, driven by despair to an inspection of the hotel book-shelves, discovered that scarcely any work they contained was complete; but this did not seem to trouble the readers, who continued to feed their leisure with mutilated fiction [. . .].[112]

Like trying to read the out-of-order volumes of old novels, hotel time is experienced not as an unfolding plot but as a series of unconnected incidents. Like the tourists driving or riding aimlessly through the countryside, the hotel guests wander through disordered fiction, experiencing the colour and movement of unfamiliar characters and scenery which will always remain distant and strange. It is a detached, deadened way of both living and reading. But Wharton has a further, more acidic critique to make, centred on the idea of *mutilation* – both of the book and of the modern mind that passively enjoys reading mutilated fiction. The strength of the word suggests some violent break with past patterns of behaviour has taken place. Our experience of time, Wharton seems to say, has taken on something of the commodified, junk quality of the abandoned Tauchnitz. We use up time and discard it. We behave, in hotel space, like amnesiac consumers of experience, barely even knowing what day it is.

The roots of this association between disposable fiction and hotel living – a metaphoric as well as a real, economic connection – can be found several decades earlier than *The Custom of the Country* in *The Reverberator* and *The Bostonians*. In *The Bostonians*, the metropolitan hotel lobbies are hothouses of publishing as well as publicity. Like the newsrooms of the daily press with which they are explicitly linked, lobbies are 'national nerve-centres', where words are generated cheaply, rumours swirl and gain voice, and the lives of individuals are broadcast to the city. We see words being churned out anonymously ('rows of shaggy-backed men in strange hats, writing letters'), surfaces covered in words ('at a table inlaid with advertisements'), words being peddled ('behind a counter [. . .] little boys [. . .] showing plans of the play-houses and offering librettos'), individuals transformed into words ('He looked with longing for the moment when Verena should be advertised among the "personals"'), and prattle being harvested (the journalist Matthias Pardon 'had begun his career, at the age of fourteen, by going the rounds of the hotels'); and all of this to the hacking sounds of spitting ('amid [. . .] the convenient spittoons'), suggestive of speech turned sour from overuse.[113] This churning cycle of words, quick and grimy and ephemeral, is reflected in the way books are traded and discarded in hotel space. Beside the boys hawking theatre tickets and librettos is a stall selling fiction: 'a counter, set apart and covered with an array of periodicals and novels in paper covers'.[114]

The pinnacle of the hotel book marketplace in Europe was the Tauchnitz edition, founded by the self-styled 'Baron' Tauchnitz in 1841, and catering to the English-speaking guests of European hotels. Tauchnitz created its own canon of English-language fiction and non-fiction, reprinting thousands of classic American and British titles, with a smattering of German, French, Latin and Greek, and offered modest royalties for doing so (something which was above and beyond its legal obligations). Its books were cheap, squat paperbacks with small type and plain white covers, bearing a somewhat endearing simplicity that influenced paperback design into the twentieth century.[115] Tauchnitz editions were distributed at major hubs like railway stations and hotels; but while they were designed for travel, the front covers warned that it was prohibited to carry a Tauchnitz into England or into any British Colony, or into the United States if the author of the book was American. This was because of international copyright treaties that Tauchnitz itself championed. For those returning to or transiting through British or American zones of control, confiscation of one's Tauchnitz was a definite possibility. Hence most editions were discarded in Europe, many of them in hotel reading-rooms. The books were cheap enough to do so without guilt.

Tauchnitz editions were just one component of a new hotel book lifecycle: from cheap publication to quiet disposal to recovery and reuse, the discards forming a ramshackle library of their own. '[T]he hotel library is limited to a volume of Klopstock and a tattered Guide to Switzerland,' complains one correspondent for *The Saturday Review*; 'the one Tauchnitz in the place is G. P. R. James's silliest novel, and even that is secured by the one other English guest.'[116] '[E]verything in the shape of literature is exhausted!' writes another in the *London Review*. 'The English girl sitting in the window has got the second volume of the Tauchnitz edition of the 'Daisy Chain,' dropped here by some former voyager! There are two odd numbers of the *Sunday at Home* of the year before last, the *Saturday Review* for one of the weeks in July, an odd volume of Schiller's works' – an array, in short, of shattered fragments and mutilated chronologies.[117] Entire hotel libraries were built not by choice and taste, but by contingency and rejection.

James was well aware that his own books were part of this lifecycle. He personally negotiated with the Baron and republished virtually his entire early catalogue through Tauchnitz, a move that provided about 5 per cent of his literary income in the late 1870s as his career was taking shape.[118] James was therefore able to concretely imagine a portion of his audience reading his work in hotel reading-rooms or in transit. In his 1884 tale 'Pandora', a German aristocrat on a steamer to New York reads a Tauchnitz edition of something that closely resembles *Daisy Miller* – a novel 'by an American author whose pages, he had been assured, would help to prepare him for some of the oddities' of the country he's visiting.[119] The transatlantic hotel-world of *Daisy Miller* or *The American* – James's 'international theme' – was perfectly suited to the Tauchnitz treatment, and James knowingly wrote himself into this marketplace.

Yet the excessive circulation suffered by Tauchnitz editions was distasteful to James. He was gently cynical about the ways in which people sourced their books – writing tartly of 'the public that subscribes, borrows, lends, that picks up in one way and another, sometimes even by purchase'.[120] The most potent expression of his distaste comes from his essay on 'The Future of the Novel': 'Almost any variety [of book] is thrown off and taken up, handled, admired, ignored by too many people, and this, precisely, is the point at which the question of its future becomes one with that of the future of the total swarm.'[121] 'Swarm' sticks out, of course, but there is a certain abject horror, too, in the word 'handled'. Every author is afraid of being 'ignored by too many people', but here James betrays his fear of the gross materiality of success, of the dirt that accumulates through market circulation, of the effect of sweaty palms and clumsy fingers on board and paper. 'Handled' summarises all the abasements suffered by the book in its new incarnation as an industrial commodity: smudged, greased, dropped, lost, ripped, dog-eared, defaced. The very process of publication – 'throw[ing] off' – is accomplished with clumsy hands, inflicting abuse from which the book never recovers.

A borrowed book is not, by virtue of being borrowed, tainted goods for James. A 'devourer of libraries' in his youth, he was fond of well-tended collections.[122] But a book borrowed from the reading-room of a hotel could feel more like borrowed leftovers, like recycled waste. In the great chain of hands imagined by James, the hotel is endmost, encouraging the reader into fractured browsing. Francie, the elder Dosson daughter, is found guilty of such reading practices in *The Reverberator*. Francie is plugged into the subterranean rhythms of the hotel, the constant disposals and abandonments that ensure everything always appears to be new. She is a Tauchnitz devotee, and in her sister Delia's mind, she is the good reader of the family:

> Had not a trail of forgotten Tauchnitzes marked the former line of travel of the party of three? The elder sister grabbed them up on leaving hotels and railway-carriages, but usually found that she had brought odd volumes.[123]

Here, disposal comes first, and after dumping her books, Francie blindly reacquires more – 'grabb[ing] them up', all hands and no discernment. The passage deliberately blurs the nature of Francie's acquisition: is she purchasing new volumes from railway bookstalls or picking up old ones from the carriage floor? Has she bought or merely 'brought'? Are the odd volumes due to neglectful selection or is she simply salvaging what's available? In other words, are we at the beginning of the lifecycle, where books are 'thrown off' by publishing companies, or at the end of the cycle, when readers throw them away? Mr Dosson, too, is prone to evaluate Francie's development in terms of the trail of debris she creates ('he believed she was cultivated up to the eyes. He had a recollection of tremendous school-bills and, in later days, during their travels, of the way she was always leaving books behind her'). She is an individual whose positive qualities are shadowed by negation ('Moreover, was not her French so good that he could not understand it?'), whose growth and education are also processes of dissolution.[124]

Francie's participation in the hotel's disposable economy sets her apart from James's obsessive hoarders and collectors. For her, culture is weightless, and can be discovered and cast off as she goes. Her unencumbered life (anticipating the 'weightlessness' of Dreiser's Carrie Meeber) might be predicated on negation, but it also carries transformative potential.[125] To be unencumbered was a peculiarly American quality for James. In a letter from 1867, the young James writes of the American artist's natural advantage over the European: 'we can deal freely with forms of civilization not our own, can pick and choose and assimilate and in short (aesthetically etc.) claim our property where we find it.'[126] The young American artist is a rambler, a rag-picker, a bricoleur; but she assimilates as well as rejects, and gradually accumulates her proprietorial identity. The space that James creates for Francie is in this sense liberating. Against the suffocating enclosure of the Probert family, the Dossons value drift, a philosophy mulled over by Mr Dosson as he sits in the court of the Hôtel de l'Univers:

> The two girls, at any rate, were the wind in his sail and the only directing, determining force he knew; they converted accident into purpose; without them, as he felt, he would have been the tail without the kite. The wind rose and fell, of course; there were lulls and there were gales; there were intervals during which he simply floated in quiet waters – cast anchor and waited. This appeared to be one of them now; but he could be patient, knowing that he should soon again inhale the brine and feel the dip of his prow.[127]

For all of James's jabs at the Dosson family's shallow thoughts and simple habits, there is something touchingly genial about Mr Dosson's vision of life and his relationship with his daughters, and something genuinely sympathetic about James's representation of them. The space in which Dosson sits is emblematic of his philosophy. He takes the emptiness at the heart of the hotel, and of the hotel reading-room in particular, and fashions it into an asset. For him, its emptiness is not a void, but an expression of what Vernon Lee called the '*margin of nothing*': a space of low significance and minor experience that gives major experiences a proper perspective and meaning. And in the meantime, floating in becalmed waters has its pleasures: a freedom (a highly privileged freedom) from the attachments and burdens of home and labour; and a freedom, too, from the heavy baggage of subjectivity. The world washes by, and washes through, the Dossons. If this makes them minor players in both Parisian society and in the Jamesian canon, it is also what gives them historical significance, as early and enthusiastic adopters of disposable culture and disposable space. With the comic register of the novel's conclusion – the couple are married, a 'happy and now reckless' Gaston is 'emancipat[ed]' from his family, and the Dossons plus Gaston prepare to move on to a new hotel, 'not at all clear as to where they were going' – *The Reverberator* represents a small triumph of disposability over settlement in a way that might be impossible in anything but a Jamesian *jeu d'esprit*.[128]

Notes

1. Henry James, 'Saratoga', in *Collected Travel Writings: Great Britain and America*, ed. Richard Howard (New York: Library of America, 1993), p. 751.
2. Mary Elizabeth Braddon, *Lady Audley's Secret* (Oxford: Oxford University Press, 2012), p. 207.
3. Anthony Trollope, *North America: Volume II* (Philadelphia: Lippincott, 1863), p. 293.
4. Blanche Willis Howard, *Tony, The Maid: A Novelette* (New York: Harper, 1887), p. 47.
5. George Augustus Sala, *My Diary in America in the Midst of War: Volume II* (London: Tinsley Brothers, 1865), p. 202.
6. Marc Augé, *Non-Places: Introduction to an Anthropology of Supermodernity*, trans. John Howe (London and New York: Verso, 1995), p. 87.
7. Robert A. Davidson, *The Hotel: Occupied Space* (Toronto: University of Toronto Press, 2018), p. 126.
8. Marc Katz, 'The Hotel Kracauer', 11 (2) *Differences* (Summer 1999), p. 147.
9. Sandoval-Strausz, *Hotel*, pp. 146–9, and Thomas A Markus, *Buildings and Power: Freedom and Control in the Origin of Modern Building Types* (London: Routledge, 1993), pp. 164–7.
10. James Whiting, *The New York Shippers' and Consignees' Guide* (New York: Butler, 1861), p. 167.
11. Barbara Penner, '"Colleges for the Teaching of Extravagance": New York Palace Hotels', 44 (2/3) *Winterthur Portfolio* (Summer/Autumn 2010), p. 173.
12. Sandoval-Strausz, *Hotel*, p. 150.
13. Braddon, *Lady Audley's Secret*, p. 207.

14. Clarence Cook, *The House Beautiful: Essays on Beds and Tables, Stools and Candlesticks* (New York: Scribner, Armstrong, 1878), pp. 307 and 308–9.
15. Kevin J. James, 'Afterword', in *Anglo-American Travelers and the Hotel Experience in Nineteenth-Century Literature*, eds Monika M. Elbert and Susanne Schmid (New York and London: Routledge, 2018), p. 271.
16. Cook, *The House Beautiful*, pp. 101–2.
17. David A. Ellison, 'Mobile Homes, Fallen Furniture, and the Dickens Cure', 108 (1) *South Atlantic Quarterly* (2009), p. 90.
18. Ibid., p. 98.
19. William Laird MacGregor, 'Hotel Life in San Francisco', 27 *Victoria Magazine* (May–October 1876), pp. 525–6.
20. Mary Elizabeth Braddon, 'From Paddington to the Land's End', 27 *Belgravia* (August 1875), p. 200.
21. G. H. Lewes, 'Recent Novels, French and English', 36 *Fraser's Magazine* (1846), pp. 686–95.
22. George Eliot, *Adam Bede* (Oxford: Oxford University Press, 1996), p. 177.
23. See Elaine Freedgood on Barthes's reality effect, in *The Ideas in Things: Fugitive Meaning in the Victorian Novel* (Chicago and London: University of Chicago Press, 2006), pp. 9–21.
24. Thad Logan, *The Victorian Parlour: A Cultural Study* (Cambridge: Cambridge University Press, 2001), p. 94.
25. Florence Caddy, *Lares and Penates: or, The Background of Life* (London: Chatto & Windus, 1881), pp. 34–5.
26. Walter Benjamin, 'Experience and Poverty', in *Walter Benjamin: Selected Writings: Volume 2, Part 2, 1931–1934*, eds Michael W. Jennings et al. (Cambridge, MA and London: Belknap Press of Harvard University Press, 1999), p. 734.
27. Walter Benjamin, *The Arcades Project*, trans. Howard Eiland and Kevin McLaughlin (Cambridge, MA and London: Belknap Press of Harvard University Press, 1999), p. 222.
28. Ibid., p. 20.
29. Paddy Ireland, 'Capitalism without the Capitalist: The Joint Stock Company Share and the Emergence of the Modern Doctrine of Separate Corporate Personality', 17 (1) *Journal of Legal History* (1996), p. 69.
30. M. E. James, *How to Decorate Our Ceilings, Walls and Floors* (London: George Bell, 1883), p. 2.
31. Anna Kornbluh, *Realizing Capital: Financial and Psychic Economies in Victorian Form* (New York: Fordham University Press, 2014), p. 12.
32. Fanny Fern, *Ginger-Snaps* (New York: Carleton, 1870), p. 247.
33. In Klimasmith's formulation, the hotel is a 'home without a history'. Betsy Klimasmith, *At Home in the City: Urban Domesticity in American Literature and Culture, 1850–1930* (Durham, NH: University of New Hampshire Press, 2005), p. 169.
34. Henry James, *Italian Hours*, in *Collected Travel Writings: The Continent*, ed. Richard Howard (New York: Library of America, 1993), p. 294.
35. Henry James, *The Portrait of a Lady*, ed. Roger Luckhurst (Oxford and New York: Oxford University Press, 2009), p. 517.

36. 'Vitreous Hotel China', in *Montgomery Ward & Co. Catalogue and Buyers' Guide, 1895: Unabridged Facsimile* (New York: Skyhorse Publishing, 2008), p. 530.
37. 'Mr. Wilde on Decorative Art: An Outline of his Observations in Wallack's Theatre Yesterday', *New York Times*, 12 May 1882, p. 8.
38. Ruth D. Reichard, 'A "National Distemper": The National Hotel Sickness of 1857, Public Health and Sanitation, and the Limits of Rationality', 15 (3) *Journal of Planning History* (2016), pp. 175–90.
39. *Buckingham Hotel, Fifth Avenue, New York.* (New York: Buckingham Hotel, 1877), p. 7.
40. Nancy Tomes, *The Gospel of Germs: Men, Women, and the Microbe in American Life* (Cambridge, MA: Harvard University Press, 1998), pp. 172–4.
41. Eileen Cleere, 'Victorian Dust Traps', in *Filth: Dirt, Disgust and Modern Life*, eds William Cohen and Ryan Johnson (Minneapolis, MN: University of Minnesota Press, 2005), p. 138.
42. *The British American Guide-Book: Being a Condensed Gazetteer, Directory and Guide, to Canada, the Western States, and Principal Cities on the Seaboard* (New York: Bailliere, 1859), p. 11.
43. M.N.S., 'How to Keep an Inn', *The Nation*, 16 June 1887, p. 508.
44. Gail Hamilton, 'The Hotel of the Future', 11 (1) *Scribner's Monthly* (November 1875), p. 110.
45. 'Hotel Hygiene', 963 *Scientific American Supplement*, 16 June 1894, p. 15393.
46. George Vivian Poore, *The Dwelling House* (New York and Bombay: Longmans, 1897), pp. 22–3.
47. 'Joint-Stock Speculations: Their Value and Prospects. No. VII. – Hotel Companies', 11 *London Review of Politics, Society, Literature, Art, and Science*, 12 August 1865, p. 169.
48. 'Floor-Cloth', *Chambers's Encyclopaedia: Volume IV* (London: Chambers, 1874), p. 379.
49. 'Encaustic Tiles', *New-York Tribune Illustrated Supplement*, 7 November 1897, p. 13. The article also describes a new paving material used in the Astoria's semi-circular entrance court. Mixed with cork, the material was 'smooth, elastic, noiseless and clean'.
50. Henry James, *The American Scene*, in *Collected Travel Writings: Great Britain and America*, ed. Richard Howard (New York: Library of America, 1993), p. 714.
51. May Sinclair, *The Immortal Moment: The Story of Kitty Tailleur* (New York: Doubleday Page, 1908), pp. 5–6 and 20–1.
52. Peter Knight, *Reading the Market: Genres of Financial Capitalism in Gilded Age America* (Baltimore, MD: Johns Hopkins University Press, 2016), p. 147.
53. Karen Halttunen, *Confidence Men and Painted Women: A Study of Middle-class Culture in America, 1830–1870* (New Haven, CT: Yale University Press, 1982), pp. 39–43.
54. Wilkie Collins, *Basil* (Oxford: Oxford University Press, 2008), p. 98.
55. Ibid., p. 53.
56. David Trotter, *Cooking with Mud: The Idea of Mess in Nineteenth-century Art and Fiction* (Oxford: Oxford University Press, 2000), p. 184.

57. Eva Badowska, 'On the Track of Things: Sensation and Modernity in Mary Elizabeth Braddon's *Lady Audley's Secret*', 37 (1) *Victorian Literature and Culture* (2009), pp. 165–6.
58. Ibid., p. 166.
59. Collins, *Basil*, p. 91.
60. Ibid., p. 99.
61. Ibid., p. 158.
62. Charles Dickens, 'An Unsettled Neighbourhood', *Selected Journalism: 1850–1870* (London: Penguin, 1997), p. 48.
63. Collins, *Basil*, p. 129.
64. Ibid., p. 137; Laurence Talairach-Vielmas, 'Modern Phantasmagorias and Visual Culture in Wilkie Collins's *Basil*', in *Monstrous Media/Spectral Subjects: Imaging Gothic Fictions from the Nineteenth Century to the Present*, eds Fred Botting and Catherine Spooner (Manchester: Manchester University Press, 2015), p. 64.
65. Mary Poovey, *Genres of the Credit Economy: Mediating Value in Eighteenth- and Nineteenth-Century Britain* (Chicago: University of Chicago Press, 2008), pp. 1–7.
66. Andrew H. Miller, 'The Discourse of Liability in the Joint Stock Companies Act of 1856 and Gaskell's *Cranford*', 61 (1) *ELH* (1994), p. 143.
67. Robbie Moore, 'Corporate Space', in *The Routledge Companion to Literature and Economics*, eds Matt Seybold and Michelle Chihara (New York: Routledge, 2019), p. 213.
68. House of Commons Select Committee on Joint Stock Companies, *First Report of the Select Committee on Joint Stock Companies, Together with the Minutes of Evidence (taken in 1841 and 1843), Appendix, and Index* (1844), p. 4.
69. Henry James, 'Guest's Confession', in *Complete Stories: 1864–1874*, ed. Jean Strouse (New York: Library of America, 1999).
70. Ibid., p. 679.
71. Ibid., p. 681.
72. Ibid., p. 679.
73. Ibid., p. 682.
74. Ibid., p. 683.
75. Ibid., p. 679.
76. For Edith Wharton – who argued fiercely against the trend of permeable, open-plan domestic architecture – a permeable sitting-room is no sitting-room at all. The typical '"little room down-stairs"' in the modern town house, with its 'inevitable yawning gap in the wall, giving on the hall close to the front door', looks 'less like a sitting-room in a private house than a waiting-room at a fashionable doctor's or dentist's'. Edith Wharton and Ogden Codman Jr, *The Decoration of Houses* (London: Batsford, 1898), p. 22.
77. James, 'Guest's Confession', p. 683.
78. Ibid., p. 686.
79. Ibid., p. 688.
80. Ibid., p. 674.
81. Ibid., p. 690.
82. Ibid., p. 684.

83. Ibid., p. 684.
84. Karen Chase and Michael Levenson, *The Spectacle of Intimacy: A Public Life for the Victorian Family* (Princeton, NJ and Oxford: Princeton University Press, 2000), p. 143.
85. Katz, 'The Hotel Kracauer', p. 143.
86. Howard, *Tony, The Maid*, p. 71.
87. Vernon Lee, 'A Hotel Sitting-Room', in *Hortus Vitae: Essays on the Gardening of Life* (London and New York: John Lane, 1904), p. 88.
88. Henry James, 'Prefaces to the New York Edition', in *Literary Criticism: French Writers, Other European Writers, The Prefaces to the New York Edition*, eds Edel and Mark Wilson (New York: Library of America, 1984), p. 1192.
89. Michael Sayeau, 'Waiting', in Restless Cities, eds Matthew Beaumont and Gregory Dart (London: Verso, 2010), pp. 281–2; and 'Work, Unemployment, and the Exhaustion of Fiction in *Heart of Darkness*', 39 (3) *Novel* (2006), p. 358.
90. Ross Posnock, *The Trial of Curiosity: Henry James, William James, and the Challenge of Modernity* (Oxford: Oxford University Press, 1991), pp. 43–5.
91. Louise Hornby, 'Downwrong: The Pose of Tiredness', 65 (1) *Modern Fiction Studies* (2019), p. 210.
92. Henry James, *The Reverberator*, in *Novels: 1886–1890*, eds Daniel Mark Fogel (New York: Library of America, 1989), p. 582.
93. Richard Salmon, *Henry James and the Culture of Publicity* (Cambridge: Cambridge University Press, 1997), p. 129.
94. James, *The Reverberator*, p. 626.
95. Ibid., pp. 557–8.
96. Ibid., p. 557.
97. Henry James, *The Ambassadors* (London: Methuen, 1903), pp. 74 and 349.
98. For another description of this reading-room, see Thomas F. Strychacz, *Modernism, Mass Culture, and Professionalism* (Cambridge: Cambridge University Press, 1993), pp. 45–6.
99. James, The *Reverberator*, p. 558.
100. Ibid., p. 557.
101. Ibid., p. 558.
102. Ibid., p. 562.
103. Ibid., p. 565.
104. Matthew Rubery, 'Wishing to Be Interviewed in Henry James's *The Reverberator*', 28 (1) *Henry James Review* (Winter 2007), p. 67.
105. James, *The Reverberator*, pp. 558 and 562.
106. Ibid., p. 562.
107. Henry James, *The Reverberator*, in *The Reverberator, Madame de Mauves, A Passionate Pilgrim, and Other Tales* (New York: Charles Scribner's Sons, 1908), p. 11.
108. Lucius M. Boomer, *Hotel Management: Principles and Practice* (New York and London: Harper, 1925), p. 294. In 1905, barely eight years after the Astoria section of the hotel was built, the former manager of the Waldorf-Astoria, George Boldt, was informed by senior staff that the rooms were 'filthy' and the 'house is

rotten'. A major clean-up and modernisation programme was undertaken, but the hotel never regained its lost custom, and was operating at a loss by 1915. Albin Pasteur Dearing, *The Elegant Inn* (Secaucus, NJ: Lyle Stuart, 1986), pp. 194–5.
109. Arthur Conan Doyle, *The Hound of the Baskervilles* (London: George Newnes, 1902), p. 67–8.
110. Edith Wharton, *The Custom of the Country*, in *Novels*, ed. R. W. B. Lewis (New York: Library of America, 1985), p. 623.
111. Ibid., p. 698.
112. Ibid., p. 860.
113. Henry James, *The Bostonians*, in *Novels: 1881–1886*, ed. William T. Stafford (New York: Library of America, 1985), pp. 894–5 and 916.
114. Ibid., p. 894.
115. Alistair McCleery, 'The Paperback Evolution: Tauchnitz, Albatross and Penguin', in *Judging a Book By Its Cover: Fans, Publishers, Designers, and the Marketing of Fiction*, eds Nicole Matthews and Nickianne Moody (Aldershot: Ashgate, 2007), pp. 5–6.
116. 'The Troubles of Tourists', 34 (881) *Saturday Review*, 14 September 1872, p. 339.
117. 'The Visitors'-Book at Our Swiss Inn', 15 (381) *London Review*, 19 October 1867, p. 428.
118. A full breakdown of James's publishing income is available in Michael Anesko's '*Friction with the Market': Henry James and the Profession of Authorship* (Oxford and New York: Oxford University Press, 1986), p. 176. For James's dealings with Tauchnitz, see pp. 57–9 of Anesko's study.
119. Henry James, 'Pandora', in *Complete Stories: 1874–1884*, ed. William L. Vance (New York: Library of America, 1999), p. 819. William James picked up a Tauchnitz edition of *Daisy Miller* while he was holidaying in Vers-chez-les-Blanc, as he notes in a letter to Henry James on 1 September 1892, in *William and Henry James: Selected Letters*, eds Ignas K. Skrupskelis and Elizabeth M. Berkeley (Charlottesville, VA: University of Virginia Press, 1997), p. 273.
120. Henry James, 'The Future of the Novel', *Literary Criticism: Essays on Literature, American Writers, English Writers*, eds Leon Edel and Mark Wilson (New York: Library of America, 1984), p. 100.
121. James, 'The Future of the Novel', p. 103.
122. From a letter from Henry James Snr to Catharine Barber James written in October 1857. Quoted in R. W. B. Lewis, *The Jameses: A Family Narrative* (New York: Farrar, Straus, Giroux, 1991), p. 89.
123. James, *The Reverberator*, p. 564.
124. Ibid., p. 570.
125. Ross Posnock, *The Trial of Curiosity: Henry James, William James, and the Challenge of Modernity* (New York and Oxford: Oxford University Press, 1991), p. 274.
126. Henry James, *Letters: Volume 1, 1843–1875*, ed. Leon Edel (Cambridge, MA: Harvard University Press, 1974–84), p. 77 (12 September 1867).
127. James, *The Reverberator*, p. 570.
128. Ibid., p. 699.

3

'RITZ': THE ROOF GARDEN

Hotels rose and fell with the tides of mobile capital. '[W]e frequently hear young men refer to a hotel twenty years old as 'an old hotel',' writes a columnist in *The Hotel World* in 1919. Recent income tax requirements, the columnist writes, had introduced new terms – obsoletion and depreciation – for describing and measuring a hotel's decline. The era's proliferating professional magazines, like *The Hotel World*, *The Hotel Monthly* and *Hotel Management*, were full of advice about calculating depreciation, amortisation and insurance, and precisely estimating 'how long [. . .] the wood or marble finishing, the style, shape, height of ceiling, etc.' will be '"up to date," modern', as well as structurally sound.[1] Twenty years seems about right: while Henry James saw the Waldorf-Astoria during his 1904 to 1905 tour of America as the apotheosis of capitalist culture and the American genius for organisation, for the young F. Scott Fitzgerald, travelling into New York from Princeton in 1916 and honeymooning with Zelda in 1920, the Waldorf was already a relic. In his short story 'The Freshest Boy', the Waldorf is a place to meet your mother; in *This Side of Paradise*, the Waldorf is associated with Amory Blaine's distant childhood.[2]

The shift from James's city to Fitzgerald's city was more than one of generations and fashion. Capitalism had changed gears. The change is encapsulated by Annabel Wharton in her analysis of the old Waldorf-Astoria (first opened in 1893, merged in 1897 and finally demolished in 1929), and the new Waldorf-Astoria (completed in 1931). The old Waldorf, she writes, was a totem; the new Waldorf was a fetish:

> The totem performs publicly to identify a clan – or in this case a class. Although a totem is generally associated with the demarcation of consanguinity, its territorial dimension has been acknowledged by anthropologists. The hotel both framed the space of monopoly capitalism and monumentally represented it in the spectacle of the city. Here, the totem not only defines the membership of a community, it also marks its domain. By 'fetish' I mean a product that provides satisfaction to its user in its representation of a false source of power. The fetish performs privately or, if publicly, for private gratification. The fetish is characteristically unstable and unterritorial.[3]

For Wharton, the hinge between these two kinds of spaces was the Depression. Where the old Waldorf spectacularised real wealth and power, the new Waldorf – which was propped up by the federal government and didn't make a profit until 1945 – staged the grand illusion of *absent* capital, its image acting as a substitute for wealth and projecting a dream of future prosperity to an impoverished mass. The terminology of totem and fetish is useful, yet Wharton's underlying distinction between real and simulated prosperity is inexact. After all, the old Waldorf was already struggling by 1905 and running at a loss by 1915; it was only a jump in patronage during the First World War that saw it limp into the 1920s.[4] The old hotel sold a fabricated dream of prosperity as much as the new one.

What really distinguished the totemic late-nineteenth-century hotel from the fetishistic early-twentieth-century hotel was a marketing apparatus. The old Waldorf's capital was tied up in its land and its machinery. Utterly immovable, it was a bureaucratic-infrastructural installation. In Zygmunt Bauman's terms, it was a monument of 'heavy modernity', concerned as it was with territory and control.[5] With the parading ground of Peacock Alley, and the Pequod-like excesses of its colonialist ornamentation, the hotel expressed its power architecturally. The nineteenth-century grand hotel paradigm, however, was stuttering and failing in the early twentieth. Making profits meant banding together in large conglomerates like the United Hotels Company, the Bowman-Biltmore Hotels Corporation, the Boomer-du Pont Properties Corporation or the Statler Hotel Company; it meant investing equity into brands, not buildings; and it meant controlling multiple rather than single properties, arranged as a loose chain through ownership, lease or management contract.[6] These loose chains moved capital rapidly, speculating freely and affiliating or disaffiliating without sentimentality: a half-built hotel development could be re-branded a Ritz-Carlton and then sold off and re-re-branded the following year.[7] Exemplars of an emergent 'light modernity' of mobile capital, the new generation hotel, coming into maturity not in the Depression but in the 1910s, projected its power as an image, as a name and as a brand.[8]

The importance of the brand grew as the architectural individuality of hotels declined. The new generation of New York hotels included the St Regis (1904) and the rebuilt Plaza (1907) uptown at the base of Central Park; and a slew of gigantic midtown hotels like the Hotel Astor (1905) at Times Square; the McAlpin (1912) and Vanderbilt (1913) close to the old Waldorf-Astoria; the Hotel Pennsylvania (1919) servicing Pennsylvania Station; and a core cluster including the Belmont (1908), Ritz-Carlton (1910), Biltmore (1913), Commodore (1919), Ambassador (1921) and Roosevelt (1924) surrounding Grand Central Station.[9] The 'Terminal City' hotels around Grand Central formed a new zone of luxury consumption to the east of the city (commenting on the blueprints, one journalist noted that 'The last generation did not consider it good form to frequent hotels near "depots"').[10] The prosaic location matched the 'modern functionalism' of their Beaux Arts design, drawing the Waldorf era of rococo extravagance to a close.[11] Many of these hotels shared the same architectural provenance: the Belmont, Biltmore, Commodore, Ambassador and Ritz, as well as the Vanderbilt and newer additions to the Plaza, were all designed by architectural firm Warren and Wetmore. And many shared financial links: the Biltmore was originally leased and managed by the United Hotels Company, which would also build the nearby Roosevelt Hotel; after the First World War, the Biltmore passed into the hands of the Bowman-Biltmore Hotels Corporation, along with the nearby Belmont and Commodore.[12] (United Hotels and Bowman-Biltmore finally merged in 1929.) For Scott and Zelda on their honeymoon in 1920, the Terminal City hotels were interchangeable. They simply checked into the Commodore after being thrown out of the Biltmore for drunken misbehaviour. Not only did those hotels share the same architect and the same management, but they shared a network of underground tunnels connecting their lobbies directly with the station concourse.[13] They were a literal interchange, a dense infrastructural knot.

What distinguished these tangled hotels, then, was their enchanted names. But while the Biltmore, Ambassador and Ritz had namesakes across the country and across the world, not all of these hotels could be considered brands in the modern sense. The concept was still an evolving one. John Jakle, Keith Schulle and Jefferson Rogers, who have written variously on gas stations, motels, parking lots and fast-food restaurants, coined the concept of 'place-product-packaging' to describe the creation of branded corporate images projected onto landscapes, involving the adoption of readily identifiable logos, colour schemes, architectural designs, and service and product mixes. Gas stations pioneered 'place-product-packaging' in the 1910s; hotel chains tentatively followed in the 1920s.[14] The lead was taken by the Statler hotel chain, which developed centralised efficiencies along with a unified aesthetic. As Statler's key architectural consultant, W. Sydney Wagner, claimed in 1917:

> This similarity in style, together with a studied similarity in the forms and arrangements of the public rooms, corridors, and guest rooms, has given to these hotels a striking family resemblance. The guest arriving at one, after having stopped at another, is immediately impressed with the fact that he is again in a Statler Hotel. There is, in addition to a definite advertising value, a good deal of sound psychology in this principle of intentional similarity; yet I know of only one other chain of hotels – the Ritz-Carlton – in which there is any evidence of its recognition and use.[15]

The multinational Ritz was the kind of chain hotel that Fitzgerald was more familiar with and more fascinated by. The form of the Ritz was, if anything, more fluid and unterritorial than the duplicable Statler. A hotel which 'put the adjective "ritzy" in common parlance and caused London bankers to realize the cash value of a name',[16] the Ritz was less a place than a fiction of global finance: a floating trademark residing temporarily in ephemeral structures. While Statler mastered the arts of centralised and Taylorised control, the Ritz was de-centred and dispersed. And while Statler grew through duplication, Ritz grew through assimilation and metamorphosis. Much like the Trump name in the era of late capitalism, 'Ritz' could take the architectural form of a hotel, an apartment block, a golfing community or a ship; it could take the commodity form of a chair, a cigar or a song. The company could generate capital not only by renting rooms, but by endorsing products, merchandising its image and franchising its brand. Where advances in managerial technologies made possible the old Waldorf-Astoria, advances in marketing and intellectual property law were prerequisites for the success of the Ritz. Fitzgerald, too (whose books, to his embarrassment, were once advertised under the tag line, 'Make it a Fitzgerald Christmas'), understood the monetary value of his own name.[17] Already himself a formidable brand, Fitzgerald identified with, hitched himself to but also critiqued this hinge-point in the history of the American corporation, when names became as valuable as real estate. Fitzgerald was well equipped to represent America's emerging branded spaces, and to think about space beyond architecture.

All that Is Solid

Corporations yearn, like Gatsby, for a transcendent identity beyond any 'stable, definable body'.[18] Yet while Gatsby's weightless self-invention transforms him, in some critical accounts, into a symbol of a greater whole – part of the 'alphabet' of America's 'collective consciousness or national subjectivity'[19] – the dematerialised corporation allegorised in Fitzgerald's novella 'The Diamond as

Big as the Ritz' (1922) signifies nothing more than its own mobility and liquidity. It signifies money.

'The Diamond as Big as the Ritz', set in rural Montana, has nothing and everything to do with the hotel of its title. A pedantic yet crucial thing to note about its title is that the diamond in question – a diamond mountain measuring a cubic mile – is much bigger than the Ritz. Among a generation of American super-hotels, the Ritz-Carlton was 'the smallest among the best hotels in New York'.[20] It was built along English lines, with a (slightly inflated) English sense of scale and an English 'idea of quietness and calm', according to its mastermind, William Harris.[21] At fourteen floors and 300 rooms, it was dwarfed by its neighbour, the Biltmore, at 26 floors and 1,000 rooms, and by the Hotel Pennsylvania, the largest hotel in the world at the time, at 22 floors and 2,200 rooms. If Fitzgerald's title was trying to evoke the gigantism of New York architecture, we would instead be reading about a Diamond as Big as the Pennsylvania; but the title is trying to measure the gigantism of international capital, and to give a (necessarily impossible) sense of material scale and value to an unstable and unterritorial corporate brand. Fitzgerald's title hovers, therefore, between the material and the immaterial, the first in a series of similes in the novella trying to imbue money with a fixed form.

Before looking at Fitzgerald's novella, it is worthwhile recounting the historical journey toward liquidity of the Ritz, in order to speak more specifically about capitalism and brand culture in the 1910s and 1920s. The Ritz name used to be attached to the body of César Ritz, who mythically began life as a Swiss goatherd, before working through the ranks of various restaurants and hotels as a bellhop, waiter, maître d' and manager. He was taken on as the manager of the Savoy in London in 1889, proving valuable not only for his know-how but for his hard-earned connections (Cornelius Vanderbilt, J. P. Morgan and the Prince of Wales were fans) and for his name-recognition in the press. At times, he was a mere figurehead for the Savoy, with interests in hotel ventures in fourteen other cities leading to frequent international travel. César formalised his international ambitions by establishing the Ritz Hotel Development Company Ltd with the intention of spawning Ritzes across the world. When the famous manager was fired from the Savoy for cultivating his interests and neglecting his everyday duties, Ritz committed his energies to building his first eponymous hotel in Paris in 1898. At the same time, he bought an interest in the Carlton in London, a hotel whose noble name (finally appended to 'Ritz' when the company invested in America) derived from its proximity to the former residence of the Prince Regent. The Ritz Hotel Development Company Ltd and the Carlton Hotel Ltd, with overlapping shareholders and boards of directors, constituted the London-based hub of César's expansionary mission. The dual companies were not to be the headquarters of a coherent, centrally organised Ritz chain. They did not fully finance or fully administer hotels. Rather, they were gatekeepers of the Ritz name: a central licensing apparatus for a loose, decentralised and self-propagating franchise of global Ritzes. Through this apparatus, 'Ritz' began to separate from the body and the labour of César, to be parcelled out among a complex network of affiliated corporations.

César collapsed in the Carlton in 1902, suffering a nervous breakdown. Stepping down from management and resigning his directorships, he had little input into the design of the new London Ritz (1906), pushed through by the boards of the Development Company Ltd and the Carlton Hotel Ltd.[22] Plans for a London Ritz were expedited, according to the chairman of the Carlton Hotel Ltd, William Harris, in order to 'secur[e] for all time the title of Ritz Hotel in London [. . .]. You must remember that we had no right to that name, but the construction of this hotel gives us the right.'[23] With César essentially incapacitated by his fragile physical and mental health, the desire to claim the Ritz name as intellectual property by deploying it in the marketplace redoubled in intensity. Harris and César's wife Marie-Louise helped forge international partnerships in which the London-based Ritz apparatus provided the expertise and the Ritz name and crest, and local investors supplied the capital. The London office sometimes offered oversight of the kitchens or other managerial assistance. They held the common stock and a controlling interest in these local Ritz companies, and drew much of their profit from such arrangements, without excessive financial exposure if the local hotels failed.[24] In this way, Ritzes were established in Madrid (1910), New York (1910), Philadelphia (1911) and Montreal (1912), with other Ritz-aligned hotels in Pittsburgh, Buenos Aires, Cairo, Johannesburg, Berlin, Hamburg, Rome, Naples, Lucerne and elsewhere. Replica Ritz-Carlton restaurants – porcelain, cutlery and all – were also installed in four gigantic Hamburg-Amerika cruise liners: the *Amerika* (1905), the *Kaiserin Auguste Victoria* (1908), the *Imperator* (1912) and the *Vaterland* (1913). Ritz was afloat.

The only impediment to Ritz was America. In 1907, the London operation registered the Ritz-Carlton Restaurant and Hotel Company Inc. as an American beachhead and as an assertion of their rights to the Ritz name in that country.[25] Chairman William Harris went to New York to speak with financier Robert Walton Goelet, who wanted to build a Ritz on his plot on Madison Avenue. He was prepared to pay for the rights to the brand and to finance the hotel's construction. The firm Warren and Wetmore would file the architectural plans.[26] The *New York Times* reported in April 1908 that plans for the hotel were 'now all approved'.[27] It seems, however, that Harris was negotiating the deal without César's consent or without his knowledge. When Harris returned from negotiations in New York, César was ill and unable to discuss the matter. When César was well enough, 'To the surprise of Chairman Harris and the Directors of the Ritz company, he then refused to allow his name to be used'; indeed, he threatened to bring injunction proceedings against anyone who tried.[28] César was asserting his power for the last time. He seems to have been concerned about quality control, and about American wages and conditions being, improbably, too high: 'The greatest difficulty, in his opinion, would be the retaining of a competent staff without the staff being spoiled by getting over rich.'[29] Perhaps pacified by the fact that his old friends Albert Keller and Auguste Escoffier were travelling to New York to enforce aristocratic standards, and perhaps weakened by his ill-health, César relented and handed over his name. That year César retired to Saint-Cloud and 'gradually sank out of life, until 1912, when, to all intents and purposes, his life finished.'[30] He spent his last years in private Swiss clinics and died in 1918.

As one speaker noted at the opening of the New York Ritz-Carlton in December 1910, this was the 'spirit of the Ritz-Carlton system brought from Europe to New York': a suitably supernatural conception of the global brand name.[31] In America, the spirit of the Ritz spread rapidly.[32] In 1917, a local realty corporation in New York, burdened with a failing apartment block diagonally opposite the new Ritz-Carlton, obtained the rights to the Ritz name for 'a tremendous sum' and rebranded their development 'Carlton Mansions – the Ritz-Carlton of Apartment Houses'. The venture was an overwhelming success, touted as 'an innovation in real-estate advertising'.[33] Another New York apartment hotel, Ritz Tower, was constructed with Hearst money in 1925 (while Fitzgerald was still writing under contract for *Hearst's International*). Further Ritzes sprang up in Atlantic City (1921), Boca Raton (1926) and Boston (1927).

The Ritz business model was also its marketing model. The Ritz advertised relatively little, instead preferring to lease out its name for merchandising and endorsements. While the London organisation set up the Ritz Carlton Cigar Company Ltd in 1919,[34] from 1915 into the 1920s the Gimbels department store on Broadway advertised a furniture suite called '"The Ritz-Carlton": An exquisite reproduction of the POOLEY-designed suite, which is found in the bedrooms of the luxurious Ritz-Carlton Hotel in New York. At an almost unbelievably low price.'[35] The Ritz name also appeared in product endorsements, a marketing technique that gained new sophistication and popularity after the First World War. The technique was popular, claimed Stanley Resor, president of advertising firm J. Walter Thompson, because 'the eternal "search for authority" led people to revere whomever in a democracy could best fill the traditional role of aristocracy.'[36] The Ritz lent their aristocratic stamp to such mundane items as Bigelow-Hartford carpets ('because to hotel men, wearing quality is of as great importance as beauty'),[37] Fatima cigarettes,[38] Sawtay nut butter ('What the World-Famous Chef of the Ritz-Carlton has to say of SAWTAY')[39] and Yuban, the Arbuckle Guest Coffee.[40] The most befitting cross-promotion was the 1918 campaign for Smirnoff's Shampoo Powder, a self-mythologising, pre-Soviet Russian brand now being manufactured under licence in America. Its advertisements simultaneously evoked hoarded Tsarist riches and vaporous modern capital by wrapping an international licensing deal in the garb of Scheherazade. The Ritz's Smirnoff's endorsement comes from Charles of the Ritz's hairdressing parlour, but it seems at first to come from the hotel itself – brought back, for a brief moment, in virtual corporeality: '"An added charm to the Hair," says the Ritz-Carlton [. . .], "improving the loveliness of its lustre. We gladly endorse and recommend it."'[41] (Or to put it another way: you too can have hair as lustrous as the Ritz.) Like the Carlton Mansions advertising strategy, it was important to sell an aspirational Ritz to 'the masses – the four million', wrote a contemporary commentator in an advertising industry magazine: because to offer something 'that all New York was talking about for smart exclusiveness would be infinitely more desirable than [a hotel] recognized merely by the wealthy.'[42]

It worked. Irving Lewis Allen describes the circulation of Ritz through the language:

> The rich and elegant of the city were collectively known as *the ritz* and *the ritzies* (collective nouns), who sometimes *ritzed* (transitive verb) their social inferiors. *Ritzy* (adjective), *ritzier* and *ritziest* (comparative adjectives), *ritziness* (abstract noun), and *ritzily* (adverb) – all mean high style and conspicuous spending. The style of the Ritz inspired several whole phrases in slang: *in the ritz* (in fat city); the complaint *this ain't the Ritz*; the reproachful observation *acting ritzy*; the gentle warning *don't get ritzy with me*; and, well, getting ritzy in *put(ting) on the ritz* was in the language by 1921.[43]

'Ritz' became an abstracted, infinitely flexible, infinitely scalable measure of value: a set of magical consonants blown like fairy-dust over ordinary objects, people, or streetscapes to make them glow with significance.[44] 'There was magic in the name Ritz', Marie-Louise Ritz observed, 'magic that was worth many thousands of pounds to many people.'[45] Just as Daisy's voice in *The Great Gatsby* is said to be 'full of money [. . .] the jingle of it, the cymbals' song of it', so 'Ritz' – moving from tongue to air from a grand, alveolar 'R' to a twinkling, sibilant 'itz' – was a song of money.[46]

Richard Godden's reading of the fetish in Fitzgerald is enlightening on this point. For Godden, it is Žižek that best captures Fitzgerald's enchanted relationship with money: 'Fitzgerald reaches for the tone of Daisy's voice; Žižek for the lexicon of the sublime.' If Ritz represents a form of currency, then it is the half-material, half-sublime currency that Žižek describes in *The Sublime Object of Ideology*:

> Žižek [. . .] suggests that we treat money as though it were double-bodied: the notes and coins in our wallets and pockets crumple and tarnish, yet their value remains unmarked, constituting what Žižek terms 'an indestructible

and immutable body [value] which persists beyond the corruption of the physical body,' a 'body within the body of money,' describable for Žižek as money's 'sublime object.'[47]

Žižek argues that the modern mind is cynical: that we all know very well there is nothing magical about money, yet in our use of money in the marketplace we act *as if* coins and notes were made of a special substance over which time has no power. What makes Fitzgerald interesting is that he does not take this alchemical relation for granted. The transformation of the physical to the immaterial in modern capitalism becomes his ultimate subject, and the transformation of architectural space into branded space, something that became conceivable with the emergence of the double-bodied Ritz, was a defining example of this Fitzgeraldian trope.

Ritz/Fitz

Fitzgerald could write authoritatively on marketing culture because he self-reflexively participated in the industry throughout the 1920s. He had a brief career at advertising agency Barron Collier in 1919; his proudest moment was the invention of the slogan for the Muscatine Steam Laundry. In 1929, with his writing career going sour and his money dwindling, he was paid $1,500 for appearing with John Barrymore and Cornelius Vanderbilt Jr in advertisements promoting a beauty contest sponsored by the Woodbury Soap company. His brief sketch 'Ten Years in the Advertising Business', published in the *Princeton Alumni Weekly* in 1929, deprecatingly illustrates these two incidents, and shows Fitzgerald making a perfunctory attempt to maintain the sanctity of his name ('it's understood that I'm in no sense to endorse this product').[48] Yet in some sense Fitzgerald's career was built on endorsements. His fiction is littered with product placement, especially luxury hotel brands, and journalists covering the Fitzgerald mystique couldn't help but buy in: 'In a pleasant corner of the Plaza tea garden he sounded like an intellectual Samson prophesying the crumbling of its marble columns.'[49] Fitz and the Ritz were allied commodities.

For the Ritz-Carlton in particular, the collected works of Fitzgerald and the legs of Fred Astaire were the most valuable endorsements it could have dreamed of. Especially so, given American publishing was emerging out of a mindset that was generally sceptical about brand names in print. What Philip Curtiss, writing in *Harper's* in 1922, called an unofficial 'John Doe law in literature' had somewhat suppressed the mention of actual persons, places and proprietary products in American fiction. Policed most vigorously by newspaper editors, it sought to keep fiction free from advertising and free from libellous content. 'Even an American writer would not hesitate to put up his hero and heroine at the Ritz in London or the Ritz in Madrid,' Curtiss complains, 'but when the unhappy couple returned to their native New York he could find them no place to lay their heads except in a shadowy structure known as "The Harlton" or "The Spitz"'.⁵⁰ A younger generation of writers, however, were paying as much attention to that convention as they were to the Volstead Act.

Yet there was a critical dimension to Fitzgerald's use of brands. Fitzgerald deploys Ritz conspiratorially, and with intent, in 'The Diamond as Big as the Ritz', even as other brands (the Rolls-Pierce automobile) or locations (the town of Hades) are gleefully fabricated in John Doe style. The Ritz-Carlton is only mentioned twice in the story, and only to reiterate the tag line of the title. Yet if you look carefully, the brand is everywhere, rhyming and vamping like an Irving Berlin lyric. The discoverer of the diamond mountain, the deceased patriarch of the Washington family, was named Fitz-Norman Culpepper Washington, a name in which Norman buttresses Fitz with connotations of an ancient bloodline in the same way that the royal Carlton buttressed Ritz to give the impression of double-barrelled gentility. Fitz-Norman's son is Braddock Tarleton Washington. Fitzgerald reused the name Tarleton in other short stories, but here it clearly echoes Carlton. From there, the eye is drawn to the hyphenation and the tell-tale 'itz' of the 'Schnlitzer-Murphys', another family of enormous wealth; then to the nonsense Italian name of the adventurer and jewel-hunter 'Critchtichiello', a kind of little Ritz, or Ritz in waiting, who eventually destroys the Washington family stronghold with a squadron of aircraft. Nearly everyone in this tale, therefore, aspires toward the divine state of 'Ritz'. But what is that state?

Clearly, in the first instance, it is to be rich. The first actual mention of the Ritz-Carlton emerges in the tale out of the obsessive repetition of 'rich', in a conversation between two boys on a train:

> [. . .] it promised rich confectionery for his curiosity when Percy invited him to spend the summer at his home 'in the West.' [. . .]
> 'My father,' he said, 'is by far the richest man in the world.' [. . .]
> 'By far the richest,' repeated Percy. [. . .]
> 'He must be very rich,' said John simply. 'I'm glad. I like very rich people. The richer a fella is, the better I like him. [. . .] I visited the Schnlitzer-Murphys last Easter. Vivian Schnlitzer-Murphy had rubies as big as hen's eggs [. . .] – '
> 'That's nothing at all. My father has a diamond bigger than the Ritz-Carlton Hotel.'⁵¹

The construction of this aural landscape is both freewheeling – unfolding according to the child logic of a rhyming game – and claustrophobically repetitive. Those two properties are interrelated. Just as it did in American culture, Ritz has become an omniscient presence in the tale through its shape-shifting liquidity. Ritz is everywhere because it is flexible enough to signify any form of capitalist desire. It functions symbolically as the disembodied spirit of capital.

Ritz can therefore be used as a hermeneutic agent – a drop of iodine in the blood – that allows us to see associations between seemingly unrelated things. In a story filled with ciphers and word games, Fitzgerald is encouraging us to read conspiratorially, and by extension, to read America in the same way. The real-world Ritz bonded together the moneyed elite (the Ritz hotel) with their aspirational middle-class imitators (Ritz-endorsed shampoo); in the same way, Fitzgerald's fictional Ritz creates imaginary connections between old, new, and emergent forms of wealth and power, from Fitz-Norman's slave-driven feudalism, to the Schnlitzer-Murphys' Gilded Age conspicuous consumption, to Critchtichiello's techno-piracy, to the overnight publishing fortune of a certain F. Scott Fitz-Gerald. In other words, the tale sketches a total order, a system, which shifts and vamps through history even as it unfolds according to a rigid, singular logic. Critchtichiello, a stand-in for the Italian anarchist archetype of the Sacco and Vanzetti era, might blow up the Fitz-Norman château, just as an anarchist was alleged to have bombed the House of Morgan on Wall Street in 1920; but the system – Ritz – will go on unimpeded, if not strengthened, in an age of delirious expansion.

The monomaniacal fetish at the centre of the novella is in fact not the diamond but this unplaceable Ritz with which the diamond is compared. The tale, then, is about capital's struggle to make the metaphoric leap encoded in the story's title: to become as big as the Ritz, to escape the physical, to become liquid and transcendent. The novella begins with the revelation of the ultimate *illiquid* commodity. The Washington family's secret diamond mountain is near impossible to exploit and trade: 'There was no valuing it by any regular computation, however, for it was *one solid diamond* – and if it were offered for sale not only would the bottom fall out of the market, but [. . .] there would not be enough gold in the world to buy a tenth part of it.'[52] What the Washington family rather unhappily controls, therefore, is a pre-modern kind of wealth: a dragon's hoard of (mostly) untouched and untouchable treasure. Nonetheless, the Washingtons work to liquidise their asset by smuggling out pieces of the diamond to international investors, and converting the proceeds into 'the rarest of all elements – radium – so that the equivalent of a billion dollars in gold could be placed in a receptacle no bigger than a cigar box'.[53] The Washingtons keep a notebook written in cipher detailing the thousand banks in which the radium has been deposited and the thousand aliases used to open the accounts. The proliferation of the word 'radiant' in the tale and the emphasis laid on the diamond's innate radiance ('the first yellow beam of the sun struck through the innumerable prisms of an immense and exquisitely chiselled diamond – and a white radiance was kindled that glowed upon the air like a fragment of the morning star') suggests that the Washingtons have not merely exchanged a mineral for a metal in trading diamonds for radium, but have disembodied their asset and turned it into light.[54] They have extracted the diamond's essence to store in safe deposit boxes. The ploy seems less like a functional financial strategy than a phantasmal metaphor for a Morgan-style international banking network, where luminescence represents the after-image of fluid capital.

WHITE SPACE

Fitzgerald's story not only allows us to think about the fluidity of the Ritz brand, but also about the fluidity of hotel space in the early twentieth century, with its emerging aesthetic of whiteness, emptiness, luminescence and translucency, epitomised in the open-air fantasia of the hotel roof garden. 'The Diamond as Big as the Ritz' represents hotel architecture through the presence of the Washingtons' marble château which stands next to the diamond mountain. Fitted out with a rooftop garden, elevators, concealed orchestras and magical conveniences (panels that slide away at the push of invisible buttons, cinema screens installed in bathrooms), the château is double-coded as both a fairytale castle and a metropolitan hotel. With its room that resembles 'a platonic conception of the ultimate prism [...] lined with an unbroken mass of diamonds', the château would have evoked for a local readership the New York Ritz, which in 1915 had installed what one advertisement described as 'the brilliant, glistening Crystal Room' as a centrepiece attraction (Figure 3.1).[55] The Ritz, like the Washington's château, glowed like a diamond. An architect from Warren and Wetmore pointed to the use of 'crystal prisms' in the hotel's intricate lighting rig, which add 'much to the diversity and brilliance of the interior – brilliance that is multiplied by a skilful but restrained use of mirrors.'[56]

The Washingtons' château-hotel deceives the eye: it is at once immovably, medievally solid ('The many towers, the slender tracery of the sloping parapets') and sublimely fluid ('the shattered softness of the intersecting planes of star-shine and blue shade'). An impenetrable fortress (with anti-aircraft guns, slaves' quarters and a prison bunker), it is also a fragrance, a sound and a shimmer of light. For John T. Unger, visiting at the invitation of his schoolfriend Percy Washington, the château emerges into view and melts in the same moment: it 'climbed in marble radiance half the height of an adjoining mountain, then melted in grace, in perfect symmetry, in translucent feminine languor'.[57] Designed by a 'moving-picture fella', the château is filled with illusory surfaces, from actual cinema screens to frames that one can tumble through ('he began to roll, startled at first, in the direction of the wall, but when he reached the wall its drapery gave way, and sliding two yards farther down a fleecy incline he plumped gently into water the same temperature as his body'), to surfaces that melt upon human touch ('There was a room where the solid, soft gold of the walls yielded to the pressure of his hand').[58] It is a space that forces the user to engage with its spatiality and scale ('he mounted a long flight of stairs') even as it melts all sense of scale with near-instantaneous navigation ('she pressed the button that shot them upward').[59] This figurative Ritz

Figure 3.1 The Crystal Room at the Hotel Ritz-Carlton, New York, c.1915 (Credit: Byron Company, New York, NY, Museum of the City of New York, 93.1.1.5390)

represents hotel space as profoundly contradictory: a monumentalisation of evanescence.

The château-hotel, like the diamond mountain it stands beside, is on its way to becoming immaterial. And like the diamond, this dissolution is associated with whiteness or 'white radiance'.⁶⁰ The château is constructed with marble and ivory as well as diamond-clad surfaces, which 'dazzled the eyes with a whiteness that could be compared only with itself'. Prismatic refractions of many colours flash across the château's surfaces, as when the floor 'flame[s] in brilliant patterns from lighting below'.⁶¹ But whiteness, and the absence this whiteness implies, is key to the space's meaning. The château, like the Ritz, is in many ways a 'white' space: in terms of its literal colour, its void-like nowhere-ness and its racial segregations, all of which are intimately entangled.

It was César Ritz himself who set the template for the early-twentieth-century hotel as a radiantly white space. Ritz was a student of sanitary reform, and during the development of the Paris Ritz he peppered the briefing note for his architect Charles Mewès with words like 'modernity', 'efficient' and 'hygienic'. He was anti-Victorian in his sympathies – no wallpaper, no ornaments, no dust-collecting plush or velvet – and white walls and white furnishings accorded with his interest in cleanliness.⁶² Unsurprisingly, therefore, one reviewer of the newly-opened Paris Ritz linked the hotel's interiors with hospital interiors:

> Were I afraid of catching tuberculosis – the most contagious of diseases – I should go to the Hôtel Ritz. Every bedroom faces south, and has wide, high windows that solicit light. There are no bed curtains. The window-curtains are of white muslin, so as to be often washed. The white walls would show the least speck of dust; so would the highly polished furniture. I cannot think of where a microbe could take refuge, unless in the carpets [. . .]. The bath is marble, and the walls are faced with Dutch tiles. The whole room might be 'scalded' with steam.⁶³

Even before the New York iteration of the Ritz-Carlton opened in 1910, the Plaza (1907) imported the white Ritz aesthetic to Fifth Avenue. The Plaza's manager, Frederick Sterry, cited the London Ritz as his inspiration for a no paintings and no murals policy. In the Plaza lobby, whiteness prevailed. There would be 'no room' for mural decorations 'as the fine Italian marble will run to within two or three feet of the ceiling'.⁶⁴ An advertisement for Enamolin paint described the hotel's interiors as 'Immaculate. The Plaza Hotel, New York, used Enamolin because of its porcelain-like beauty and perfect whiteness.'⁶⁵ A journalist at its opening described the 'quiet rose and green tints' of the sofas as giving the lobby 'its only colour'.⁶⁶

The whiteness of the Ritz and the Plaza was inevitably charged with race. '[T]he Grand Hotel's association with an ineffable *bel mondo*', writes James

Hay on the escapist 'white telephone' films of fascist Italy, 'was easily articulated to its racialization of exclusivity and even beauty as a Light or White space of leisure.'[67] It was not simply the predominance of white surfaces, but the concomitant bareness and restraint of the interiors that fed into this racialisation of grand hotel architecture. The 'philosophical basis for the ideal of the denuded modern surface', writes Anne Anlin Cheng, can be found in Adolf Loos's essay 'Ornament and Crime' (1908). A polemic directed at nineteenth-century bourgeois culture and its desire to embellish and encase surfaces and objects, Loos's essay explicitly racialises the treatment of architectural surfaces in a social evolutionary framework. Loos argues that modernity has evolved beyond the need for ornament. In this essay and elsewhere, he suggests that modernity has taken root most securely in America (where he briefly lived and studied during the 1890s, and where he became interested in the permeability of hotel lobbies).[68] Loos regards the compulsion to revive ornamentation as a degenerate return to the pre-modern. Comparing heavily decorated interiors with the tattoos of Papuan peoples, Loos argues that excessive ornamentation belongs to a primitive stage of cultural development – characterised by uncontrolled eroticism, feminine adornment, infantile babbling and criminality – a stage that the superego of 'modern man' must outgrow and restrain. As Cheng argues, the 'ideal of architectural purity – defined as specifically the liberation from "primitive" and "feminine" inclinations – is inextricably bound to the twin ideals of culture and civilization.'[69] Loos dreams of a civilised space of perfect whiteness: 'Soon the streets of the cities will shine like white walls! Like Zion, the Holy City, Heaven's capital.'[70] He thereby provides, Cheng writes, 'the basis for a long trajectory of Modernist preoccupation with the idea of clean surfaces, culminating in Le Corbusier's [. . .] resolute call for the ubiquity of a coat of opaque whitewash'.[71]

We can detect a similar racialisation of elaborately ornate spaces in Henry James's late short story 'A Round of Visits' (1910). The original Waldorf-Astoria, built in the 1890s, is fictionalised in the tale as the Hotel Pocahontas, named after the figure of colonial mythography. Its excessiveness is represented as a savage jungle of ornaments: 'the heavy heat, the luxuriance, the extravagance, the quantity, the colour, gave the impression of some wondrous tropical forest, where vociferous, bright-eyed, and feathered creatures, of every variety of size and hue, were half smothered between undergrowths of velvet and tapestry and ramifications of marble and bronze.'[72] The Pocahontas is not only architecturally excessive, but architecturally miscellaneous. Like the riotous polystylism of the Waldorf-Astoria – with its Second Empire mansard roof, its Austrian Baroque onion domes and turrets, and its themed rooms (the East India Suite, the Colonial Bedroom, the Pompeiian Bedroom, the Marie Antoinette Room, the Turkish Room, the Russian Baths) – the Pocahontas in 'A Round of Visits' also shifts from 'one portentous "period" of decoration [. . .] to another', a quality which makes the space appear racially suspect: the narratorial eye notes the 'rich confused complexion of the Pocahontas'.[73] The language of confused complexions echoes a thread of early-twentieth-century American architectural discourse that expressed a suspicion of *fin de siècle* architectural eclecticism in racist terms. As analysed in Adrienne Brown's monograph *The Black Skyscraper*, figures including Louis Sullivan decried architectural eclecticism as 'miscegenation', and associated the style with artistic sterility and perversity.[74] The architect John Beverley Robinson criticised buildings that joined together two formally or stylistically dissimilar parts (like the combined Waldorf and Astoria itself), as these combinations created 'an unequally matched pair, of hostile race and alien feeling'. This is, he directly states, a case of 'architectural miscegenation'.[75] In place of eclecticism, Robinson advocated instead for a 'purity' of architectural form; for Sullivan, the solution was a virile, modern, national style.[76]

It was this racialised language of purity, coolness and control that was invoked by advocates of the new white hotel aesthetic. Reviews and commentaries frequently referred to the Ritz's 'cool' and 'restrained' interiors (bordering on 'severity'),[77] and its 'pure and delicate beauty', with its walls 'painted white and rubbed down to the smoothness of ivory'.[78] By extension, a guest in this kind of space was a more self-possessed and self-restrained subject than the loud and creaturely jungle-dwellers in James's 'A Round of Visits'. If, as Brown argues, whiteness was constructed as a distinct category of affective experience – 'an identity historically yoked to self-sovereignty and a heightened capacity for bodily and emotional control' – then the restrained Ritz was a space in which the white subject imagined themselves to be more white.[79] One reviewer in *Good Furniture* magazine writes of the 'restful effect of free, uninterrupted expanses of wall' in hotels like the Ritz; another noted the Ritz's 'cool' and 'restful' colour scheme.[80] Similarly, Mary Doyle, a former hotel newspaper stand manager, recollected that the architectural 'hodgepodge' of the old Waldorf generated 'noisy, jostling throngs'; yet in the 'cool and quiet foyer of the Plaza', some of the 'noisiest and more carefree of the Waldorf's patrons had become models of restrained propriety'.[81] Doyle imagines, therefore, that the Plaza's white spaces exerted a disciplinary effect, cooling and taming the multitudinous crowds of the urban jungle. While Peacock Alley, the central connective spine of the old Waldorf-Astoria, functioned as another boisterous, beplumed boulevard for the promenading bourgeois, the white spaces of the Ritz and Plaza tried to negate urban space. '[Q]uietness and calm' were the stated ideals of the New York Ritz, such that 'tired and jaded New Yorkers may enjoy tranquillity and peace in a hotel and forget that they are in a great bustling city.'[82] This new hotel aesthetic represented an escape into whiteness.

It is no coincidence, then, that Daisy Buchanan in *The Great Gatsby* (herself surrounded by a cluster of white imagery) is drawn to the Plaza as the site of the climactic confrontation of the novel. The Plaza seems to be the 'white palace' that Nick Carraway fantasises her inhabiting ('High in a white palace the king's daughter, the golden girl . . .').[83] Nor is it a coincidence that Jordan Baker responds to Tom Buchanan's tirade in the Plaza suite about the fall of family institutions and the rise of miscegenation by murmuring 'We're all white here'.[84] This was a space that very much belonged to a white elite. And given that the 'spatial dimensions of Jim Crow' metastasised into a 'basically national system' in the early-twentieth century, as 'urban territory was racialized in new and more intense ways', the white space of the hotel can be read not simply as an architectural construct, but as a socio-legal construct as well, that actively elided the presence of Black guests and workers.[85] Garrett Bridger Gilmore argues that 'the racial structure that subtends [*The Great Gatsby*]'s economic class structures points us towards the ultimate source of value – black labor – that Nick does not bring into discourse'.[86] The racial logic of white space, in other words, necessitated a disavowal of the value created by Black bodies. This is manifest in 'The Diamond as Big as the Ritz', in which the fortune of the Washingtons is founded on enslaved Black workers 'who had never realized that slavery was abolished'.[87] The process of liquifying the diamond is therefore a process of laundering expropriated wealth, turning Black labour into white luminescence. Guests of the Washingtons' château-hotel, furthermore, 'are granted a leisured lethargy akin to sedated deliquescence, founded on the barely visible work of Washington's slaves' who operate the building's magical contraptions for pampering white bodies.[88]

Historically, the white space of the Plaza in *Gatsby* was also founded on elided and exploited Black labour. While James noted the lounging Black waiters in Reconstruction-era Saratoga, Black workers would be displaced from much of the hospitality sector in New York by the end of the nineteenth century, particularly in high-end hotels and restaurants, through a combination of racism, new sources of cheap immigrant labour and an inability to gain full access to white-controlled hospitality unions. As a correspondent to the Black newspaper the *New York Age* reported in 1905, 'It is quite safe to say that in the last fifteen years the colored people have lost about every occupation that was regarded as peculiarly their own.'[89] However, during the New York City waiters' strike of 1912, in which thousands of hotel workers took to the streets to demand basic conditions, the Plaza took the lead in recruiting thousands of Black workers from the south as strike-breakers. 'The first appearance of colored waiters in the first-class hotels in New York, after an absence of many years, took place last Thursday,' reported the *New York Age*, 'when the Plaza, regarded as the leading hotel in the city, discharged all the floor waiters who were making demands and filled their places with trained colored waiters.'[90] Frederick Sterry, who still managed the Plaza, offered to supply the other hotels of the city with up to 10,000 more Black workers: or to 'ship negroes', as the *Boston Globe* revealingly phrased it.[91] A labour squeeze during the First World War, and a further waiters' strike in 1918, meant that Black workers continued to be employed at the Plaza.[92] The position of such workers, hired in such a fashion, was precarious. They occupied marginal roles and were almost certainly underpaid in comparison with their white colleagues, a phenomenon documented contemporaneously by Black scholars looking at labour conditions in the American service industry, from W. E. B. Du Bois in *The Philadelphia Negro* (1899) to Lorenzo J. Greene and Carter G. Woodson in *The Negro Wage Earner* (1930).[93] Concomitant with their marginal roles, Black workers occupied marginal spaces in interwar grand hotels – much like Black guests, if they were accommodated at all. Though New York hotels were 'among the most cosmopolitan in America', writes Scott Nearing, the city's establishments commonly refused service to Black guests, or ensured that Black visitors or musicians were made as invisible as possible by only allowing them to ride in the rear service elevators. 'Negroes do not ride in passenger elevators of Fifth Avenue Hotels,' one hotel manager declared.[94] Black hotel workers likewise tended to occupy less prominent or non-public spaces, which meant they couldn't be tipped for their work and struggled on their base wages.[95] In the Plaza, reports in the *Age* show that Black waiters were not employed in the prestige zone of the main dining room, but were instead restricted to spaces like the pantry or used as floor waiters to deliver room service.[96] It is therefore possible to imagine that the unnamed and unremarked floor waiter who knocks on the door of the Plaza suite in *Gatsby* is one of the Plaza's precarious Black employees. His arrival is accompanied by historically resonant symbols of Black exploitation: he carries the fixings for a mint julep, a cocktail associated with the Old South, while jazz (likely appropriated by white musicians) reverberates from the ballroom below. The waiter's brief appearance is an occasion to consider what is not seen in order to make the illusion of white space possible: of everything that happens, as if by magic, between Tom placing a call to room service and the eventual knock at the door.

For Fitzgerald's white protagonists, the white space of the hotel represents the possibility of negation and dissolution, a strangely desirable anywhere or nowhere into which the privileged white subject can regain their sense of separateness and self-sovereignty, away from the multiplicity of the city. During a decade in which 'the end of whiteness – white dominance of the world – became a widespread cultural obsession', this mode of escape into nowhere was a historical prefiguration of post-war 'white flight' into isolated and segregated white communities.[97] Jess Row argues that this white flight was accompanied by a flight into psychological isolation in white American fiction: into a state of imaginative autonomy which 'often feels like vacancy'.[98] The illusion of white autonomy in post-war American fiction is carefully constructed, Row suggests. The trope in American minimalist fiction of the white subject alone 'in vacant space, like an Edward Hopper painting', for instance, is achieved through a strategic 'social erasure' that foregrounds the lonely figure and empties the background. 'The city is not actually empty,' Row writes; 'the viewer is primed by the image to imagine it is. The social world has not collapsed; the viewer just wants to believe that it has.'[99] Imaginative autonomy that 'feels like vacancy' is a state of mind that can be discerned in Fitzgerald's short story 'May Day', which concludes with two 'glowing souls' 'taking form dimly' in the back of a taxi cab at dawn, with its roof open.[100] These souls are Peter Himmel and Philip Dean, two rich white Yale graduates who are in New York for a college fraternity dance. The city is theirs, and they have rebranded themselves Mr In and Mr Out by removing their coats and hanging stolen 'In' and 'Out' signs from a restaurant around their necks. Unencumbered by identity ('Mr. In and Mr. Out are not listed by the census-taker. [. . .] Oblivion has swallowed them and the testimony that they ever existed at all is vague and shadowy'), they float around like points of light, the bleary representatives of a class with total mobility.[101] Despite their disreputable appearance, they gain access everywhere, into the white spaces of the wealthy (Delmonicos, the Commodore, the Biltmore), consuming whiteness and nothingness ('The waiter drew the cork with an enormous *pop* – and their glasses immediately foamed with pale yellow froth') and then getting out and drifting on, paying for cabs along the way.[102] Entering the Biltmore Hotel, they sidestep a melee of brawling bodies in the lobby and escape into an elevator. The tumult of the social world fades: 'They heard loud voices; they saw the stout man spring; the picture suddenly blurred. Then they were in an elevator bound skyward.' Here, their restless search for white spaces reaches a terminal limit:

> 'What floor, please?' said the elevator man.
> 'Any floor,' said Mr. In.
> 'Top floor,' said Mr. Out.
> 'This is the top floor,' said the elevator man.
> 'Have another floor put on,' said Mr. Out.
> 'Higher,' said Mr. In.
> 'Heaven,' said Mr. Out.[103]

In 'May Day', the calmness, separateness, and pleasurable nowhereness of white space slips easily into deathliness. The freedom of white space turns out to be terrible and sublime: an escape from the terrestrial which is indistinguishable from the afterlife. Positioned just before the short story's coda, which features a trapped man in a dim hotel room deciding to shoot himself with a revolver, Mr In and Mr Out's journey into heavenly oblivion at the top of the Biltmore also reads as a figurative skyscraper suicide. White space in Fitzgerald consolidates and annihilates the white subject.

Rooftop Delirium

If Mr In and Mr Out explored the top floor of the Biltmore, they might have found the hotel's roof garden. Roof gardens are key white spaces in Fitzgerald's work, their moonlit forms portending both pleasure and death. Roof gardens sprang up in the theatre district of Manhattan in the late-nineteenth century as a place for outdoor summer cabarets; by the 1920s, they were more associated with hotels and the culture of dance bands.[104] In 'My Lost City', an essay about returning to Manhattan after a long absence, roof gardens are a crucial component of Fitzgerald's imaginary metropolis. He notes that 'it had been a tradition of mine to climb to the Plaza Roof to take leave of the beautiful city, extending as far as eyes could reach.' He mentions, too, an evening when an ex-lover, Ginevra King, 'made luminous the Ritz Roof on a brief passage through'.[105] The romance of a skyscraper roof vista, writes David E. Nye, derives from its presentation of a unified and ordered cityscape, or a 'capitalist "romance" [. . .] of rationalization, abstraction, and growth'. Atop a skyscraper, Nye argues, 'one momentarily adopts the perspective of the captain of industry', or 'the panopticon of corporate power.'[106] But the rooftop was also a space of giddiness and disorientation. The vertical movement up to these spaces was felt both as an escape and a loss, as Hans Ulrich Gumbrecht writes in his account of the spatial obsessions of the mid-1920s:

> This movement conquers, on the other hand, a spatial dimension that eliminates the claustrophobia – suffered by the workers in Metropolis – of living on an overcrowded surface. This is why roof gardens become the setting for an earthly paradise. If, however, rising above the ground in an elevator frees the passengers from the limitations of the human body as controlled by inertia and gravity, a price has to be paid for this redemption. Those who are redeemed must give up their claim to subjecthood [. . .].

'[R]ising above the ground', Gumbrecht suggests, 'is inevitably accompanied by the fear of losing the firm foundation under one's feet'.[107] Adrienne Brown argues that losing one's subjecthood in the upper reaches of a skyscraper was a specifically white anxiety in 1920s fiction. 'The self-sovereignty of the white men in these narratives, historically imagined to be their special providence,' Brown writes, 'appears frayed by the overwhelming vertical built environments of Jazz Age cities.' Brown argues that in the work of Fitzgerald, Mary Borden and Le Corbusier, the heavenly peaks of American skyscrapers

> stan[d] accused of turning once self-sovereign virile white agents into dwarfed and distracted subjects whose personal breakdowns in and around skyscrapers foretell whiteness's broader impending collapse as

a category alleged to be exceptional, superior or even distinct. Whereas racial minorities, viewed by these texts as purely corporeal beings, are rendered immune to the skyscraper's mesmerizing presence, white metropolitans appear swallowed, disoriented, disarmed, entranced and unnerved by it.[108]

Roof gardens were especially mesmerising and disorienting spaces because they could be any spaces. While hotels like the Ritz strove for the illusion of translucence within interior spaces ('The cheerful palm room beyond has a decidedly out-of-doors feeling that has been produced without the assistance of [. . .] electric lights hidden in bunches of grapes'), that desire was only truly achieved in the roof garden, where surfaces evaporated and elaborately landscaped scenery stood naked under the stars.[109] A reproduction German farmyard was set up on the roof of the Ritz in 1913 (the German-born manager liked to ascend to the roof and 'imagin[e] himself on the Alte Schloss'),[110] while a Japanese garden was installed on the three hundred metre-long roof of the Hotel Astor (the landscape artist Takeo Shiota explained his technique of tricking the eye: 'If we put a bridge on a low part we imagine there is a brook where there is no brook. If we put a boat on the white sand we imagine it is a shore') (Figure 3.2).[111] This was a space of fantasy: tennis matches were played on the roof of the Ritz;[112] Rudolph Valentino challenged a journalist to a boxing match on the roof of the Ambassador;[113] fashion shows, technology shows and dog shows were staged here. As Meir Wigoder

Figure 3.2 Drawing of the Hotel Astor roof garden and environs, 1905 (Credit: Byron Company, New York, NY, Museum of the City of New York, 93.1.1.5390)

argues, roof gardens were 'heterotopias', or places which are outside of all places, and which represent and invert the real world as if in a convex mirror:

> The heterotopian character of these gardens relied on three crucial principles: because they copied the horizontal experience of the streets, they enabled people to be above while feeling that they were actually below; they allowed visitors to imagine themselves in different settings – from the domestic garden to the countryside – without leaving the city; and, third, they offered the possibility of standing at the edge of the roof and looking down at the city as if it were a sublime, romantic view enjoyed from a mountain crag.[114]

When Fitzgerald comes to represent such spaces, descriptive details evaporate. In *The Beautiful and Damned*, a gathering of men for dinner on the Ritz roof garden is represented using dialogue organised as a theatrical script, with description relegated to bracketed asides. In a novel heavy with saturated detail and incident, it is a moment of carefully engineered lightness. The device is deployed again in *The Great Gatsby*, when Jordan Baker reports the backstory of Gatsby and Daisy's romance, and Daisy's eventual engagement to Tom Buchanan. The story is presented without speech marks in the first person, unfolding as a monologue in white space – not this time on the roof, but in one of the Plaza's translucent indoor-outdoor spaces: 'One October day in nineteen-seventeen – (said Jordan Baker that afternoon, sitting up very straight on a straight chair in the tea-garden at the Plaza Hotel) – I was walking along from one place to another half on the sidewalks and half on the lawns.'[115] Before Jordan locates her tale in the suburbs of Louisville, we are suspended with Jordan's voice in a void, drifting 'from one place to another'. The connection between the disembodied voice and white space makes sense in the context of technological history: the white space of the hotel was a key site for early amplification technologies and radio broadcasting.[116] A demonstration of new radio technologies on the roof garden of the Hotel Pennsylvania, including remote control and a transatlantic transmitter, caused a near stampede in March 1921. The press reaction to the event was just as supercharged: it was 'Without question [. . .] the most spectacular, mystifying, and gripping exhibition which New York has ever witnessed.'[117] The event 'radiated considerable verbal energy of various frequencies'.[118] To ascend to the top of a tower in the 1920s, then, was to be at one with the currents and whispers of the air.

Fitzgerald moves easily from the roof garden as a space of pleasurable disembodiment to the roof garden as a realm of the spirits. The dialogue on the Ritz roof garden in *The Beautiful and Damned* turns quickly, if jokingly, toward death. Between ordering and the arrival of the soup, Anthony Blaine launches facetiously into an argument about the meaninglessness of art and the tedium of the theatre. Everything is ephemeral, he suggests (as the text highlights the 'iridescent surface of sheer gloss' in his finely-combed hair); to write for the theatre is to 'pla[y] before a grand stand peopled with ghosts'.[119] The scene fulfils Anthony's prophecy of artistic impermanence by concluding mid-stream: '*(Here the soup arrives and what MAURY might have gone on to say is lost for all time)*'.[120] Shortly after the dialogue at the Ritz, a scene in the same theatrical manner presents a dialogue set in the white void of 'Paradise', implicitly linking the two spaces. The Paradise tableau features a dialogue between 'Beauty', the soon to be reincarnated spirit of Gloria Gilbert, and a 'Voice' in the wind. Paradise, described as '*a sort of outdoor waiting room through which blew gusts of white wind and occasionally a breathless hurried star*', is white space in its purest form: a transcendental waiting room strongly reminiscent of a hotel roof garden.[121] The fantasy scene is, after all, not that far removed from the kinds of entertainments commonly staged on hotel roofs. Just as Gloria is ceremonially reincarnated in Paradise as 'a ragtime kid, a flapper, a jazz-baby, and a baby vamp',[122] so a fashion show on the roof garden of the Hotel Pennsylvania featured 'a black satin outfit [. . .] worn by a little girl with gray eyes. She was billed as the "Little Vamp" and she did a Spanish dance with castanets.'[123] The rendering of Paradise as a roof garden also resonates with the finale of 'The Diamond as Big as the Ritz', when John T. Unger and the Washington sisters climb up to the château's roof garden at night to watch the aerial attack on the Washingtons' garrison. Like Paradise, here too we find a vacant space as white as the stars, but with the heavenly host replaced by a squadron of bombers:

> A minute later they had stepped out upon the star-white platform. Above, under the misty moon, sliding in and out of the patches of cloud that eddied below it, floated a dozen dark-winged bodies in a constant circling course. From here and there in the valley flashes of fire leaped toward them, followed by sharp detonations.[124]

Just as roof gardens could be styled to look like anywhere, so these spaces in Fitzgerald's fiction are unmoored from realist mimesis and become conduits to the fantastical in a variety of forms: from the comic fantasy of Paradise to the dystopian fantasy of 'The Diamond as Big as the Ritz'. In one text, the roof garden gives birth to Beauty; in the other, to fire and death. Yet they are both of a piece: in both, the roof garden is at the threshold of another world.

WRECKING BALL

The dark-winged bombers portend the end of Braddock Washington's regime. He gathers together his slaves and commits a horrific mass murder-suicide in a vast explosion that evaporates the diamond in a flash of iridescence. The château-hotel also implodes, leaving a smoking ruin: 'There was no fire – what smoke there was drifted off mingling with the sunshine, and for a few minutes longer a powdery dust of marble drifted from the great featureless pile that had once been the house of jewels.'[125] The implosion of the Washington château is reminiscent of the fate of many New York hotels in the age of mobile capital – those which succumbed to outmodedness, unprofitability, ruination and demolition. Demolition had already been the fate of the U.S. Hotel, the Fifth Avenue, the Metropolitan, the Park Avenue, the once mighty St Nicholas, the James family's beloved Astor House, the Windsor and the old Plaza Hotel, and was soon to be the fate of the Buckingham, the New Netherland, the Savoy and the old Waldorf-Astoria, which would become the site of the Empire State Building.[126] (The old Ritz itself survived the wrecking ball until 1951.) Like all monuments to bourgeois culture, the pathos of the modern hotel 'is that [its] material strength and solidity actually count for nothing and carry no weight at all,' writes Marshall Berman:

> Even the most beautiful and impressive bourgeois buildings and public works are disposable, capitalized for fast depreciation and planned to be obsolete, closer in their social functions to tents and encampments than to 'Egyptian pyramids, Roman aqueducts, Gothic cathedrals'.[127]

Indeed, Rem Koolhaas suggests that New York hotels were only fully realised when they were pulled down, liberating their spirit – their brand – for reincarnation:

> The Waldorf has instigated a paradoxical *tradition of the last word* (in creature comfort, supportive technologies, decor, entertainments, metropolitan lifestyles, etc.) which, to preserve itself, is forced continuously to self-destruct, eternally to shed its latest incarnation. Any architectural container that fixes it to a site degenerates sooner or later into a battery of outdated technical and atmospheric apparatus that prevents the hasty surrender to change that is the tradition's *raison d'être*.[128]

Though the old Waldorf was obliterated, 'the spirit of the Waldorf will, once more, survive physical destruction to reappear triumphantly on another location in the Grid.'[129] Hotel brands like the Ritz, their structures reduced to rubble and their human namesakes committed to the ground, achieved a kind of vampiric deathlessness beyond material bounds. It was part of the nowhereness of a white space like the Ritz that its architectural container was fungible and disposable, while its 'spirit' – the intangible property of its brand – lived on. The roof garden was the purest expression of this evanescent quality of New York hotels: an architectural frame that was also an escape from architecture;

an anywhere and a nowhere whose white luminescence foretold the dynamite of the demolition crew.

NOTES

1. '1939 – Your Hotel in Twenty Years', 88 (14) *Hotel World* (April 1919), p. 33.
2. F. Scott Fitzgerald, 'The Freshest Boy', in *The Basil, Josephine, and Gwen Stories*, ed. James L. W. West (Cambridge: Cambridge University Press, 2009), p. 67; F. Scott Fitzgerald, *This Side of Paradise*, ed. James L. W. West (Cambridge: Cambridge University Press, 1995), p. 12.
3. Annabel Wharton, 'Two Waldorf-Astorias: Spatial Economies as Totem and Fetish', 85 (3) *The Art Bulletin* (September 2003), p. 524.
4. Albin Pasteur Dearing, *The Elegant Inn* (Secaucus, NJ: Lyle Stuart, 1986), p. 195.
5. Zygmunt Bauman, *Liquid Modernity* (Cambridge: Polity Press, 2000), pp. 901–29.
6. The immediate post-war years unleashed a boom of hotel construction and company consolidation, documented in 'The Battle of the Giants', 27 (310) *Hotel Monthly*, (January 1919), p. 53. See John A. Jakle, Keith A. Schulle and Jefferson S. Rogers, *The Motel in America* (Baltimore, MD: Johns Hopkins University Press, 1996), p. 122.
7. This was the experience of the Boca Raton Resort and Club, Florida, originally the Castillo del Rey, then briefly the Ritz-Carlton Cloister Inn (alongside the Ritz-Carlton Park residential golfing community) after the Ritz-Carlton Investment Corporation staked a claim in 1926. Sally J. Ling, *A History of Boca Raton* (Charleston, SC: History Press, 2007), p. 24.
8. Bauman, *Liquid Modernity*, pp. 91–129.
9. These midtown hotels belonged to a group of 90 in the Times Square theatre district, bounded by Twenty-Eighth and Forty-Eighth Streets, Park and Eighth Avenues, in which 30,000 guests registered every week in 1920. Norman S. Hayner, 'Hotel Life and Personality', 33 (5) *American Journal of Sociology* (March 1928), p. 791.
10. 'Growth of Hotel Luxury', *Evening World*, 27 July 1904, p. 10.
11. Jeff Hirsch, *Manhattan Hotels: 1880–1920* (Charleston, SC: Arcadia, 1997), p. 80.
12. Kurt C. Schlichting, *Grand Central Terminal: Railroads, Engineering, and Architecture in New York City* (Baltimore, MD: Johns Hopkins University Press, 2001), p. 162.
13. Schlichting, *Grand Central Terminal*, p. 62.
14. John Jakle and Keith Sculle, *The Gas Station in America* (Baltimore, MD: Johns Hopkins University Press, 1994), pp. 18–47; Jakle et al., *The Motel in America*, esp. pp. 120–5.
15. W. Sydney Wagner, 'The Statler Idea in Hotel Planning and Equipment', 27 (5) *Architectural Forum* (November 1917), p. 118. See also Lisa Pfueller Davidson, 'Early Twentieth-Century Hotel Architects and the Origins of Standardization', 25 *Journal of Decorative and Propaganda Arts: The American Hotel* (2005), p. 85.
16. Walter Monfried, 'Swank, by Ritz: Swiss Peasant Lad Introduced World to Luxury in Hotels', *Decatur Herald*, 16 October 1939, p. 4.
17. F. Scott Fitzgerald, 'To: Maxwell Perkins', in *F. Scott Fitzgerald On Authorship*, eds Matthew J. Bruccoli and Judith Baughman (Columbia, SC: University of South Carolina, 1996), p. 103.

18. Betsy Nies, *Eugenic Fantasies: Racial Ideology in the Literature and Popular Culture of the 1920s* (New York: Routledge, 2002), p. 102.
19. Mitchell Breitwieser, 'Jazz Fractures: F. Scott Fitzgerald and Epochal Representation', 12 (3) *American Literary History* (Autumn 2000), p. 361.
20. 'A New Hotel on 5th Avenue', *The Sun* (New York), 3 September 1908, p. 1.
21. 'Quiet London Style for New Hotel Here', *New York Times* 12 April 1908, p. 1.
22. Marie-Louise Ritz, *César Ritz: Host to the World* (London: George G. Harrap, 1938), pp. 293–4.
23. From the minutes of the annual meeting of the Carlton Hotel Limited board, in 'Carlton Hotel, Limited', 3298 *The Economist*, 10 November 1906, p. 1837.
24. That these arrangements were quite novel is shown by the baffled and sceptical questions put to William Harris during annual meetings of the board.
25. Details of the fairly well advanced negotiations for an American Ritz are found in Carlton Hotel, Limited', 3350 *The Economist*, 9 November 1907, p. 1934.
26. 'Ritz-Carlton Plans: Hotel to Cost "2,000,000"', *New-York Daily Tribune*, 11 July 1908, p. 13.
27. 'Quiet London Style for New Hotel Here', *New York Times*, 12 April 1908, p. 1.
28. 'No Ritz Hotel Here: European Restaurateur Will Not Permit His Name to Be Used', *New York Times*, 9 July 1908, p. 1.
29. 'No Ritz Hotel Here', p. 1.
30. Ritz, *César Ritz*, p. 304.
31. 'New Ritz-Carlton Formally Opened', *New York Times*, 15 December 1910, p. 9.
32. A merger with the United Hotel Company and Vanderbilt hotel interests was discussed in 1910. The deal might have established the Ritz as an actual American chain rather than a loose franchise, but it fell through. 'Plans Chain of Hotels', *New-York Tribune*, 3 June 1910, p. 5; and 'Hotel Syndicate Plans Big Merger', 8 (19) *New York Hotel Record*, 14 June 1910, p. 4.
33. R. Leigh, 'Securing Apartment House Tenants through National Advertising', 27 *Advertising and Selling* (December 1917), pp. 13 and 39.
34. 'Carlton Hotel (Limited): A Record Year', *The Times*, 27 November 1919, p. 25.
35. 'Gimbels', *New York Times*, 26 July 1915, p. 5.
36. Roland Marchand, *Advertising the American Dream: Making Way for Modernity, 1920–1940* (Berkeley, CA: University of California Press, 1985), p. 96.
37. 'Bigelow-Harford', *New-York Tribune*, 12 June 1921, p. 90.
38. 'Fatima', *New-York Tribune*, 20 February 1920, p. 10.
39. 'Sawtay', *Evening Public Ledger* (Philadelphia), 15 January 1918, p. 6.
40. 'Yuban', *The Sun* (New York) Pictorial Magazine, 29 August 1915, p. 40.
41. 'A New Toilet Companion', *New-York Tribune*, 7 July 1918, p. 12.
42. Leigh, 'Securing Apartment House Tenants', p. 13.
43. Irving Lewis Allen, *The City in Slang: New York Life and Popular Speech* (Oxford and New York: Oxford University Press, 1993), p. 122.
44. As one advertisement for the Philadelphia Ritz put it: 'The name "Ritz-Carlton" has always stood as the hallmark of "Best." The terms are interchangeable.' 'Ritz-Carlton', *Evening Public Ledger* (Philadelphia), 3 June 1918, p. 3.
45. Ritz, *César Ritz*, p. 294.

46. F. Scott Fitzgerald, *The Great Gatsby*, ed. Matthew J. Bruccoli (Cambridge: Cambridge University Press, 1991), p. 94.
47. Richard Godden, 'A Diamond Bigger Than the Ritz: F. Scott Fitzgerald and the Gold Standard', 77 *ELH* (2010), p. 591.
48. F. Scott Fitzgerald, 'Ten Years in the Advertising Business', in *Last Kiss*, ed. James L. W. West (Cambridge: Cambridge University Press, 2017), p. 415.
49. Harry Salpeter, 'Fitzgerald, Spenglerian', in *F. Scott Fitzgerald on Authorship*, eds Matthew J. Bruccoli and Judith Baughman (Columbia, SC: University of South Carolina, 1996), p. 111.
50. Philip Curtiss, 'When Is a Ford Not a Ford?', 145 (867) *Harper's* (August 1922), pp. 407–10.
51. F. Scott Fitzgerald, 'The Diamond as Big as the Ritz', in *Tales of the Jazz Age*, ed. James L. W. West (Cambridge: Cambridge University Press, 2002), p. 129–30.
52. Ibid., p. 140.
53. Ibid., p. 141.
54. Ibid., p. 161.
55. Fitzgerald, 'The Diamond as Big as the Ritz', p. 135; 'Crystal Room of the Ritz-Carlton', *New York Tribune*, 27 November 1921, p. 4.
56. Matlack Price, 'Great Modern Hotels of America: Architectural Distinction in the Ritz Hotels', 20 (3) *Arts and Decoration* (July 1924), p.40.
57. Fitzgerald, 'The Diamond as Big as the Ritz', p. 134.
58. Ibid., pp. 152, 137 and 135.
59. Ibid., p. 158.
60. Ibid., p. 161.
61. Ibid., p. 135.
62. Ritz, *César Ritz*, pp. 208–9; Hugh Montgomery-Massingberd and David Watkin, *The London Ritz: A Social and Architectural History* (London: Aurum, 1980), p. 51.
63. Quoted in Ritz, *César Ritz*, p. 77.
64. 'No Paintings in New Plaza Hotel. Manager Says Patrons These Days Have a Preference for Simplicity', *New-York Daily Tribune*, 1 August 1907, p. 7.
65. 'Enamolin', 29 (4) *House and Garden* (April 1916), p. 81.
66. 'Another Fine Hotel Now on the City's List', *New York Times*, 29 September 1907, p. 3.
67. James Hay, 'Revisiting the Grand Hotel (and Its Place within the Cultural Economy of Fascist Italy)', in David B. Clarke and Marcus A. Doel, *Moving Pictures/ Stopping Places: Hotels and Motels on Film*, eds David B. Clarke, Valerie Crawford Pfannhauser and Marcus A. Doel (Lanham, MD: Lexington Books, 2009), p. 45.
68. Rajesh Heynickx, 'Tracing Tracks: Illusion and Reality at Work in the Lobby', in *Hotel Lobbies and Lounges: The Architecture of Professional Hospitality*, eds Anne Massey and Tom Avermaete (Abingdon and New York: Routledge, 2013), p. 113.
69. Anne Anlin Cheng, *Second Skin: Josephine Baker and the Modern Surface* (Oxford and New York: Oxford University Press, 2011), pp. 24–5.
70. Adolf Loos, 'Ornament and Crime', in *Ornament and Crime: Selected Essays*, trans. Michael Mitchell (Riverside, CA: Ariadne Press, 1998), p. 168.

71. Cheng, *Second Skin*, pp. 24–5.
72. Henry James, 'A Round of Visits', in *Complete Stories: 1898–1910*, ed. Denis Donoghue (New York: Library of America, 1996), p. 899.
73. Ibid., pp. 899 and 910.
74. Adrienne Brown, *The Black Skyscraper: Architecture and the Perception of Race* (Baltimore, MD: Johns Hopkins University Press, 2017), pp. 93–6.
75. John Beverley Robinson, *Architectural Composition: An Attempt to Order and Phrase Ideas which Hitherto Have Been Only Felt by the Instinctive Taste of Designers* (New York: Van Nostrand, 1908), p. 68.
76. Ibid., p. 214.
77. Mary Doyle, *Life Was Like That* (Boston and New York: Houghton Mifflin, 1936), p. 49.
78. 'The Ritz-Carlton Hotel', 5 (1) *New York Architect* (January 1911), p. 11.
79. Brown, *The Black Skyscraper*, p. 158.
80. H. Donaldson Eberlein and Abbot McClure, 'The Modern Hotel and Its Furniture', *Good Furniture* (May 1916), p. 279; Price, 'Great Modern Hotels of America', p. 40.
81. Doyle, *Life Was Like That*, p. 52.
82. 'Quiet London Style for New Hotel Here', *New York Times*, 12 April 1908, p. 1.
83. Fitzgerald, *The Great Gatsby*, p. 94.
84. Ibid., p. 101.
85. James Smethurst, *The African American Roots of Modernism: From Reconstruction to the Harlem Renaissance* (Chapel Hill, NC: University of North Carolina Press, 2011), p. 13.
86. Garrett Bridger Gilmore, 'Refracting Blackness: Slavery and Fitzgerald's Historical Consciousness', 70/71 (2) *Mississippi Quarterly* (Spring 2017), p. 199.
87. Fitzgerald, 'The Diamond as Big as the Ritz', p. 140.
88. Godden, 'A Diamond Bigger than the Ritz', p. 606.
89. Quoted in Lorenzo J. Greene and Carter G. Woodson, *The Negro Wage Earner* (Washington, DC: Association for the Study of Negro Life and History, 1930), p. 94.
90. 'Negro Waiters in Best Hotels', *New York Age*, 6 June 1912, p. 1.
91. 'Negro Help for Hotels', *Boston Globe*, 31 May 1912, p. 9.
92. 'Call Out 500 from Two More Hotels', *New York Times*, 10 November 1918, p. 12.
93. Greene and Woodson, *The Negro Wage Earner*; W. E. B. Du Bois, *The Philadelphia Negro: A Social Study* (Philadelphia, PA: University of Pennsylvania Press, 1996).
94. Scott Nearing, *Black America* (New York: Vanguard Press, 1929), pp. 166–7.
95. Lorenzo J. Greene and Myra Colson Callis, *The Employment of Negroes in the District of Columbia* (Washington, DC: Association for the Study of Negro Life and History, 1936), p. 28.
96. 'Negro Waiters in Best Hotels', p. 1.
97. Jess Row, *White Flights: Race, Fiction, and the American Imagination* (Minneapolis, MN: Graywolf Press, 2019), p. 249.
98. Ibid., p. 84.
99. Ibid., pp. 134–5.

100. F. Scott Fitzgerald, 'May Day', in *Tales of the Jazz Age*, ed. James L. W. West (Cambridge: Cambridge University Press, 2002), p. 107.
101. Ibid., p. 107.
102. Ibid., p. 111.
103. Ibid., p. 113.
104. Theodore Osmundson, *Roof Gardens: History, Design, and Construction* (New York: Norton, 1999), pp. 122–4.
105. F. Scott Fitzgerald, 'My Lost City', in *My Lost City: Personal Essays, 1920–1940*, ed. James L. W. West (Cambridge: Cambridge University Press, 2005), p. 114 and p. 107.
106. David E. Nye, 'The Sublime and the Skyline: The New York Skyscraper', in *The American Skyscraper: Cultural Histories*, ed. Roberta Moudry (Cambridge: Cambridge University Press, 2005), p. 265.
107. Hans Gumbrecht, *In 1926: Living at the Edge of Time* (Cambridge, MA and London: Harvard University Press, 1997), p. 78.
108. Adrienne Brown, *The Black Skyscraper: Architecture and the Perception of Race* (Baltimore, MD, Johns Hopkins University Press, 2017), p. 159.
109. 'The Ritz-Carlton Hotel, New York', 99 (1832) *American Architect* (February 1911), p. 46.
110. 'Farmyard on a Hotel Roof', *New York Times*, 31 August 1913, p. 9.
111. 'Japanese Garden Atop Hotel Astor', *New York Times*, 4 March 1923, p. 14.
112. 'To Inaugurate Roof Garden Tennis at the Ritz-Carlton', *New York Times*, 17 December 1921, p. 21.
113. Hans Ulrich Gumbrecht, *In 1926: Living at the Edge of Time* (Cambridge, MA and London: Harvard University Press, 1997), p. 201.
114. Meir Wigoder, 'The "Solar Eye" of Vision: Emergence of the Skyscraper-Viewer in the Discourse on Heights in New York City, 1890–1920', 61 (2) *Journal of the Society of Architectural Historians* (June 2002), p. 159.
115. Fitzgerald, *The Great Gatsby*, p. 59.
116. In 1921, New York's first official radio station, the Westinghouse-owned WSJ, set up its studios in the Waldorf-Astoria, connected via a Western Union telephone wire to a transmitter in Newark. NBC marked its entry into radio with a gala broadcast from the Waldorf-Astoria in 1926. Jim Cox, *American Radio Networks: A History* (Jefferson, NC: McFarland, 2009), pp. 94 and 133.
117. 'New York's Amateur Show', 9 (7) *Wireless Age* (April 1922), p. 17.
118. 'Future Unfolds as Radio Show Opens on Roof', *New-York Tribune*, 8 March 1922, p. 22.
119. Fitzgerald, *The Beautiful and Damned*, pp. 23 and 27.
120. Ibid., p. 27.
121. Ibid., p. 30.
122. Ibid., p. 32.
123. 'Fashion in Review Exhibits Eyelashes: Aside from This Artificiality, There Is a Display of Chinese Bathing Suits', *New York Times*, 27 February 1921, p. 15.
124. Fitzgerald, 'The Diamond as Big as the Ritz', p. 158–9.
125. Ibid., p. 166.

126. Nathan Silver, *Lost New York* (New York: Houghton Mifflin, 2000), pp. 62–71.
127. Marshall Berman, *All That Is Solid Melts into Air: The Experience of Modernity* (London: Verso, 1983), p. 99, incorporating a partial quote from *The Communist Manifesto*.
128. Rem Koolhaas, *Delirious New York: A Retroactive Manifesto for Manhattan* (New York: Monacelli Press, 1994), p. 143.
129. Ibid., p. 138.

4

HOTEL ANGST: THE CORRIDOR AND ELEVATOR

At the centre of Elizabeth Bowen's debut novel, *The Hotel* (1927), is an anonymous establishment on the Italian Riviera over which no one seems to be in charge. There is an unnamed manager and a Madame, and a collection of hotel workers including a concierge, chambermaid, head waiter, junior waiters and the 'boots' (a porter), but the influence of this governing body over the space of the hotel is diffuse. Each figure is seen, or mentioned, only fleetingly. No one answers the bell for assistance when the lift breaks down, nor, as a backup, can the head waiter be found in the dining room. The manager and the Madame are occasionally invoked but never called. On several occasions, the guests approach an empty concierge desk: in one scene, a guest looks through the absent concierge's letter-rack; in another, packets of lunch for a picnic are set out on his desk; in a third, someone has left the afternoon post scattered all over it. Something more is going on than an account of poor service in an Italian hotel. Bowen goes to great lengths to keep the staff at a remove, by fitting them into the frame as an afterthought ('He arrived late, having dined on the train, and few people were at hand to witness the arrival: a big man talking Italian above the folds of a muffler and making abundant, baulked gestures at the boots and concierge'), or by veiling them in figurative language ('From behind a screen that hid the service-lift the waiters with their steaming dishes debouched suddenly and sped like bees to distribute themselves among the tables').[1] Consigned to a zone behind locked doors, screens and service lifts, and to a linguistic space just out of focus, the trace of hotel workers and hotel management is barely visible amid the traffic of circulating guests.

Accounting for this absence goes some of the way toward understanding the aesthetic and social concerns of Bowen's novel. *The Hotel* has been wrongly dismissed as juvenilia, and as a diminished pastiche of the hotel fiction of James, Forster (*A Room With a View* (1908)) and Woolf (*The Voyage Out* [1915]).[2] For all its literary debts, *The Hotel* also directly responds to its new cultural moment. It rethinks and estranges the idea of the hotel via an aesthetic that is significantly inspired, I argue, by the cinema. The nexus of hotel and cinema is propitious. Written just after the release of F. W. Murnau's hotel film, *Der Letzte Mann* (*The Last Laugh*), Bowen's roaming camera-eye glides through *The Hotel*, like Murnau with his innovative crane- and tracking-shots, down empty corridors and elevator shafts. The hotels of Bowen and Murnau are mechanistic spaces, mechanistically perceived. While Bowen's manager and Madame have little influence over the scenes playing out under their roof, the machinery of the hotel itself seems to direct the action. The genteel guests discover themselves to be comic bit-players and dupes in a merciless architectonic engine. In this way, *The Hotel* reimagines the hierarchical social world of its literary predecessors in a post-war, post-Edwardian context of class anxiety and *déclassement*.

A Room without a View

What makes *The Hotel* so different to its predecessors is that it begins to enunciate Bowen's unusual conception of the individual's relationship to objects: to the architecture, furniture, fashion, machinery and miscellanea that constitute the collected stuff of existence in her fiction. Bowen stood against a prevailing current of modernism that wanted to rid fiction of the material baggage of nineteenth-century realism. Virginia Woolf, in 'Mr Bennett and Mrs Brown' (1924), sought to distinguish her generation from materialist writers who 'laid an enormous stress upon the fabric of things'. Novels, Woolf argues, 'are in the first place about people, and only in the second about the houses they live in'.[3] Willa Cather pursued a similar argument in 'The Novel Démeublé' (1922), describing the novel as being historically 'over-furnished'. Cather wanted to redeem fiction not merely from furniture, but from labour, technology, commerce, commodities and the physical body, to 'select the eternal material of art' from out of the stream of everyday events. 'How wonderful it would be if we could throw all the furniture out of the window [. . .] and leave the room as bare as the stage of a Greek theatre, or as that house into which the glory of Pentecost descended; leave the scene bare for the play of emotions, great and little'.[4] Bowen's work can be read, however, as the novel radically re-furnished. Rather than elevating individual consciousness and the play of emotions, Bowen's characters stand almost on an equal footing with objects. While human faces in her novels often appear flat, void, unreadable, her objects flash with life.

For Maud Ellmann, Bowen's relation to things is what fundamentally sets her apart from Woolf:

> Woolf treats the object as a grain of sand to be surrounded in a pearl of thought. In Bowen, on the contrary, things behave like thoughts and thoughts like things, thus impugning the supremacy of consciousness. [. . .] In Woolf, consciousness exists in opposition to the object; in Bowen, consciousness escapes into the object, leaving human beings [. . .] vacant.[5]

While Bowen's characters use and think with objects, they do not possess or master them. Objects have a life and an affective glimmer of their own. They are 'too "over-charged" to be transcended', Ellmann writes.[6] For this reason, a hotel, full of corporate objects that do not proclaim the taste of the individual or bear the individual's trace – objects which belong to no one, over which no one is in charge – is the ideal setting for a preliminary novelistic thought-experiment about the relationship between humans and matter in the age of mechanical reproduction. The absence at the heart of the hotel is an absence of possessive control, and it forces the hotel guests to interact with rented objects that are stubborn and troublemaking.

It is crucial, then, that Bowen's hotel *is* a hotel and not an Italian *pensione* – as in her short story 'The Secession' (1926), written shortly before *The Hotel*, or as in Forster's *A Room With a View* (1908), of which *The Hotel* is, according to Ellmann, both 'homage and satire'.[7] The *pensione*, like the hotel, offered writers a structure for the enactment of brief, accidental, trans-cultural encounters. But it differed from the hotel in being family-owned, in having a family-centred labour structure and in having an essentially domestic scale and form. Whereas a hotel's management, as Bowen underscores, is diffuse and partially invisible, a *pensione* is presided over by a proprietor-matriarch or a proprietor-patriarch. Their ownership makes a dramatic difference to the way that guests interact with and interpret the furnishings and the space. In the *pensione*, the values and personality of the proprietor loom large. The proprietor-matriarch of the Pension Bertolini in *A Room With a View* symbolically overdetermines the meaning of the establishment. Signora Bertolini, a Cockney émigré, is for Forster a deeply suspect member of the lower-middle class, not because she strives upwards, but because she fails to change at all. She refuses the middle-class ideal that one should be transformed by foreign adventure. Though she has married an Italian, she has named her children Victoria and Henry and cocoons them in Englishness. Forster happily blames Signora Bertolini for the pension's inauthenticity, for its stalwart Victorian style (with its 'portraits of the late Queen and the late Poet Laureate'), and for its attempt to 'rival the solid comfort of a Bloomsbury boarding-house'.[8] There is a thick imprint of national, historical and class-based anxieties in these rooms, such that the Pension Bertolini becomes not merely a place to stay, but a way of seeing the world and a way of living in it: it is a room with an (ideological) view. The function of the Signora and the Pension Bertolini is to create a stronghold of stiffness and falsity out of which the heroine, Lucy Honeychurch, must emerge into naturalness and authenticity. When Lucy daydreams of the wonders of Italy, it is not merely 'The Cockney Signora' but 'her works' – her material domain – which 'vanished like a bad dream'.[9] With the Signora as figurehead and interpretive key, the pension is an easy space for Forster's characters to read, negotiate and, eventually, transcend. It is, in both senses of the word, *familiar*. And it slots easily into a framework of romanticised spatial oppositions that structure the novel – drawing-room and Sacred Lake, England and Italy, confinement and a view.

In *The Hotel*, Bowen is concerned with more ambivalent spaces. Bowen drew on her own experience of a dreary winter in a grand hotel in Bordighera, on the Italian Riviera near the border with France. The seaside town was no quaint backwater. Hooked into Europe's rail network, it was 'an important winter resort with a large English colony', according to a 1924 Muirhead's guidebook, featuring a casino, a theatre presenting English plays, lawn tennis and croquet club, golf course and British Consulate.[10] Bowen, escaping a complicated romantic situation at home, stayed with her aunt and uncle, George and Edie Colley, members of the Irish landed gentry who themselves had decamped to Bordighera to escape the War of Independence. Bowen spent much of her time gloomily babysitting her young Colley cousins. The Colleys had the resources to rent the entire top floor of an Art Nouveau edifice called, magnificently, the Hotel Angst, named after its original Swiss-German proprietor, Adolph Angst (Figure 4.1).[11] It was 'one of the largest hotels on the Riviera, first class in every respect', assured the Standard Italian Travel Association,[12] and was an exemplar of the Riviera's increasingly professionalised and internationalised tourist industry.[13] Bowen's novel uses the everyday banalities of the seaside resort to explore the impersonality and unfamiliarity of modern objects and spaces, dismissing as illusory the possibility floated by Forster of breaking free into a realm of authenticity.

Bowen's desacralised approach to thinking about space was influenced by the cinema and by the cinematographic quality of Proustian *mise-en-scène*. 'I know the idea of a hotel scene came from Proust', Bowen wrote in a letter to Charles Ritchie in 1949, recalling the composition of *The Hotel*.

> I was reading the Balbec hotel part in *À l'Ombre [des] Jeunes Filles en Fleur* when I suddenly remembered the (at the time) appalling hotel at Bordighera where I had spent a winter, 3 years before [in 1921], with the Colleys. Never was I more bored and depressed – never have I been since – than during that Bordighera winter. But I afterwards saw this was a case of what Proust says about boredom being (subsequently) fruitful.[14]

Figure 4.1 Postcard from the Hotel Angst, Bordighera, Italy, c.1910

In *À l'Ombre des Jeunes Filles en Fleur*, Marcel undertakes several pages of descriptive and cognitive work to adjust to his hotel room. While he perceives his 'things' in his Paris home as 'merely extensions of my organs, an enlargement of myself', Marcel's new hotel 'things' appear strange and unassimilable. Literally imprinted with a corporate identity ('holding in one hand the starched, unyielding towel, with the name of the hotel printed upon it, with which I was making futile efforts to dry myself'), hotel things do not react to the human body, or soften against its contours.[15] In fact they actively rebel against human presence, forcing him into

> a position as cramped and comfortless (even if I had stretched out my legs) as that of Cardinal La Balue in the cage in which he could neither stand nor sit. Space there was none for me in my bedroom (mine in name only) at Balbec; it was full of things which did not know me, which flung back at me the distrustful look that I had cast at them [. . .]. The clock [. . .] continued without a moment's interruption to utter, in an unknown tongue, a series of observations which must have been most uncomplimentary to myself, for the violet curtains listened to them without replying, but in an attitude such as people adopt who shrug their shoulders to indicate that the sight of a third person irritates them.[16]

The paragraph represents a catalogue of images and effects that Bowen would also attempt in *The Hotel*: from talking furniture ('She looked up for a moment and – "She has so absolutely given you the go-by," the room repeated, catching her unawares. The shapes of the furniture, everything that she looked at, said it again'),[17] and objects that come uncannily to life ('trying to write a letter with a Hotel pen that screeched and staggered'),[18] to the collusion of objects and the watchfulness of objects ('He looked round at the armchairs all facing one way with awful intelligence'),[19] to a sense of being physically and psychically crowded in by hotel objects ('He took in enough of his No. 19, when the chambermaid switched the lights up, to know that it [. . .] was so furnished as to confuse thought, distract contemplation and impede the movements of the body'),[20] to hotel space as a cage ('One had a sense of being caged into this crowded emptiness').[21]

Proust was a starting point, therefore, for Bowen's interest in corporate aesthetics. In her 1928 essay on 'Modern Lighting', Bowen writes of 'that intolerable high-up Balbec bedroom' which is 'glazed with sea-reflections', and the 'almost agonising' effect of its blazing intensity. Proust, argues Bowen, is not interested in the 'cheerful glow' of the fireplace, the 'universal mild exposure of day' or the 'diffused mild rosiness' of Edwardian drawing-rooms (a kind of light which Bowen deems to be 'out of date'). Rather, Proustian light is electrical, 'modern' and hyper-real, 'a sinister energy' that can be manipulated to compel one's attention and work upon one's nerves. *The Hotel*, too, is bathed in sinister light: with its gleaming mirrors, white tiles and plate glass. '[T]his affectability of ours' toward engineered light 'has been recognised commercially,' Bowen notes, implicitly linking Proust to modern shop interiors (which are 'now bright with secretive, pleated shades which can space a whole room out into coloured islands').[22] Bowen thereby rejected the critical commonplace that linked illumination in Proust with deep recesses of private memory and affect – like the French reviewer in 1922 who encouraged readers to adjust to Proust as 'deep sea fish' adjust to the darkness, and pointed them 'towards the vague fringes of light that make up the halo of the soul, towards the dark zones that constitute the infra-red and the ultra-violet of the heart'[23] – and instead connected Proustian aesthetics with the euphoric intensity of corporate surfaces.

Waiting the Camera

In its 5 July 1924 edition, *The Spectator* published Bowen's short story 'Ann Lee's'. The publication was something of a breakthrough in Bowen's early career, with three more of her stories being accepted at various British publications in the following months, and two more being published in *Everybody's Magazine* in America. One of *The Spectator*'s young reviewers, L. P. Hartley, became an early and vocal champion of her work. After these small successes, Bowen began drafting *The Hotel*.[24]

The Spectator in 1924 was a new venue for short stories; it was also becoming known as a venue for intellectual film criticism through the columns of Iris Barry. Barry and John Strachey, *The Spectator*'s editor, were part of a growing movement in English highbrow circles in the mid-1920s that was trying to promote cinema as a serious art form. That movement culminated in the formation of the London Film Society in 1925, of which Barry and Strachey were founding members.[25] It is not surprising, then, that when Strachey accepted 'Ann Lee's', Bowen recalls that 'he urged me to go (or, rather, resume going) to the cinema, just then emerging from disrepute. There was much, he remarked, to be learned from new screen technique. I in part learned it.'[26]

Bowen was living on the northern outskirts of Northampton at the time – not a great centre for film – but frequently took the train to London, where cinema culture was booming. Whether Bowen actually started patronising cinemas more frequently in 1924 (like the bank clerk in her story 'Dead Mabelle' (1929), who decides to go to the movies after 'a man with important-looking initials mentioned it in a weekly review as an "art-form"') is difficult to tell.[27] Bowen had already been a keen cinema-goer since her childhood, while her father was an 'ardent cinema-goer some years before the movies became the thing'.[28] Bowen grew up in Dublin right next to the Abbey Theatre at the time of the Irish literary revival, but she, like her father, never had a fondness for theatre: 'No, really I like the cinema more', Bowen told an interviewer in 1959. 'It would be idiotic not ever to go to the theatre, but a cinema is more like pure pleasure to me.'[29] Bowen would eventually join the London Film Society and publish a film review in *Sight and Sound* (1936) and an essay on 'Why I Go to the Cinema' in *Footnotes to the Film* (1938).[30] At a time when film was 'emerging from disrepute' and becoming 'the thing', many of Bowen's associates were naturally cinema enthusiasts too, including Alan Cameron, whom she married in 1923. Cameron worked for the newly formed British Film Institute as well as the BBC for several decades until his death in 1952. It is generally acknowledged that by the time of her major novels of the late-1930s, Bowen's fiction was being influenced by film in some way. Yet relatively little critical work has been undertaken on Bowen and the cinema,[31] and almost none looks back to the 1920s – even to her 1929 story 'Dead Mabelle', described by David Trotter as 'one of the finest short stories ever written about movie-going'.[32]

Bowen's interest in film, space and the object-world was by no means unique. It was a reflection of the tastes and preoccupations of the period. *Mise-en-scène* was a star attraction in early film theory and criticism. German films in particular, with their elaborate architectural stage sets and lighting, had found a niche in London in the mid-1920s, both within the Film Society and in commercial cinemas like the Marble Arch Pavilion.[33] Before some of the leaders of English alternative film culture shifted their affections to Soviet montage, German films represented the pinnacle of international cinema and the avant-garde. The German emphasis on construction and world-building was mirrored in English film criticism of the time. In the Film Society's programme notes, for example, German films were particularly praised for their achievements in design. In the notes for the Film Society's opening night, Ivor Montagu wrote of Paul Leni's *Waxworks* (1924) that its merits were 'partly architectural – the sets and groupings of Dr Leni are of great pictorial beauty'.[34] In 1926, the Society formalised its interest in cinematic architecture and *mise-en-scène* with a public exhibition of Leni's movie set designs. Iris Barry, writing for *The Spectator* in 1924, two months before the publication of 'Ann Lee's', expressed this interest in a strikingly Bowen-like manner. The cinema, she wrote, offered

> an infinite variety of scenes, endless angles of vision and of focuses: you can look down on the action, or up to it, from behind or before. It also includes as part of itself all the riches of landscape or architecture, which are not, as they are in the theatre, mere conventionalized hints. [. . .] [T]he camera brings out an enormous and dramatic significance in natural objects. Chairs and tables, collar-studs, kitchenware and flowers take on a function which they have lost, save for young children, since we abandoned animism in the accumulating sophistications of civilization.[35]

Bowen, too, reflected on the way the camera could make visible, and give meaning to, ordinary objects and ordinary spaces that the human eye overlooked. In 'Why I Go to the Cinema', written in 1938 from the perspective of the sound era, Bowen complains that the

> frumpy and unsatirical flatness of the average English stage-set is almost always transferred to the screen. The French make *genre* films in which every vase, tassel and door-handle thickens the atmosphere, makes for verisimilitude and adds more to the story: why cannot we do the same?[36]

Too many English filmmakers (with the exception, she writes, of Hitchcock and Asquith) short-circuit that process of thickening. Rather than building atmosphere through detail, they signal locality through symbolically conventional establishing shots: of 'Westminster Bridge, crazy gables stuck with oak beams, corners of (apparently) Oxford colleges masquerading as Great Homes [. . .] and those desolating, unconvincing, always-the-same rooms'.[37] Truly redolent stage sets would draw attention to the particularity of ordinary things: vases, tassels, door-handles – things that are troubling in their very ordinariness. Calling on English film to value visual detail, Bowen creates a counter-catalogue of cinematic objects in the English landscape:

> All over this country, indoors and out, a photographable drama of national temperament is going on, and every object has character. Bypasses, trees on skylines, small country town streets with big buses pushing along them, village Sundays, gasometers showing behind seaside towns, half-built new estates, Midland canals, the lounges of private hotels, stucco houses with verandas, rectory tea-tables, the suburban shopping rush, garden fêtes and the abstract perspectives of flyblown, semi-submerged London are all waiting the camera and are very dramatic.[38]

What is recognisable in this assemblage is Bowen's characteristic visual aesthetic: a flattening out of the social and a compensatory fascination with details, with vernacular architecture (including, significantly, private hotel lounges) and with empty structures that literally bypass the social. Bowen not only argues that background details are important, but that the movie camera can, and should, realign our relationship with the background. English cinema does not just need better *mise-en-scène*; it should in some respects be about *mise-en-scène*.

Leo Mellor and Ian Walker have alluded to the similarities between Bowen's camera-eye and Bill Brandt's Blitz-period photographs of a depopulated London – that comparison is useful here.[39] Bowen was Brandt's favourite writer, and his portrait of Bowen appeared in the American edition of *Harper's Bazaar* next to her short story 'Mysterious Kôr'.[40] Both Bowen and Brandt were interested in aftermaths, or the no-longer-quite-present; both entertained elements of the ghostly. Both, too, entertained elements of the surreal. Their form of surrealism resonates with a passage by Walter Benjamin describing the photography of Eugène Atget, whose work inspired Brandt's own:

> Remarkably, however, almost all [of Atget's Parisian photographs] are empty. [. . .] They are not lonely, merely without mood; the city in these pictures looks cleared out, like a lodging that has not yet found a new tenant. It is in these achievements that surrealist photography sets the scene for a salutary estrangement between man and his surroundings. It gives free play to the politically educated eye, under whose gaze all intimacies are sacrificed to the illumination of detail.[41]

Bowen's camera-eye, like Atget's and Brandt's, uses the absence of the human subject as a way of bringing detail into focus. Separating objects from their habitual function, she unsettles our habitual, semi-conscious way of looking at the world. The world is revealed in its 'thingness', its strangeness, and its malignity. This aesthetic was not born in the Blitz, nor in Bowen's visit to the International Surrealist Exhibition of 1936,[42] nor in the maturity of her great novels of the 1930s. It was there from the start in *The Hotel* and 'Dead Mabelle', and it was shaped, in some measure, by a union of hotels and movie-going.

There is a key scene towards the middle of *The Hotel* that brings together a meditation on the film image with a meditation on hotel objects. Sydney Warren, the novel's young, disaffected heroine, and James Milton, an English clergyman who pursues her, are walking back to the hotel at dusk. Night compresses the landscape, producing the optical illusion of a hill which 'loomed, by some *trompe-l'œil* of twilight seemed to topple, above the larger hotels'.[43] But this play of light and shadow is a cinematic rather than painterly *trompe-l'œil*, as in the feigned depth of the cityscape in Murnau's *Der Letzte Mann*. The hotel not only appears as a large-scale stage set, but as an array of illuminated cinema screens: 'They could hear forgotten windows being slammed indignantly, while lights springing up behind the curtains brought them out in hundreds in their uniformity, with here and there some figure passing regularly as a pendulum to and fro across the screen of lace'.[44] Watching this cinematic vista, Sydney speculates on what is behind the plasterboard and floodlights:

> She said, 'I have often thought it would be interesting if the front of any house, but of an hotel especially, could be swung open on a hinge like the front of a doll's house. Imagine the hundreds of rooms with their walls lit up and the real-looking staircase and all the people surprised doing appropriate things in appropriate attitudes as though they had been put there to represent something and had never moved in their lives.'[45]

With a directorial, or perhaps art-directorial, eye, Sydney conceives of society as a collection of extras, performing 'appropriate things in appropriate attitudes' according to their obligatory position within the *mise-en-scène*. Sydney is here developing what film archivist Henri Langlois called (in reference to the architectural achievements of German set designers) a 'metaphysics of décor'.[46] Sydney's is a metaphysics in which architecture makes people rather than the other way around, a more deterministic iteration of views Bowen herself expressed in 'Notes on Writing a Novel' (1945): 'Nothing can happen nowhere. The locale of the happening always colours the happening, and often, to a degree, shapes it.'[47] Hotels, with their simulated domesticity and hired furniture, exemplify Sydney's worldview:

> 'If one could see them like that,' she continued, 'one could see them so clearly as living under the compulsion of their furniture – or the furniture they happen to have hired. It would seem very doubtful, I dare say, whether men were not, after all, made for the Sabbath; and worse, for

beds and dinner-tables and washstands, just to discharge the obligations all those have created. [. . .] Though it may have been an Idea in the first place that made churches be built, it was the churches already existing, with rows of pews for people to sit in and a pulpit and things all ready that had to be filled, that made you into a parson.'[48]

Milton is bemused and Sydney recants, yet *The Hotel* plays like a trial run of this philosophy. It is the 'rigid sofa pasted square to the wall of a drawing-room',[49] the 'isolating vastness' of the 'grouped furniture' in the lounge,[50] and the 'trysting place' provided by 'Each armchair, each palm or bureau'[51] that transforms the ordinary people of this novel into hotel creatures, doing appropriate hotel things in appropriate hotel places. Indeed, with its absence of staff, the hotel looks less like a working institution and more like Sydney's vision of a film set for people to perform in. The guests are more or less conscious of this fact: looking around an empty drawing-room, one of them begins to find 'the *mise en scène* queerly important'.[52]

The Landscape Walks Through Us

Bowen not only unsettles our relation with things. Perhaps more importantly, she unsettles our relation with space itself. Given its setting on the Italian Riviera, there is much about *The Hotel* that is painterly and neoclassical: we are taken in one scene 'down the suggestive cul-de-sac away from the sea, walled in steeply and vanishing at a succession of angles round the palm-tufted bases of the hills'.[53] Bowen evokes a painterly spatial order – with its contemplative distance, stable perspective and stable sense of foreground and background – only to disrupt it with an immersive and mobile form of cinematic perception. This disruption has important political consequences.

The guests in *The Hotel* all believe themselves to be foreground figures, yet historically they are fading into the background. Bowen sketches a collection of Victorian middle-class throw-backs (country vicars, London doctors, officers, old administrators of the Indian empire), most of them comfortable and middle-aged, or else retired or nearly retired. One of the younger representatives of this class, Victor Ammering, is leapt upon and 'appropriated for general use' as a potential match for single daughters; yet despite his pedigree ('Public School and University education, active, keen sportsman, good general capacities'), Ammering exudes only desuetude.[54] A veteran of the war, he is now unemployed and listless. The war has wounded Ammering's future and the future of the social order he represents. Not only was this old middle class in the 1920s being squeezed by a new kind of middle class – a 'technical-scientific-commercial-managerial' class – it was also deeply anxious about its position relative to the working class after the social realignments of the war.[55] As Ross McKibbin writes:

> The active fear of the working class in the 1920s; the sense that there was a lower depth which could sweep away property, decorum, the constitution; these were all Edwardian panic-fantasies which the early 1920s, unlike the Edwardian years themselves, contrived to make reality for much of the middle class.[56]

These resentments culminated in 1926 with the General Strike, when some of the old order organised against the strike to protect their class interests.

In formal as well as historical terms, the foreground status of these characters is precarious. Bowen's idiosyncratic narrative technique, already quite developed in *The Hotel*, was a technique of selective intimacy. Some of her characters are given close, foreground attention while others remain blank and distant. In 'Notes on Writing a Novel', Bowen discussed this technique in cinematic terms, with reference to the novelist's 'visual angle': 'Where is the camera-eye to be located? [. . .] In the breast or brow of *one* of the characters?' Bowen writes that this angle 'imposes on the novel the limitations of the "I" – whether the first person is explicitly used or not.' Bowen prefers the camera-eye to be located in an 'omniscient story-teller (the novelist)'. Not only does this allow for 'entry, at will, into any of the characters', but it also allows the opposite: 'the gain in necessary effect, for some characters, of their remaining *seen* – their remaining closed, apparently, even to the omniscience of the novelist.'[57] Bowen's technique of selective intimacy spatialises the social order, granting focus and fullness to the few and blankness to the many. However, her technique also creates the conditions for the destabilisation of that spatial order, with an excess of nameless figures and a willingness to shift focus 'at will'.

The social world of Bowen's novels, as Ellmann demonstrates, is defined by abstraction and a geometric logic. Bowen's protagonists form triangular or rectangular relations of desire, functioning in 'constellations rather than as independent agents'.[58] They are placed within an abstract pattern and made to behave in accordance with the logic of that pattern. In a similar way, Shawna Ross points to the 'pre-written scripts of hotel life and hotel fiction' that press Bowen's hotel guests into traditional patterns and relations (heterosexual romance and the family unit), even as the hotel opens up 'temporary autonomous zones' of freedom and leisure beyond traditional norms.[59] The geometric structure that fixes *The Hotel* in place centres on the dyad of Sydney Warren and Mrs Kerr. Sydney, suffering nervous exhaustion and taking a forced holiday from her medical studies, is romantically drawn to the older, impassive and imperious Mrs Kerr. But when Mrs Kerr's prodigal son, Ronald, joins his mother at the hotel and replaces Sydney in his mother's affections, Sydney strategically reaches out to James Milton, the vicar, to play him off against Mrs Kerr. Sydney cannot escape from the script of hotel romance, and hastily accepts Milton's proposal of marriage, solidifying a romantic rectangle. But as soon as one point of the rectangle collapses, as it does with Sydney's abrupt change of heart and her rejection of Milton, the knot of relations and the novel itself dissolves, as the travellers begin to stream out of the hotel towards home.

The geometric logic or pre-scripted quality of hotel space is also visible among the minor, background figures in *The Hotel*. Major and minor figures in the novel band together in impromptu groups to dine, walk, smoke, dance, embroider, play tennis or play cards. Friends, strangers – anyone who dares wander around unoccupied is press-ganged into these groups, often to fill a precise quota. The group's structure, in other words, is more significant than the group's personnel. Mrs Hillier asks Sydney to 'stay down here and make up the second four for bridge [. . .]. You see there are only seven of us; we'll be going down directly'; earlier, Sydney completes the quota for a game of mixed-doubles tennis.[60] Six join Mr and Mrs Lee-Mittison for a walk and a picnic, setting off after a head-count and some 'quick calculations'.[61] The picnic goes the way of the novel's central rectangle, however, when the uninvited ninth guest, Victor Ammering, upsets the geometric equilibrium and causes a scandal by publicly kissing one of the young women. In embarrassment, the others go off for walks in different directions, while Mr and Mrs Lee-Mittison retreat back to the hotel.

While Bowen's camera-eye gives us a more intimate portrait of her core constellation of characters, her wider social constellations, filled out with bit players, retain an air of anonymity. The anonymity of the circle of bridge players, for instance, is immediately striking. Their gossip in the drawing-room is choric, their speech repeatedly attributed to 'one', 'another', 'a lady' and 'somebody else', even though most of the women have been previously introduced to the reader and are named and noted as present.[62] At the Lee-Mittisons' picnic, furthermore, there are 'Two other girls, a pair of pale Miss Bransomes' who make very little impact on the proceedings and whose individual opinions are attributed merely to 'one of the Bransomes'.[63] Twinning is no doubt a very old literary trope, but with the Bransomes as well as two Lawrence sisters at the picnic, and the bridge players trying to form not one but two sets of four, Bowen through sheer excess seems to be underlining the duplicability and redundancy of her creations. Bowen is using hotel space, in essence, as a factory for the production of minor characters.

Knowing who is influential and who is not in this novel is a spatial question. This is always the case in a hotel: in Joseph Roth's *Hotel Savoy* (1924), the cheap rooms are on the sixth floor, where the roof slopes low and steam pours from the laundry, while each layer downward, each turn of the central stairs, reveals thicker carpets, and more elaborate room number signs. Even the clocks run slower down on the third floor, 'because the rich have time'.[64] In Bowen's hotel, a guest's place in the spatial order is reflected in what Alex Woloch calls their 'character-space'.[65] Woloch argues that the fate of a character in a novel – whether they gain significance as a major figure or irrelevance as a minor one – is a product of their implied human personality (their 'character') as well as the space they are allocated within the narrative discourse. Some characters are squeezed into peripheral scenes or broken up into fragments and scattered through the text; others fight their way into the centre of things. Depending on the novel's genre, those characters that move to the centre have the room to develop psychological depth and complexity, while squeezed or fragmented characters will invariably have a flattened and simplified human personality. Their place in the narrative discourse leaves them 'compress[ed]', 'externaliz[ed]', 'abstracted' and 'distort[ed]'.[66]

In *The Hotel*, such effects are crucial. Central characters are only important if they command the intimacy of the camera-eye; characters become minor when they shift into the background and move out of focus. In the dining room at lunchtime, for instance, Sydney watches guests as they swim into focus, transforming from background into foreground figures: 'Beyond, down the long perspective to the foot of the stairs, one could see visitors take form with blank faces, then compose and poise themselves for an entrance.'[67] In a description loaded with significance, Bowen pinpoints the exact location – the threshold between the public lobby and the semi-public dining-room – where individuals become conscious of themselves as characters. By drawing this boundary, Bowen economically demarcates two forms of narrative space: one in which familiar characters consolidate their identities and further their plot lines, and another populated by a constant circulation of unfamiliar figures in which incidental activities are carried out. From her table, Sydney keeps glancing between her fellow diners, rich with potential narrative – the parading Mr Lee-Mittison, the scarlet-eyed Miss Pym, the quietly dignified Mrs and Miss Pinkerton – and the anonymous comings and goings in the next room. Through her gaze, she constructs the hotel's social hierarchy:

> Beyond the dining-room, along the expanses of the lounge, people risen early from their tables were awaiting one another, meek under the rule of precedent, to fulfil a hundred small engagements. Leisure, so linked up with ennui, had been sedulously barred away. Each armchair, each palm and bureau had become a trysting-place where couples met to hurry off or groups were reunited.[68]

The creeping pathology of this hotel, however, is a fear of tumbling into the background, of losing one's sense of foreground importance. An excess of blank minor characters is a symptom of, but in some ways also a solution to, this middle-class paranoia. Minorness, like perspective, is an artificial effect of representation. Part of the work performed by minor characters is simply to reinforce the comparative depth and complexity of major characters. Set in relief against the blank bit players of the hotel, the central figures of Bowen's drama gain a false three-dimensionality that hotel space itself threatens to erase. The attachment of the major characters to neoclassical models of spatiality – Milton is presumed to have lectured on the Renaissance at the National Gallery – seems, therefore, to have deep ideological roots. Distanced contemplation is not merely an aesthetic preference, but a class survival strategy.

Tom Gunning, in his work on cinema and landscape, demonstrates how the movie camera radically overturned the centuries-long tradition of distanced contemplation. Gunning's focus is the 'phantom ride', a peculiarity of the pre-narrative 'cinema of attractions' era during the 1890s and 1900s, in which cameras were attached to trains moving through dramatic landscapes. The train was a symbol of territorial conquest and the dominion of technology over nature, but Gunning does not read these films as an extension of the magisterial gaze.

> [A]nother experience seems dominant, one prompted by physical sensations of vertigo [. . .]. The vanishing point, the fixed convergence of classical perspective, its point of coherence, becomes in the phantom ride a point of constant transformation and instability. [. . .] The reversal reworks perspective's inherent sense of visual dominance into an experience of an abject subjection to the course of movement and the logic of the track.[69]

Phantom ride films were unique phenomena, but their effects were representative of a more general rupture enacted by cinema – which could equally be seen in films where motion was aimed at a fixed camera (in its purest form, in the Lumières' famous *Arrival of a Train at Ciotat*). Both kinds of film burst through the frame, abolishing the safe distance between spectator and spectacle, immersing the spectator in a new form of dynamic spatiality. Dorothy Richardson, writing in *Close Up* in 1931, described the sensation of being the 'motionless, observing centre', sitting before the 'moving reality' of the cinema screen: 'In life, we contemplate a landscape from one point, or walking through it, break it into bits. The film, by setting the landscape in motion and keeping us still, allows it to walk through us.'[70]

The landscape-in-motion is explored in Bowen's short story 'Dead Mabelle'. The story tells of William Stickford, a 'cinema-shy' bank-clerk who is drawn into the world of the picture house through his obsession with a rising Hollywood silent film star, Mabelle Pacey.[71] On news reports of Mabelle's sudden death, Stickford goes to see the final screening of a film Mabelle made in 1923, *The White Rider*, at the Bijou Picturedrome. As Stickford walks into the movie theatre, he sees an empty filmic landscape waiting for Mabelle to occupy it:

> He looked down a long perspective, a flickering arcade of shadow. For twenty seconds or so there was no one – the trees' fretful movements, the dazzlingly white breaking-through of the sky. The orchestra wound off their tune with a flourish and sharply, more noticeably, were silent down in their red-lighted pit. The flutter and click of the machinery streamed out across the theatre, like the terrified wings of a bird imprisoned between two window-panes – it gave him the same stretched sensation of horror and helplessness. A foreign whiteness, a figure, more than a figure appeared; a white-coated girl on a white horse drawn sideways across the distant end of the drive. She listened, all tense, to that same urgent flutter and clicking, then wheeled the horse round and dashed forward into the audience, shadows streaming over her.[72]

Written by Bowen on the cusp of the talkies era, this moment in the narrative seems to return to the dim, early history of cinema, where vehicles charged toward the camera in an elemental landscape. By inserting a twenty-second glitch in the flow of time, Bowen heightens the moment just before Mabelle enters the screen. The moment underlines Mabelle's absolute, ontological absence, and the deathliness of the cinema image, with its X-ray aesthetic and its mechanised reproduction (represented by the grinding projector and the broken orchestra running out of music and winding down). But even here, even in a moment of ghostly absence, Bowen also underlines the connective and immersive aspects of film: the way it activates the space between viewer and screen, transforming it into a three-dimensional extension of the flat image. Instead of providing a stable viewing platform for the contemplation of a distant scene, the Picturedrome theatre is part of the scene. Stickford might either be looking down at the theatre or up at *The White Rider* when he enters. The 'long perspective, a flickering arcade of shadow', could ambiguously refer to an interior or an exterior arcade, to the rows and aisles of the Picturedrome, raking toward the screen and bathed in projected light, or to the arcade of trees that continues that line into the far-distance of the image. The two spaces are as one. Stickford's sensory alertness to the mechanics of the illusion confirms his detachment from the image, and yet his awareness of the room and its flicker and click also creates the sensation of standing *within* the dimensionalised image. Stickford imagines the sound of the film projector that 'streamed out across the theatre' reaching Mabelle's ear; it seems to summon her forth. When Mabelle dashes 'forward into the audience, shadows streaming over her', the Picturedrome and *The White Rider* become a single stream of sensation. Stickford, agitated, feels neither inside nor outside the screen, but both simultaneously, trapped and 'stretched' in an impossible in-between, as if 'between two window-panes'.

This cinematic landscape-in-motion is also a crucial effect in *The Hotel*, in competition with the painterly. The novel begins not with a room and a view, nor in any localisable space, but with 'Miss Fitzgerald hurr[ying] out of the Hotel into the road'.[73] We are inserted *in media res* not only into the plot, but into space. The feeling of being constantly in the middle, constantly on the move, characterises Bowen's camera-eye. Miss Pym goes in wary pursuit of Miss Fitzgerald and the camera follows her:

> She listened; she clung to the bannisters – tense for retreat at every turn of the staircase. The lift-shaft rose direct from the lounge and the stairs bent round and round it: she stared down for a long time through the wire netting case of the shaft to assure herself that the lounge was empty. It was. There was not a soul down there; not a movement among the shadows, it was eleven o'clock and everybody would have gone out to the shops or the library, up to the hills or down to the tennis courts. Not a shadow crossed the veiled glass doors of the drawing-room to interrupt the glitter from the sea. Not a sound came up from the smoking-room. Miss Fitzgerald was not there.[74]

The hotel lobby is doubly empty, because what we are seeing is not the subjective observation of a human character. The passage is detached from a human perspective, describing things that Miss Pym peering down from the stairs could not see. By the time we reach the glittering doors of the drawing-room, the perspective has become that of a mobile camera-eye, and not a human eye, wandering the ground floor alone.

The camera creeping through hotel corridors recalls the mobile camera of *Der Letzte Mann*, a hotel film released in London in March 1925 while Bowen was drafting *The Hotel*. In notes prepared for a newspaper article in 1922 or 1923 and later uncovered by historian Lotte Eisner, the director F. W. Murnau spoke of creating an 'architectural' film:

> What I refer to is the fluid architecture of bodies with blood in their veins moving through mobile space; the interplay of lines rising, falling, disappearing; the encounter of surfaces, stimulation and its opposite, calm; construction and collapse; the formation and destruction of a hitherto unsuspected life; [. . .] the *play of pure movement*, vigorous and abundant. All this we shall be able to create when the camera has at last been de-materialized.[75]

Created through the partnership of cinematographer Karl Freund, designer Robert Herlth, and screenplay writer Carl Mayer at the Ufa Studios in Berlin, *Der Letzte Mann* concerns a hotel porter who loses his job, his magnificent coat and the respect of his working-class neighbourhood after becoming too old and tired to carry heavy luggage. The film has virtually no inter-titles and tells its story through the expressiveness of its shots and *mise-en-scène*. Freund's camera was 'unchained' from its tripod and mounted on a wagon and a bicycle, hung from a gondola and carried up ladders. One famous shot replicates the drunkenness of the porter by having Freund himself stagger around wildly with the camera attached to his chest. Yet overall the cinematography does not seek to evoke subjective impressions. Rather, *Der Letzte Mann* extends and exceeds human perception through mechanical means. Freund's bicycle-mounted camera does not just follow the porter through the hotel corridors, but glides swiftly beyond him to focus on another group of men at the far end of the lobby. The opening shot of *Der Letzte Mann* directly foregrounds its mechanical nature by mounting the camera behind the grille of a descending elevator. The smooth movements of the travelling camera are from this moment encoded with the hotel's smooth mechanisms of circulation. From the elevator we momentarily slide forward, as if pushed by a bellhop on a luggage trolley; after a cut, we slide toward the revolving doors, introducing us to the porter on the street through the door's flashing glass surfaces. The hotel is the ideal mobile space for a mobile camera: in the hotel's long lines and rhythms, the camera finds its home. In a scene set at night, while the porter is trying to steal back his confiscated coat, a security guard with a flashlight strapped to his chest approaches the camera – which will itself be strapped to the chest of Freund in a later scene. Two functionaries of the hotel and the cinema look back at each other: they are allies, both prosthetic extensions of the mechanical systems they represent.

There are indications that Bowen and Murnau, too, are aesthetic allies, especially in Bowen's highly self-conscious allusion to German expressionism in *The Hotel*:

> The glass doors behind and beside her flashing as they opened and shut, the staircase going up and down and doubling off at angles into oblivion, and the way the lift came sliding down the shaft to wait behind the latticed gates were all like so much expressionist scenery, emphasizing the effect she gave of being distracted, mechanical and at a standstill.[76]

Der Letzte Mann was not an obscurity in Britain: one of Ufa's rare international successes, its London release was a high-profile cultural event. It ran for three weeks to sell-out crowds and enthusiastic reviews, with a promotional boost from star Emil Jannings, who arrived in London for the occasion.[77] Nonetheless, a lack of documentary evidence for the early period of Bowen's life means it is not possible to confirm which precise films influenced *The Hotel* or whether she did indeed see *Der Letzte Mann*. But it seems plausible that Murnau was an inspiration for Bowen's mechanisation of narrative point of view and her denaturalisation of the hotel's visual order.

The cinematic aesthetic clashes directly with the painterly during a hilltop picnic in *The Hotel*. Overlooking an old villino, the commanding view unfurls like a picturesque landscape. Milton describes it as 'out of some background looked at, you know, through an arch of the slit of a window' – but then is anxious 'not to appear unduly familiar with the National Gallery or the Uffizi'.[78] The clergyman, like Jane Austen's leading men, is trained in aesthetics and is inclined to gloss a landscape for the benefit of female company. Yet while Mrs Lee-Mittison gazes in reverie at the picturesque details of Italian rural life, she snaps back to an image of the hotel corridor in a sudden eruption of the cinematic:

> The villino suddenly dropped away from her eye as though she had put down a telescope, and as her life sprang back into focus she must have been dizzy, for she felt sick at the thought of their hotel bedrooms that stretched, only interposed with the spare rooms of friends, in unbroken succession before and behind her.[79]

The superimposition of two realities joined by a dizzying focal effect brings to mind a scene from *Der Letzte Mann*, when the demoted porter returns to the hotel and sees his younger replacement working in his old position. The dawning horror of the porter is represented by a tracking shot that moves in on his younger replacement, while slowly slipping into focus. Through her own focal effect, Bowen suggests that perspective, and the harmonious relationship between foreground and background, are neither natural nor static, but manipulable, mobile and collapsible. The social order that depends on a stable foreground and background is thereby imperilled. It is this sense of social peril that makes Mrs Lee-Mittison swoon.

Pratfalls

For good reason, the corridors and elevator are the most cinematic but also the most anxious and paranoid elements of Bowen's hotel. In *The Hotel*, double-loaded corridors cross the upper floors of the hotel from end to end. 'Five times across the Hotel, each on a floor, these corridors ran – dark, thickly carpeted, panelled with bedroom doors'.[80] The long perspective forms a narrowed, closed-off tunnel. The image of the corridor, with its 'view of many individual lives standardized by the identical spatial distribution of cellular private lives along a semi-public passageway', provides an instant demonstration of the individual's relativity, or a 'sense of transience, of easy substitution', as Roger Luckhurst writes.[81] This experience, which Luckhurst calls 'corridor dread', is deeply unsettling for Bowen's middle-class guests (Figure 4.2).

The double-loaded corridor, with standardised rooms coming off both sides of a single, central circulation space, was a major feature of rationalised institutional

Figure 4.2 The first-floor corridor in the Midland Adelphi Hotel, Liverpool, 1912 (Source: Historic England Archive)

design.[82] Allowing for a more efficiently organised floor plan, it became part of the architectural vernacular in hotels, apartment blocks, offices, schools, prisons and hospitals in the mid-nineteenth century. The corridor replaced older forms of circulation with communicating doors between chambers, instead allowing for private and enclosed chambers which were separated from zones of circulation. The corridor, argues Kate Marshall, 'simultaneously makes possible and constantly irritates' privacy and interiority, as bodies and information nonetheless circulate freely just beyond the threshold of the private chamber.[83] 'The corridor differentiates, separates and divides', writes Luckhurst, 'but it also unnervingly makes linking things together much easier: genders and classes, family and strangers'.[84] This is certainly the case in hotel corridors, which forced strangers occupying the same floor to interact with each other in the same space, as well as aligning opposing doorways in unintentionally intimate pairings.

Double-loaded corridors had long attracted filmmakers of the silent era as spaces of threat, violation, promiscuity and disorientation: from the first instalment of Feuillade's *Fantômas* (1914) to Monca's *La Proie* (1917), Stroheim's *Blind Husbands* (1919) and *Foolish Wives* (1921), Lang's *Dr Mabuse, der Spieler* (1922), Dupont's *Variety* (1925) and Stiller's *Hotel Imperial* (1927) (Figure 4.3). The corridor was intensely filmic not just – as Lotte Eisner notes of Weimar cinema's 'obsession' with corridors and staircases – because it presented ideal opportunities for chiaroscuro.[85] Vanishing into the obscure reaches of the cinema frame,

Figure 4.3 Still from *Variety*, directed by Ewald André Dupont, Ufa, 1925

corridors gave cinema the illusion of exploring deep, infinitely interconnected space, promising new, random, anonymous and possibly dangerous encounters beyond the flat plane of everyday life. Fritz Lang, for instance, was 'fascinated by passageways, the intermediary spaces which join up other spaces, transitory spaces, [. . .] corridors and elevators', writes Tom Gunning, because they connected together hierarchised layers of architectural space, 'undermin[ing] these divisions or bring[ing] them into contact'.[86] For precisely the same reason, double-loaded corridors were also ideal spaces for film comedy. Hotel slapstick was a virtual sub-genre in itself. All of the major silent-era comics did stints as hotel bellboys, doormen or rowdy hotel guests. Harold Lloyd made a string of bellboy films; Fatty Arbuckle and Buster Keaton worked at the Elk's Head Hotel in *The Bell Boy* (1918); Laurel and Hardy worked as a doorman and footman in the silent short *Double Whoopee* (1929); while the Marx Brothers translated their hotel-based vaudeville routines into talkies in *The Cocoanuts* (1929). The template was set down by Charlie Chaplin at Keystone, a studio that frequently used hotels as its basic comic location. The Keystone productions *Mabel's Strange Predicament* (1914), *Caught in the Rain* (1914) and *The Rounders* (1914), and the Essanay production *A Night Out* (1915), were variations on the same plot: Charlie returns to his hotel drunk, and either stumbles into the room of the woman who lives across the corridor, or finds the woman across the corridor accidentally locked in his own room, or is berated by his wife and hurled into the room across the corridor, in which he finds another drunk husband being berated by his wife – or else some combination of the above. That the various hotel rooms mocked up in the studio look the same, both within the same film and across different films, is almost part of the joke: this was infinitely duplicable film comedy, generated out of the architectural tension between two duplicated rooms joined by a single corridor (Figures 4.4 and 4.5).

Figure 4.4 Corridor trouble. Still from *Caught in the Rain*, directed by Charlie Chaplin, Keystone, 1914

Figure 4.5 Corridor trouble. Still from *Caught in the Rain*, directed by Charlie Chaplin, Keystone, 1914

Bowen also finds an irresistible comic tension in the double-loaded corridor. 'The important thing about *The Hotel*', writes Bowen biographer Victoria Glendinning, 'is that it is very, very funny.'[87] Yet the novel's breeziness is heavily tempered. 'Comedy in Elizabeth Bowen may cut very deep indeed,' Neil Corcoran argues in reference to *The Last September*, 'with a laughter on the other side of hysteria'.[88] The comic business that goes on in Bowen's hotel corridors and elevators is an anxious comedy, a comedy of corridor dread, motivated by fears of decline and dissolution. Bowen uses two set-piece comedy routines to breach the slender boundary between public and private space, and to collapse the boundary between classes of hotel guest (not to mention the genre boundaries of her novel). Her comic routines begin with a set of dupes who assume a status of superiority and centrality; they end with those claims being trashed. Mrs and Miss Pinkerton, widow and sister of the deceased Lord Pinkerton, establish the parameters of the first routine by trying to short-circuit the relativity of the corridor. They have paid a large excess to claim private usage of the bathroom across the hall. Other guests respect this privilege – it has 'a certain beauty for them, the accretion of prestige' – and bathe instead at the far end of the hall or upstairs.[89] But the Pinkertons' 'occupation' of the bathroom is shallow, as all occupation of hotel space must be; it consists only of Shetlands hanging on the radiator, bath salts, loofahs and a verbal agreement with the hotel manager. Nevertheless, with this piece of real estate the Pinkertons effectively control one end of the first floor, just as Bowen's wealthy relatives reserved an entire floor of the Hotel Angst. With the space nicely rationalised, they experience a 'comfortable feeling of enclosedness'.[90] James Milton, newly arrived at the hotel after a long rail trip, also believes he can overcome the blankness of the corridor: he claims the innate hotel literacy of a well-travelled gentleman. Milton deals with the staff matter of factly; he quickly inspects his room; he scoops up his bathing paraphernalia and calls out to the chambermaid in three languages that he plans to take a bath. 'He was an independent man with a bump of locality on which he had grown with years increasingly reliant, and he brought himself without difficulty to the door of a hospitable-looking bathroom.'[91]

All are mistaken. The corridor is not the space that either the Pinkertons or James Milton imagines. As lusty singing begins to flow from the Pinkertons' bathroom, the women hold an urgent conference with Sydney and her cousin Tessa – who in these desperate circumstances are the first guests to cross the threshold into the Pinkertons' hotel bedroom. The scene concludes with Milton – damp, boiled and cheerful – opening the bathroom door in his dressing-gown; Sydney and Tessa – also in her dressing-gown – coming face to face with Milton on their way out of the Pinkertons'; Tessa fleeing; Sydney staring; Milton, unnerved, bowing gravely; and behind Sydney, the Pinkertons sticking horrified faces out of their door before slamming it closed again. The interchange is perfectly timed, and it demonstrates just how rapidly pretensions of order and mastery can fall into disorder in a hotel. Milton instantly loses his calm, *au fait* air, and never recovers it. He enters the bathroom sure of his place within the hotel hierarchy and emerges from the bathroom rebirthed as a stranger. Through the simultaneous opening of two doors, the Pinkertons' careful rationalisation of space suffers a dizzy collapse: a stranger looks into their bedroom and they into the bathroom of a stranger.

Bowen stages a second set-piece in an elevator, with Milton and two nameless bit players. Entering the lobby, the trio are watched by a few scattered people sitting and talking in the lounge. Many in this audience have already tried and failed to get the lift to work; it's out of order.

> [T]hree people in mackintoshes, two women and a man, came in rustling and dripping from the porch. Their collars were turned up and over these they looked repudiatingly at one another. They had not been for their walks together, and they did not wish anybody to suppose they had. They had followed one another for some kilometres along a streaming road, to close up unavoidably on the Hotel doorstep. Among them was James Milton, wondering why he had ever come abroad, cold, weary, amazed by the weather. Dripping audibly, they all got into the lift and slammed the gates upon their undesired contiguity. Here they remained for some moments shut up in silence.[92]

An onlooker in the lounge shouts out that the lift is out of order; the trio, freed from the logic of a cruel cosmic joke, open the lift gates and scatter. This routine calls into being two completely blank figures, unnamed and undescribed except for their gender, their common costume (the mackintosh) and their shared irritation. The joke relies on the trio's proud assertion of separateness and free will. It undercuts them gleefully with every 'they' and 'their', collectivising every repudiating glance and every repudiating thought. Tethered together, the three are the purified essence of Bowen's geometric form. Here Milton's individuality balances on a knife-edge. He is singled out and granted an interior perspective, even if that perspective is barely imprinted with individuality and could equally apply to his companions. As a mirror image of two strangers, Milton's selfhood takes a vertiginous plunge.

With Bowen's elision of labour, English class tensions (and Irish civil strife) might seem far removed from this Italian resort hotel. ('"I mean, of course, there is always Politics"', says one of the guests, unfurling her Continental *Daily Mail*, '"but that goes on and on and on, so one begins to lose interest. Especially out here where one cannot see what effect they are having, though one does doubt really whether they do have any effect."')[93] Yet if the guests are not confronted by an unruly working class, they are confronted by unruly *mise-en-scène*. The mechanism of the hotel itself portends the doom of the old order. The hotel may be a stopping place, a place where lives are 'stilled, immovably, catatonically', and a place where Bowen's plots can assemble, jam and fall apart.[94] But the hotel itself, and Bowen's mode of representing it, is metamorphic and works to undercut her guests' rigid sense of privacy, self-possession and hierarchy. Together, cinematic effects and hotel space conspire to make Bowen's major characters look like minor characters, and to make the important seem like nameless extras in a comic routine.

Notes

1. Elizabeth Bowen, *The Hotel* (London: Vintage, 2003), pp. 27 and 24.
2. Hermione Lee, *Elizabeth Bowen* (London: Vintage, 1999), pp. 58–9. *The Hotel* is completely set aside in renée c hoogland's Bowen study, *Elizabeth Bowen: A Reputation in Writing* (New York and London: New York University Press, 1994).
3. Virginia Woolf, 'Mr Bennett and Mrs Brown', in *Selected Essays*, ed David Bradshaw (Oxford and New York: Oxford University Press, 2008), p. 49.
4. Willa Cather, 'The Novel Démeublé', 30 *New Republic* (12 April 1922), pp. 5–6.
5. Maud Ellmann, *Elizabeth Bowen: The Shadow Across the Page* (Edinburgh: Edinburgh University Press, 2004), p. 7.
6. Ibid., p. 7.
7. Ibid., p. 80.
8. E. M. Forster, *A Room with a View*, ed. Malcolm Bradbury (New York and London: Penguin, 2000), pp. 3 and 7.
9. Ibid., p. 15.
10. L. V. Bertarelli, *Northern Italy: From the Alps to Rome*, ed. Findlay Muirhead (London: Macmillan, 1924), pp. 2–3.

11. Turtle Bunbury, 'Colley of Corkagh House, Clondalkin', *Turtle Bunbury Histories*, <www.turtlebunbury.com/family/bunburyfamily_related/bunbury_family_related_colley.html>.
12. Standard Italian Travel Association, *The Standard Guide to Italy* (New York: Standard Italian Travel Association, 1912), p. 44.
13. Andrea Zanini, 'La promozione turistica durante la Belle Époque: il caso della Riviera ligure', in *Pensar con la historia desde el siglo XXI: actas del XII Congreso de la Asociación de Historia Contemporánea*, eds Pilar Folguera and Juan Carlos Pereira (Madrid: UAM Ediciones, 2015), pp. 365–81.
14. Elizabeth Bowen, *Love's Civil War: Elizabeth Bowen and Charles Ritchie: Letters and Diaries 1941–1973*, ed. Victoria Glendinning (Toronto: Emblem, 2009), pp. 139–40 (2 September 1949).
15. Marcel Proust, *Within a Budding Grove*, trans. C. K. Scott Moncrieff (New York: Modern Library, 1951), p. 351.
16. Ibid., pp. 342–3.
17. Bowen, *The Hotel*, p. 118.
18. Ibid., p. 53.
19. Ibid., p. 106.
20. Ibid., p. 27.
21. Ibid., p. 108.
22. Elizabeth Bowen, 'Modern Lighting', in *People, Places, Things: Essays by Elizabeth Bowen*, ed. Allan Hepburn (Edinburgh: Edinburgh University Press, 2008) p. 28.
23. René Rousseau, 'René Rousseau on Proust's Psychology and Art: *Le Mercure de France*, January 1922', in *Marcel Proust: The Critical Heritage*, ed. Leighton Hodson (London: Routledge, 1989), p. 178. Edith Wharton, reclaiming Proust as a traditional novelist, uses the same imagery to dispute these kinds of Freudian readings. Proust 'never loses himself in the submarine jungle in which his lantern gropes'; his real object is 'man's conscious and purposive behaviour rather than its dim unfathomable sources'. In *The Writing of Fiction* (London: Scribner's Sons, 1925), pp. 155–6.
24. Victoria Glendinning, *Elizabeth Bowen: Portrait of a Writer* (London: Weidenfeld & Nicolson, 1977), pp. 51–2.
25. Jamie Sexton, 'The Film Society and the Creation of an Alternative British Film Culture in the 1920s', in *Young and Innocent? Cinema and Britain 1896–1930*, ed. Andrew Higson (Exeter: Exeter University Press, 2002), pp. 291–305.
26. Elizabeth Bowen, *Afterthought: Pieces about Writing* (London: Longmans, 1962), p. 90.
27. Elizabeth Bowen, 'Dead Mabelle', in *Collected Stories* (London: Vintage, 1999), p. 277.
28. Elizabeth Bowen, *Bowen's Court* (London: Longmans, 1964), p. 401.
29. Elizabeth Bowen, 'Frankly Speaking: Interview, 1959', in *Listening In: Broadcasts, Speeches, and Interviews by Elizabeth Bowen*, ed. Allan Hepburn (Edinburgh: Edinburgh University Press, 2010), p. 339.
30. Bowen is described as a member of the Film Society in a biographic note that accompanied her essay, 'Why I Go to the Cinema' (1938), in *Footnotes to the Film*, ed. Charles Davy (London: Lovat Dickson, 1938), p. 323. Due to the incompleteness

of the membership records in the Film Society Collection held by the British Film Institute, it remains unclear when Bowen joined, but presumably much earlier than 1938. She is not listed among members of the Society in 1927, but it is possible that she was a temporary member before this date.

31. One of the more extended pieces on Bowen and the cinema can be found in Lara Feigel's *Literature, Cinema and Politics*, but even here Feigel inserts the caveat that Bowen's '1930s work was only loosely cinematic'. Lara Feigel, *Literature, Cinema and Politics, 1930–1945: Reading between the Frames* (Edinburgh: Edinburgh University Press, 2010), p. 5.
32. David Trotter, *Cinema and Modernism* (Malden, MA: Blackwell, 2007), p. 1.
33. The Marble Arch Pavilion ran a selection of German productions throughout the 1920s, from *The Cabinet of Dr Caligari* to the Fritz Lang films *Metropolis* and *Spione* and several early Lubitsch films. This was aided by an Anglo-German film distribution deal signed by the Ufa Company and the Gaumont-British Picture Corporation, which controlled the Marble Arch. ('Anglo-German Film Agreement. Mutual Distribution', *The Times*, 12 December 1927, p. 19.) The New Gallery Regent Street showed Lang's *Dr Mabuse, der Spieler* in 1923, while Murnau's *The Last Laugh* played for three weeks in the Capitol in Haymarket in 1925. The Film Society showed works by Leni, Lang, Wiene, Pabst, Richter and Ruttman.
34. Gerry Turvey, 'Towards a Critical Practice: Ivor Montagu and British Film Culture in the 1920s', in *Young and Innocent?*, pp. 306–20.
35. Iris Barry, *Let's Go to the Pictures* (London: Chatto & Windus, 1926), p. 27.
36. Bowen, *Listening In*, p. 200.
37. Ibid., p. 200.
38. Ibid.
39. Leo Mellor, *Reading the Ruins: Modernism, Bombsites and British Culture* (Cambridge: Cambridge University Press, 2011), pp. 139–40; Ian Walker, *So Exotic, So Homemade: Surrealism, Englishness and Documentary Photography* (Manchester: Manchester University Press, 2007), p. 140.
40. Walker, *So Exotic, So Homemade*, p. 140.
41. Walter Benjamin, 'Little History of Photography', in *Selected Writings: 1927–1934*, eds Michael W. Jennings, Howard Eiland and Gary Smith (Cambridge, MA: Harvard University Press, 1999), p. 519.
42. Keri Walsh, 'Elizabeth Bowen, Surrealist', 42 (3/4) *Éire-Ireland* (2007), pp. 126–47.
43. Bowen, *The Hotel*, p. 78.
44. Ibid., p. 78.
45. Ibid., pp. 78–9.
46. Klaus Kreimeier, *The Ufa Story: A History of Germany's Greatest Film Company, 1918–1945* (Berkeley, CA and London: University of California Press, 1999), p. 104.
47. Elizabeth Bowen, 'Notes on Writing a Novel', in *Pictures and Conversations* (London: Allen Lane, 1975), p. 37.
48. Bowen, *The Hotel*, p. 79.
49. Ibid., p. 105.
50. Ibid., p. 53.
51. Ibid., p. 24.

52. Ibid., p. 105. The use of the term 'mise-en-scène' is intriguing: a term still in common use to refer to theatrical sets, but also increasingly used in newspaper film reviews and in film journals like *The Bioscope* by the 1920s.
53. Bowen, *The Hotel*, p. 98.
54. Ibid., p. 22.
55. Ross McKibbin, *Classes and Cultures: England 1918–1951* (Oxford and New York: Oxford University Press, 2008), p. 49.
56. Ibid., p. 67.
57. Bowen, 'Notes on Writing a Novel', pp. 182–4.
58. Ellmann, *Elizabeth Bowen*, 23.
59. Shawna Ross, 'The Two Hotels of Elizabeth Bowen: Utopian Leisure in the Age of Mechanized Hospitality', in *Utopianism, Modernism, and Literature in the Twentieth Century*, eds Alice Reeve-Tucker and Nathan Waddell (Basingstoke: Palgrave Macmillan, 2013), pp. 156 and 157.
60. Bowen, *The Hotel*, p. 64.
61. Ibid., p. 33.
62. Ibid., pp. 58–62.
63. Ibid., p. 35 and p. 45.
64. Joseph Roth, *Hotel Savoy*, trans. John Hoare (London: Picador, 1988), p. 13.
65. Alex Woloch, *The One vs. the Many: Minor Characters and the Space of the Protagonist in the Novel* (Princeton, NJ and Oxford: Princeton University Press, 2003), pp. 12–14.
66. Ibid., p. 145.
67. Bowen, *The Hotel*, p. 21.
68. Ibid., p. 24.
69. Tom Gunning, 'Landscape and the Fantasy of Moving Pictures: Early Cinema's Phantom Rides', in *Cinema and Landscape*, eds Graeme Harper and Jonathan Rayner (Bristol and Chicago: Intellect, 2010), p. 59.
70. Dorothy Richardson, 'Continuous Performance: Narcissus', in *Red Velvet Seat: Women's Writings on the First Fifty Years of Cinema*, eds Antonia Lant and Ingrid Periz (London and New York: Verso, 2006), pp. 238–9.
71. Bowen, 'Dead Mabelle', p. 277.
72. Ibid., p. 282.
73. Bowen, *The Hotel*, p. 7.
74. Ibid., p. 7.
75. Lotte H. Eisner, *Murnau* (London: Secker & Warburg, 1973), p. 84.
76. Bowen, *The Hotel*, pp. 137–8.
77. Kreimeier, *The Ufa Story*, p. 145.
78. Bowen, *The Hotel*, p. 40.
79. Ibid., p. 42.
80. Ibid., p. 26.
81. Roger Luckhurst, *Corridors: Passages of Modernity* (London: Reaktion Books, 2019), p. 127.
82. A. K. Sandoval-Strausz, *Hotel: An American History* (New Haven, CT and London: Yale University Press, 2007), pp. 147–9.

83. Kate Marshall, *Corridor: Media Architectures in American Fiction* (Minneapolis, MN: Minnesota University Press, 2013), p. 70.
84. Luckhurst, *Corridors*, p. 39.
85. Lotte H. Eisner, *The Haunted Screen: Expressionism in the German Cinema and the Influence of Max Reinhardt*, trans. Roger Greaves (Berkeley, CA and Los Angeles: University of California Press, 2008), p. 119.
86. Tom Gunning, *The Films of Fritz Lang: Allegories of Vision and Modernity* (London: British Film Institute, 2000), pp. 474 and 371.
87. Glendinning, *Elizabeth Bowen*, p. 62.
88. Neil Corcoran, *Elizabeth Bowen: The Enforced Return* (Oxford and New York: Oxford University Press, 2004), p. 42.
89. Bowen, *The Hotel*, p. 26.
90. Ibid., p. 28.
91. Ibid., p. 27.
92. Ibid., p. 57.
93. Ibid., p. 136.
94. Andrew Bennett and Nicholas Royle, *Elizabeth Bowen and the Dissolution of the Novel: Still Lives* (Basingstoke: Macmillan, 1995), p. 14.

5

THE HOTEL AUTEUR: THE MANAGER'S OFFICE

In the short trick film *Hôtel Électrique* (1905), a couple walk into a hotel filled with magical electrical conveniences. They blithely look on as their luggage moves itself into the elevator, brings itself to their hotel room and unpacks itself. In their suite, automatic brushes and razors groom the pair, while an automatic pen writes a letter informing their relatives they have been *installés comfortablement* in the hotel. The film takes a turn when a drunk hotel attendant below stairs leans on a panel of electrical levers, sending the system into meltdown and hurling furniture and bodies around the hotel suite. With its disjunctive narrative broken up by extended stop-motion sequences, the film focuses attention on the uncannily animate objects that occupy much of the screen time. The hotel guests who are groomed and then attacked by these objects are the real-life couple Julienne Mathieu and Segundo de Chomón. The couple collaborated on the film (Mathieu bringing her expertise in special effects and Chomón directing) as well as performing as the duped guests. As the filmmakers, they orchestrate the scene invisibly. But as actors, Mathieu and Chomón must remain impassive, stiff-armed and blank-faced as the props shuttle around them, in order to preserve the continuity of the stop-motion animation. In these moments they do not perform as charismatic magicians, seducing and misdirecting the audience, as live performers would; instead, they are puppets of technology, their creative power ceded to the hotel and the camera. Their position recalls another short film attributed to Chomón, *Le Roi des Dollars*, which evokes the traditional sleight of hand tricks of theatrical conjurers, with coins appearing and disappearing from a pair of hands shot in close-up, and then pouring from the mouth of an assistant. But *Le Roi des Dollars*, like *Hôtel Électrique*, displaces the conjurer's power:

> The film concludes when the two hands clasp one another at the top of the frame as the 'dollar king', whose face and [. . .] body remain offscreen, congratulates himself. Who exactly is being congratulated here? The end of *Le Roi des Dollars* draws the viewer's eyes upward, but never reveals the face of the person who seems to have accomplished this rapid series of marvelous tricks, leaving the identity of the onscreen magician anonymous. Yet, by directing one's eyes past the edges of the frame, it also hints at the important, but largely unseen, role of trick photographers like Chomón, whose clever manipulations of cinematic technology in various trick films yielded an avalanche of coin for Pathé.[1]

These films are really about the hidden hands that conjure the tricks. In *Hôtel Électrique*, those hands belong to the filmmakers and to Pathé Frères Phonographes et Cinématographes, but within the diegesis, those hands belong to the hotel manager who greets the couple and who operates a switchboard that transports the couple's bags upstairs in the elevator. By pulling the levers to initiate the mechanism, the manager acts as the director's shadowy double. Through the mesmeric influence of electricity, the manager superintends every aspect of his guests' private lives, and transforms hotel labour into apparently agentless spectacle. He is 'the brain piece of the whole machinery, the power house of cables of the hotel, the latent motor of the whole operation', as an 1897 article in *The Hotel World* describes modern hotel management.[2] The hotel in *Hôtel Électrique* is itself a cinema of attractions and its manager is the director of its visual effects.

The figure of the hotel manager gradually found a place in the transatlantic imagination during the first decades of the new century. The data visualisation tool, Google Ngram, shows the older term 'hotelkeeping' (combined with its textual variants, 'hotel-keeping' and 'hotel keeping') peaking and falling in frequency in Google's corpus of English texts from the 1890s, as the term 'hotel management' starts to gain in prominence.[3] 'Hotel management' soars above 'keeping' in frequency in the 1910s and 1920s – although 'management' takes firmer hold in America, while 'keeping' retains near parity with 'management' much longer in Britain, where the managerial ethos was still nascent.[4] 'Keeping' connoted a more traditional trade. It put the hotelkeeper in company with the non-professionalised innkeeper, alehouse keeper, shopkeeper and housekeeper, activities that were alternatively romanticised and derided in gendered and classed terms (seen in the Victorian coinages 'shopkeepery' and 'shopkeeperish'). Hotelkeepers becoming 'managers' was an assertion of specialised knowledge and expertise, underlining the technical complexity of the institution being managed. It shifted the class position of the occupation, aligning it with an emergent administrative class, and shifted the gendering of the role as well, in a very real sense. As Ross McKibbin writes, women lost ground as the interwar British economy was professionalised: 'It was the old story: as hotels replaced boarding-houses or as better restaurants replaced inferior ones, men replaced women in their management.'[5] Lucius M. Boomer, celebrity co-manager of the Waldorf-Astoria Hotel with his wife Jørgine Boomer, acknowledges that women exist in hotel management, but claims that men have been 'the builders, the creative force, of business. Perhaps their particular kind of intellect will continue to direct this phase of business development.'[6] The rhetoric expressed during an address to the American Hotel Association in 1924 is typical of this moment: 'a great modern hotel requires scientifically trained minds. If hotelmen live up to the real and ancient dignity of the *profession*, it must be by the best that can be put into it; the best education, the skill, the standards of the *professional man*.'[7]

As indices of this professionalisation, the late-nineteenth and early-twentieth centuries saw new professional societies for hotel managers (the American Hotel Association, founded in 1910, and the Incorporated Association of Hotels and Restaurants, founded in Britain in the same year), hotel management schools and qualifications (starting with the Cornell Hotel School, founded in 1922), trade journals (from *Hotel World* (1895) to *Hotel Management* (1922)) and executive manuals (including Boomer's *Hotel Management: Principles and Practice* (1925), John Dismukes Green's *The Back of the House* (1925), and Ralph Hitz's *Standard Practice Manuals for Hotel Operation* (1936)). Hotel managerialism gained its legitimacy and cultural authority through the rhetoric of rationalisation and science. According to Boomer's executive manual, 'Management makes constant use of formulas, routine, appropriate accounting data and statistics, a staff and line organization. Methods of vitalizing and disciplining personnel are used. All of this [. . .] constitute[s] a *science* of hotel management.'[8] His tome is itself filled with scores of sample revenue reports, receipts, card systems, billing machine forms, inventory forms, organisational charts and standardised routines. As George Sweeney, the managing director of the Hotel Commodore, told an international hotel conference in 1921, this was an industry in which 'the manager has no time for [. . .] civilities', compared to the 'manager of yesterday' who 'made a point of meeting his guests' and 'attending personally to his creature comforts'. Now the manager 'has not less than four assistants to carry on the work for him', allowing him to remain 'at his desk [. . .] like a banker or the head of any other great institution.' The interwar hotel was 'a great machine which the manager must keep properly lubricated so that there may be no slipping of the cogs.'[9] But Boomer insists, too, that 'there is also the *art* of hotel-keeping' – switching here, significantly, to the older nomenclature. Managers provide 'comfort and beauty', 'cloth[ing] the commercial aspects of the hotel with perfection of service' and 'embellish[ing] it with pleasant details and refinements.' The hotel in Boomer's account is a machine that generates aesthetic effects and atmospheres: that stage-manages social scenes through disciplined forms of aesthetic labour, producing the 'good taste', 'morals' and 'manners' of the society it assembles together.[10] The hotel is a work of corporate art.

This chapter thinks about this troublesome coalescence of scientific management and art, and the increasingly fraught figuration of the hotel manager as artist. From Henry James's curious account of the Waldorf-Astoria's management as a rival author, to Arnold Bennett's and Sinclair Lewis's manager-poets and the managerial eye of MGM's *Grand Hotel*, the chapter considers the hotel manager as a classed and gendered fantasy of total authorial power, a fantasy that is then undone by the traffic, fog and crowds of Henry Green's *Party Going* (1939).

Master-Spirits of Management

Henry James visited the Waldorf-Astoria (before Boomer's tenure as manager) in 1905, during his return to America after two decades' absence. In his account of this journey, *The American Scene* (1907), James positions the Waldorf as a metonym for American modernity: 'one is verily tempted to ask if the hotel-spirit may not just be the American spirit most seeking and most finding itself'.[11] The Waldorf was metonymic, James argues, because it was a bureaucratic-managerial machine, exhibiting 'the American genius for organization':

> There are a thousand forms of this ubiquitous American force, [. . .] but there was often no resisting a vivid view of the form it may take, on occasion, under pressure of the native conception of the hotel. Encountered embodiments of the gift, in this connection, master-spirits of management whose influence was as the very air, the very expensive air, one breathed, abide with me as the intensest examples of American character [. . .].[12]

The master-spirit does not appear in fleshly form in *The American Scene*, other than as a metaphor. In this passage, the master-spirit's invisible, ambient 'influence' is in the ether. Hotel lobbies had long been represented by James as immanently telegraphic spaces, from the Dosson's lobby in *The Reverberator* with its 'rich hum',[13] to Strether's hotel in *The Ambassadors* with its 'sounds and suggestions, vibrations of the air'[14] – vibrations which sensitive devices, like the hotel-haunting journalist George Flack, could receive: 'knowledge came to him by a kind of intuition, by the voices of the air, by indefinable and unteachable processes'.[15] When James walked into the Waldorf-Astoria, he would have found a space that was literally a telecommunications interchange. By the time of his visit in January 1905, the Waldorf claimed to have more telephones under one roof (1,120, taking half a million calls every year) than any other building in the world, with banks of public phones set up along the central corridor, Peacock Alley.[16] The entire Waldorf system was interwoven with electric technology, including a 'network of hushed but authoritative buzzers'.[17] Western Union and the Postal Telegraph Company set up telegraph offices in the hotel during the 1890s.[18] Multiple news and stock tickers were placed in public rooms. On the evening of President McKinley's assassination, 'a crowd hung over a ticker with such weight that it broke the glass globe of the machine.'[19] By 1909, the hotel had installed a pair of 25-metre United Wireless towers on its roof, communicating with markets in Chicago and ships in the Atlantic.[20] So it is not surprising that James imagines the Waldorf, too, as a space of signals and noise, with the manager as its switchboard. '[T]he place speaks', he writes, and there is 'violence in the whole communication'. 'The air swarms, to intensity', humming with 'the loud New York story' which is 'shrieking [. . .] into one's ears' as soon as James sets foot inside, with 'all its aspects and voices'. The guests 'walked and talked' and 'listened and danced to music', moved by 'some inimitable New York tune'. And yet these sounds resolve to a tonic note: the place speaks 'as great constructed and achieved harmonies mostly speak'; there is 'unanimity' in all its aspects and voices, and the swarming air seems to impart some singular essence or moral, swarming 'with the *characteristic*, the characteristic condensed and accumulated as he rarely elsewhere has had the luck to find it'.[21] The condensation and accumulation of American voices, James suggests, is the function of management, and his catalogue builds to an image of noise coming under the control of a central intelligence, with the master-spirit transfigured as a conductor:

> I see the whole thing overswept as by the colossal extended arms, waving the magical baton, of some high-stationed orchestral leader, the absolute presiding power, conscious of every note of every instrument, controlling and commanding the whole volume of sound, keeping the whole effect together and making it what it is.[22]

This episode is intriguingly self-reflexive. The language recalls James's essay 'The Art of Fiction' (1884), and its discussion of writers as sensitive receivers and perceivers, catching all the glinting 'air-borne particle[s]' of experience that drift within the 'chamber of consciousness' and the 'very atmosphere of the mind'. '[W]hen the mind is imaginative – much more when it happens to be that of a man of genius – it takes to itself the faintest hints of life, it converts the very pulses of the air into revelations,' James writes.[23] In *The American Scene*, the hotel lobby itself has become the chamber of consciousness, with the manager a suprapersonal mind that receives and harmonises impressions.[24] In James's account, then, the hotel management's primary function is authorial. It doesn't run the Waldorf: it writes the Waldorf. Management is a kind of machine-artist, a collective consciousness imbued with creative powers and a 'technical imagination'. 'What may one say of such a spirit,' James writes, 'if not that he understands, so to speak, the forces he sways, understands his boundless American material and plays with it like a master indeed?'[25] The literary master looks with curiosity upon this fellow master of American material.

This conception of management, writes Ross Posnock, 'would be repugnant to stern men of science' like Frederick Winslow Taylor, the pre-eminent theorist of scientific management in the first decade of the century.[26] In Posnock's reading of this episode, *The American Scene* represents hotel management not as the neutral machinery of rational administration, but as a cultural force analogous to the popular press, in the way it 'organize[s] desires and attitudes into ready-made forms' and 'inculcates obedience to preordained standards'.[27] Waldorf society is thereby rendered homogenous by managerial organisation. But at the same time, we also see the vastness, noise and promiscuity of hotel society – qualities familiar from James's earliest hotel writings – pull against those organising structures. There is 'the organized' but also 'the extemporized'; there is 'the element of ingenuous joy below' as well as 'consummate management above'. The 'contrary dynamics' of this episode in *The American Scene*, writes Kevin R. McNamara, vacillate between 'management and enjoyment, between insidious imperatives to adapt one's patterns of consumption to a new norm and the possibility of an ingenuous joy in picking one's way through social products that promise plenitude.'[28] For Anna Despotopoulou, the Waldorf 'exemplifies an irresolvable conflict between progress and mindless repetition, pluralism and homogenization, mobility and stasis, freedom and captivity'.[29]

James returns again to the image of elastic as a way of figuring the push and pull of expansion and control in Waldorf society, describing 'the play and range, the practical elasticity, of the social sameness, in America'. 'One becomes aware,' he later writes of a vast university hospital in Baltimore

> wherever one turns, both of the tension and of the resistance; everything and everyone, all objects and elements, all systems, arrangements, institutions, functions, persons, reputations, give the sense of their pulling hard at the india-rubber: almost always, wonderfully, without breaking it off, yet never quite with the effect of causing it to lie thick.[30]

James frequently reaches for 'huge' and 'hugely', or 'immense' and 'immensity', as his favoured markers of scale in *The American Scene*; but he just as often uses 'simple' and 'simplified'. He sets out to examine not only the stretch of the American elastic – its skyscraping progress upward and outward – but also the snap of its resistant tension. Underlying America's expansion, he suggests, is a process of organisation, rationalisation and simplification. The immensity and the simplification of Waldorf society exemplified these tendencies.

This dialectic recalls what James Beniger called 'preprocessing', or the simplified and standardised expression of expansive phenomena in industrial capitalist economies.[31] In *The Control Revolution*, Beniger argues that from the 1870s to the early-twentieth century, industrial America gained mastery over information through bureaucratic means. In the initial stages of industrialisation, forces had been unleashed that could not be accounted for. The accelerated production and distribution processes made possible by steam power outpaced the ability of managers to monitor and organise those processes. This 'crisis of control' brought about a wave of innovations affecting the way that information was collected, stored, processed and communicated. Preprocessing reduced the amount of information that needed to be processed by fitting data sets into patterns that matched pre-existing structures. Standardised weights and grades for farm products were early and basic examples of preprocessing. Through this procedure, information could be slotted into standardised forms like timetables, contracts, catalogues and memos. '[R]ationalization might be defined', Beniger writes, 'as the destruction or ignoring of information in order to facilitate its processing.'[32]

James imagines the preprocessing function of the hotel in textual terms. The managerial apparatus edits or abridges social life: in an elaborate conceit, the hotel guest becomes 'but an instalment, a current number, like that of the morning paper, a specimen of a type in course of serialization like the hero of the magazine novel, by the highly-successful author, the climax of which is still far off.'[33] For this reason, hotel managers and journalists are twinned figures in James's work. Both edit and abridge a vast array of human stories and dramatis personae, and both transform the social into consumable texts, images or spectacles. The journalist figures in James's fiction from the 1880s are prototypical preprocessing machines, anticipating the critique of hotel managerialism that James mounted in *The American Scene*. Matthias Pardon from *The Bostonians*, 'the most brilliant young interviewer on the Boston Press', is James's most talented exponent of social preprocessing.[34] Pardon originally acquired his skills in a hotel lobby, beginning his career 'at the age of fourteen, by going the rounds of the hotels, to cull flowers from the big, greasy registers which lie on the marble counters'.[35] His 'flowers' are pungent, short-lived stories – society gossip and extra-marital affairs especially – which flourish in the hotel hothouse. With the right pair of eyes, they are easily harvested from traces (a coincidence of names, a known alias, a feigned spouse) left in the guest book. (George Flack in *The Reverberator* has the same talent: he 'skimmed [guest lists] and found what he wanted in the flash of an eye'.) Pardon prefers to work with 'fragment[s]' or 'little personal items' – incidental details harvested through snooping or casual chat and recorded as 'memoranda' in a notebook.[36] We are told that Pardon has 'condensed into shorthand many of the most celebrated women of his time', a particularly notable achievement since 'some of these daughters of fame were very voluminous'.[37] The burdensome complexity of one's biography, one's personal identity, must be discarded in order for the individual to become a preprocessed media image. To circulate in the press means to travel light.

In *The American Scene*, James makes a visceral connection between journalistic condensation and the hotel's reductive art. The central courtyard of his Virginian hotel becomes the drum of a rotary press or mimeograph, pressing out guests as pure, freshly printed sheets of information:

> The strong vertical light of a fine domed and glazed cortile, the spacious and agreeable dining-hall of the inn, had rested on the human scene as with an effect of mechanical pressure. If the scene constituted evidence, the evidence might have been in course of being pressed out, in this shining form, by the application of a weight and the turn of a screw. There it was, accordingly; there was the social, the readable page, with its more or less complete report of the conditions.[38]

The powers of the press, then, have been subsumed and generalised within hotel systems. Notable hotel guests could often find themselves in the social pages, or in the 'Prominent Arrivals at the Hotels' lists regularly published by papers like the *New-York Tribune* ('IMPERIAL – Judge W. M. Titus, of Massachusetts. MANHATTAN – Hugh Hastings, State Historian, of Albany. WALDORF-ASTORIA – Thomas M. McKee, of Pittsburg'), but in the hotel dining-hall the guests already appear in preprocessed form as a 'report' for the observer to browse.[39] Just as Pardon's prime donne need to be abbreviated in order to freely circulate as images within media networks, so the hotel guest is abbreviated as a precondition of their entry into the hotel's grand circulations. In this way, hotel society becomes 'a world of cameo appearances', borrowing a phrase from Mark Goble's reading of James's *The American Scene* and MGM's *Grand Hotel*: a world 'where a traditional poetics of character has given way to one based on speed and scale.'[40] Or as Goble writes elsewhere, 'where we experience everything in passing, in abbreviated gestures of familiarity and recognition that put precious little on display in showing us just what we want to see.'[41]

James shows hotel management performing three tangible abbreviations. Firstly, management imposes social homogeneity through screening, the 'high pecuniary tax' and the need to appear 'respectable' keeping out the undesirables.[42] Secondly, the hotel guest becomes a data point in the bureaucracy, through registration and the assignation of a room number. Finally, the guest is reduced to various serviceable desires, which are (in James's words) 'anticipate[d]', 'pluck[ed] [. . .] forth' and 'expensively sated' by different labelled rooms and departments of the hotel administration.[43] James's fellow hotel guests in Palm Beach, Florida, clearly show signs of bureaucratisation, with a resemblance to floating numerals:

> The elements of difference, whatever they might latently have been, struck me as throughout forcibly simplified by the conditions of the place; this prompt reducibility of a thousand figures to a common denominator having been in fact, to my sense, the very moral of the picture.[44]

Disburdened of some of the heavy weight of personal identity, the hotel guest's primary drive, like the publicised prime donne, is circulation. '[I]t walked and talked,' James writes, 'and ate and drank, and listened and danced to music, and otherwise revelled and roamed, and bought and sold, and came and went there, all on its own splendid terms and with an encompassing material splendour.'[45] James's construction of an easy, free-moving sentence out of clipped clauses and simple pairs of verbs serves to emphasise his point: that social simplification produces frictionless circulation. The hotel guests circulate as easily as the money that paves their way. In some sense, the guests circulate *as* money. In another mobile assemblage of clauses, James directly connects circulation with pecuniary power: 'you had to be financially more or less at your ease to enjoy the privileges of the Royal Poinciana at all; enjoy them through their extended range of saloons and galleries, fields of high publicity all; pursue them from dining-halls to music-rooms, to ball-rooms, to card-rooms, to writing-rooms [. . .].'[46] The subjects doing the circulating are vaguely announced by James's sentences ('it', and 'you'). Instead, what we see is a 'golden gorgeous blur' of ambient money.

By provocatively representing the hotel manager as an artist and 'master' superintending the narrative world of the hotel, James considered his complicity with this figure. As a social novelist, conscious that social relations 'really, universally, [. . .] stop nowhere', and that 'the exquisite problem of the artist is eternally but to draw, by a geometry of his own, the circle within which they shall happily *appear* to do so', James was interested in theorising his own acts of preprocessing, and the power wielded by those with a 'geometry of [one's] own'.[47] As James Purdon argues in his account of informatics and the turn-of-the century novel:

> The delimitation of the 'literary' as a subset of writing constitutes a preprocessing system of its own, and one which gains much of its power from the increasing need to distinguish between competing axiological claims in an increasingly complex world of literacy, information, and communication.
>
> Novels, no less than empires, seek to manage their own coherence and security by a careful organization of those contingent factors which are the conditions of the real before they become the effects of realism. [. . .] Novels [. . .] simultaneously diminish and celebrate the contingencies of 'real' relations so as to make meaning out of those contingencies.[48]

Mark Seltzer's influential reading of *The American Scene* explores precisely this territory, arguing that James finds a kindred spirit in the Waldorf's narrative machinery: 'Like the novelist whose narrative authority is at once omniscient and immanent, the presiding power [of the Waldorf] exerts a comprehensive supervision over his characters while perpetuating the ruse of their freedom.'[49] A stroll through the Waldorf, Seltzer suggests, is really a stroll through James's own 'house of fiction', a realisation in stone and marble of the theory of literary form outlined in his Prefaces. James's 'criticism of the Victorian novelist's loose and baggy monsters' and his 'formalizing of a poetics of narrative' are acts of novelistic management akin to the management of a hotel-world.[50] The link Seltzer draws between artist and machine-artist, however, is too close. The managerial aesthetic is radical simplification, reducing society to types and reducing difference to a play of surfaces and styles. This is far from the late Jamesian aesthetic of friction, complication and ambiguity.[51] In any case, as Gert Buelens argues, James foregoes the possessive, mastering impulse inside the Waldorf-Astoria. He sets aside the analytic mode; he does not organise or classify the desiring bodies circulating in the general promiscuity. Refusing a vertical perspective, James instead 'rhapsodizes the metonymic contiguity [. . .] of the constituent parts of the social and sexual sameness [. . .]. These are arranged, "in positively stable equilibrium," on the horizontal, syntagmatic axis of "circulation"'.[52] In the frisson James enjoys in this space, he finds pleasure both in the hotel's 'gorgeous golden blur' and in its 'consummate management': these elements are 'melted together' in his account of the Waldorf-Astoria, and leave him 'uncertain which of them one was, at a given turn of the maze, most admiring'. James relates to American managerialism as he did to Matthias Pardon: with a mix of fascination and suspicion in the face of a ruthlessly efficient rival, whose capacity to synthesise and represent the modern social scene challenges his own.

The Manager-Poet

The hotel manager takes human form and becomes a protagonist and a point of view – a managerial eye – in the hotel novels of Arnold Bennett: *The Grand Babylon Hotel* (1902) and *Imperial Palace* (1930). In *The Grand Babylon Hotel*, the manager does not yet have the omnipotent power of James's conductor. The novel opens with the eponymous owner, Félix Babylon, hastily selling his hotel and warning its new owner that the institution is, by design, unknowable:

> Do you not perceive that the roof which habitually shelters all the force, all the authority of the world, must necessarily also shelter nameless and numberless plotters, schemers, evil-doers, and workers of mischief? [. . .] I never know by whom I am surrounded. I never know what is going forward. Only sometimes I get hints, glimpses of strange acts and strange secrets.[53]

If Babylon 'occupies an authorial role' over this cast of hotel characters, observes Randi Saloman, 'he is far from omniscient, attending to the surface of things, rather than invading the privacy of his employees and thus delving into unpleasantries.'[54] The new American owner, millionaire Theodore Racksole, is not a professional hotel manager; he buys up the hotel on a whim when a waiter scoffs at his request for steak and beer. Racksole is an adventurer rather than an administrator. He soon asserts his mastery over hotel space by moving through it, orienting himself, unlocking secret spaces and plotting routes.[55] These efforts to map the hotel draw the novel into the detective genre, but there are undertones, too, of the imperial Gothic, as Racksole stalks through the 'vast, uncanny, deserted' hotel with a revolver, into its 'remote corners' to investigate 'night-prowling' figures,[56] and later returning 'to his original post of observation, that he might survey the place anew from the vantage ground.'[57] His movements are coded in colonial terms as an 'explor[ation]' and a 'hunt';[58] at one point, he silently stalks the duplicitous chef, Rocco, who turns on him 'with the swiftness of a startled tiger'.[59] Bringing this wild Babylonian province under control requires the physical prowess of its adventuring manager – an assertion of order grounded on the supposed natural authority of the white, masculine body.

In Bennett's later hotel novel, *Imperial Palace* (1930), the managerial apparatus is sophisticated and ubiquitous. Historically, this development could be linked to requirements legislated during the First World War, which galvanised a managerial tendency in British hotels that had long been emerging. As Kevin J. James writes, 'Wartime regimes of guest documentation coincided with the increasing systematisation of hotel management and record-keeping, with large-scale hotels often employing retinues of staff and a broad range of textual materials to record extensive transactions.'[60] There is a concomitant shift in form between *The Grand Babylon Hotel* and *Imperial Palace*. The earlier novel's light-footedness, and its playful genre appropriations – features which contributed to its prodigious popular success – are not replicated in the latter text, and the whimsical portrait of management is gone. *Imperial Palace* opts for the form of a sprawling social novel of 'indolent luxury' and 'feverish labour', structured around an upstairs-downstairs romance, using an intricate account of the hotel's daily operations and its many departments and functionaries to represent a vision of social totality.[61] The hotel in this later novel seeks outward rather than inward colonial conquest, through a proposed merger that would create a chain of Imperial Palaces beyond Britain. (We are told that the hotel was originally the 'Royal Palace', and was renamed 'Imperial' when Queen Victoria became Empress of India.)[62] The hotel itself projects an image of control: 'Even a vacuum-cleaner, at work on the crimson carpet, seemed to purr like a tiger tamed and domesticated to the uses of the lords of the earth.'[63] The information technologies that support this empire are obsessively enumerated: 'statistics, balance-sheets, valuations, estimates, reports', along with contracts, minute books, transfer books, bill forms, order checks, repair slips, graphs of consumption trends, telephones, telegraphs, typewriters, pneumatic tubes, card indexes and filing cabinets.[64] These information systems mediate relationships between staff and monitor the lives of guests. The reception manager, for instance, 'had a file-record of every guest, including the dubious, with particulars of his sojourns, desires, eccentricities, rate of spending, payments – even to dishonoured cheques',[65] while the hotel's managing director, Evelyn Orcham, 'had in his office a private card-index of all the company's principal employees. He rarely forgot anything once learnt, and now he had no difficulty in recalling that Miss Powler lived in Battersea, the daughter of a town-traveller in tinned comestibles'.[66] Almost everyone in the hotel has been processed as data, their biographies and habits instrumentalised in order to manage them more efficiently.

Imperial Palace accumulates unpoetical details in a way that, for some critics, uncomfortably made visible Bennett's own labour of novel-writing: 'it may well be asked whether the theme was worth so much labour, so much industry,' wrote Bennett biographer George Lafourcade, the redundant repetition enacting the novel's own laborious elaborations.[67] Margaret Drabble in her later biography was more sympathetic, while noting that Bennett 'works very obviously to a schedule, as though the mere recitation of room numbers and prosaic details were necessary to shore up his intentions'.[68] Yet while *Imperial Palace* is filled with labour and laboriousness, with lists and data ('Suite 365. Time, 1.51. Two bottles 43. [. . .] One Mattoni. One China tea. One kummel. One consommé. Six haddock Côte d'Azur'),[69] descriptions of business procedures and digressions into the 'prosaic industrial environment[s]' in the bowels of the hotel ('Nine fires. Oil-fed. Twenty-five tons of oil a day. Equal to fifty of coal. Yes. And here's the turbine. 4,500 revs., miss'),[70] the novel nonetheless insists on the poetic nature of modern hotel managerialism. Orcham, the managing director, protagonist and central focaliser of the third-person narrative, self-identifies as an artist and a creator (the Imperial Palace is 'the majestic and brilliant offspring of his creative imagination and of his organising brain'), and he is repeatedly flattered by a love interest in these same terms.[71] On seeing the Imperial Palace rising out of the gloom during an evening stroll, Gracie Savott, the daughter of Orcham's potential business partner, pronounces the hotel 'marvellous': '"I do admire you for that. You're a poet"', she adds.[72] Later, Orcham is 'excited by the flattery of the word "artist," which [Gracie] had so stimulatingly pronounced. She understood him: that was it. Yes, he was a creative artist, in *his* way.'[73] The hotel is rendered as an artwork, brought into being by its manager, a master of systems and texts. At the same time that Bennett's novel, a vast edifice of organisation and enumeration, yearns to be managerial, its manager-hero yearns to be an author.

To be a manager ('a marvellous manager [. . .] utterly reliable, utterly exact and with habits of order'),[74] or to be 'managing' ('he could "manage," [. . .] he could "make things do"'),[75] is a high compliment in Bennett's work. It means to be competent, practical, organised, to 'get on', to 'make things do'. Indeed, 'management' was an ethic that Bennett applied broadly to his life: to the management of the self (as the author of the self-improvement book, *Self and Self-Management* (1918)), and to the management of the household (through domestic advice columns like 'Home as a Business Concern' (1928)). Managing, furthermore, was Bennett's highest professional ambition: 'When I told the best interviewer in the United States that my secret ambition had always been to be the manager of a grand hotel, I was quite sincere,' he wrote in *Those United States* (1912).[76] So Bennett's rhetorical construction of the manager-poet was not about redeeming the disreputable activity of management in the vestments of transcendent art. Instead, *Imperial Palace* refuses to hierarchise art and business, finding continuities between both. As John Nash argues:

> It is in the sphere of manufacture, rather than that of art, where Bennett's narrators provide more specific knowledge: descriptions of the workings of an apparatus are vaguely compared to 'a poem' and 'a picture.' Greater attention is paid to the means of heating than to rumination on artistic form. One effect of this is that the self-consciously aesthetic is out of place in Bennett's fictional worlds, and in this regard he differs from some other Edwardian writers. [. . .] Whereas these other writers dramatize art and commerce into an opposition that is then partially overcome, Bennett's outlook does not conceive of the two as an opposition in the first place.[77]

The vague comparison of the Imperial Palace to a poem, then, is less an aesthetic judgment of the institution's beauty and more an assertion of Evelyn Orcham's intellectual property rights. The managing director claims authorship, and therefore ownership, over the hotel. During Orcham's speech to shareholders at the annual general meeting of the Imperial Hotel Company, the reader is presented with Orcham's internal monologue, which asserts that ownership is vested neither in the corporate body, nor in the shareholders who own a share of it. The shareholders, he internally rages, are mere 'Barbarians!' and 'Benighted savages!' True ownership, he believes, flows from the Romantic capacity for 'creation' and 'passion' that resides in the individual personality:

> Your hotels? Good God! They aren't your hotels. You couldn't have started them. You couldn't run them. You don't understand them. You've no idea what wonderful, romantic things they are. [. . .] You didn't buy shares because you are interested in hotels; only because you believed that you could squeeze a bit of money out of them. Whereas 'your' hotels are my creation. I live for them. I have a passion for them. [. . .] 'Your' hotels are mine [. . .].[78]

During this meeting the board pushes through a resolution that limits shareholder voting rights in order to shore up the position of the existing directors. Orcham therefore rhapsodises the manager-poet while his board effects a very real power grab on behalf of management.

Sinclair Lewis, Bennett's American acquaintance and admirer, explores similar ideas in his own hotel novel, *Work of Art* (1934). Lewis's core audience, which helped drive the unprecedented commercial success of *Main Street* (1920), *Babbitt* (1922) and *Arrowsmith* (1925), was the rising professional-managerial class. Lewis believed, argues Michael Augspurger, that these new professions 'promised an escape from traditional class conflicts and offered the hope of a fair, rationally planned society', yet their 'traditional professional ideals of autonomy, civic responsibility, and anti-commercialism were difficult to practice in an economy increasingly dominated by corporate organization'.[79] Linking the 'adversary professional and the autonomous artist' with the pioneer and the frontier, Lewis's blockbuster novels of the 1920s presented romantic parables of masculine escape for the claustrophobic, bureaucratised interwar professional.[80] If, as Augspurger suggests, Lewis's most popular novels located an escape hatch out of the corporation, *Work of Art* instead attempted a symbolic reconciliation of the corporation and the autonomous professional.

It did so via the ascension of Myron Weagle, a humble boarding house bellhop who becomes a corporate hotel manager, a rise described (winkingly) by his brother Ora as 'a regular Horatio Alger Rags-to-Riches' story.[81] While the bohemian Ora dreams of writing the great American novel, Myron is consumed by the dream of the Perfect Inn – his own work of art. But Myron himself is no aesthete. If the object of the novel's longing is from a *künstlerroman*, the process of attainment is from Horatio Alger. The novel is much more interested in work than in art. Derided by his brother as having 'no imagination, no pride, no sense of beauty', the earnest and industrious Myron has some passing interest in the aesthetics of hotel service, particularly in the presentation of fine dining.[82] He is absorbed by a steward's handbook which contains 'Handsome Styles and Diagrams' of napkin-folding, which seem like 'the masterpieces of a napkinate Michael Angelo'.[83] The handbook describes 'literary novelties' like a menu appended with quotes from 'the choicest poets'.[84] But the point of this reading is not to refine Myron's aesthetic sensibilities or to burnish the smithy of his soul; the point is to master every task in every department of the hotel. Myron rises in the hotel world by soberly learning all the hotel arts, from napkin-folding to cooking, plumbing, night-clerking, storekeeping, housekeeping, accounts and chain purchasing, learnt through apprenticeships as well as through the new infrastructure of managerial professionalisation – handbooks, trade journals and colleges. Myron believes that a 'hotel-keeper had to be a combination of nursery-governess, financier, steam-fitter, detective, upholsterer, architect, dietitian, garbage-handler, ventilation-engineer, lawyer, orchestra-director, psychiatrist, florist'.[85] Douglas Tallack compares Myron's rags to riches story to Gatsby, but the closer comparison is to Robinson Crusoe, who also believed that 'every Man may be in time Master of every mechanick Art'.[86] Crusoe and the hotel manager both claim total mastery over a small, contained, autarchic economy – island and hotel – where domains of knowledge fragmented by the capitalist mode of production are united again under the eye of the master. Myron is acutely aware throughout his hotel career that he is 'part of a machine, as helpless' as the staff he hires and ruthlessly fires.[87] It is only through finally building, owning and managing his own hotel, his Perfect Inn, that he believes his alienated labour can become meaningful and whole again. 'Art' in Lewis's novel is this attainment of wholeness: a vision of authorial control over one's own labours, transforming Myron's work into 'his Works'.[88] Amid the calamity of the Depression, this conception of the manager-poet offered a liberal fantasy of meaningful work and individual agency inside the corporation.

Directors and Chorus Girls

Bennett's survey of the managerial apparatus in *Imperial Palace* reflects his increasing involvement with the corporate form during the 1920s through his work in the British and American film industries. Bennett dabbled in screenwriting throughout the decade, chasing rumours of huge commissions paid to big-name authors. But his experience was disorienting. In 1920, Bennett was offered US$5,000 to develop a script for the Hollywood-based Famous Players-Lasky Corporation. According to Bennett's account, the vice president in charge of production, Jesse Lasky himself, wooed the author by insisting that his company wanted to 'break away from the star system, in order to give more importance to the author'.[89] But the project was then delegated to three successive story editors, who suggested major changes to the plot, characters and locations (more country houses, make the heroine an aristocrat, add a car race), which Bennett mostly assented to, before the project was scrapped.[90] (In *The North American Review* in the same year, Lasky wrote that 'Critics often raise their voices in condemnation because in translating a drama or a novel for the screen we make changes in the original story', but these changes are 'invariably necessary. Even plays, the saying goes, are "rewritten, rather than written".'[91]) In a separate incident, Bennett claims he was approached by two 'film-kings' and a story editor who prescriptively outlined 'the sort of story you ought to write', an approach which also bore no fruit.[92] In the summer of 1929, Bennett sat down with a young Alfred Hitchcock and the general manager of British International Pictures (BIP), J. A. Thorpe, to pitch a film-story called *Punch and Judy* which Bennett had been wrestling with for nearly a year. Thorpe was supportive and pushed for a deal, but Hitchcock was resistant. The director (who Bennett characterised in his journal as being

'Intelligent in his own way, but . . . a crude way', though with 'some creative fire in him') thought Bennett's story lacked directness and colour, and suggested sweeping alterations. A financier character might be better as a circus ringmaster, Hitchcock suggested – perhaps the whole film should be set in a circus. In the wake of the meeting, weeks went by without any further word from the studios and the project was quietly abandoned.[93] But Bennett did find success in 1929 with his screenwriting work on *Piccadilly* for BIP. Being part of this production, and seeing inside the blazing Elstree Studios crammed with extras, gave Bennett a sense of his subsidiary role in the industrial storytelling process. The opening credits of *Piccadilly* appear as advertisements on passing buses; the name of the studio and the director, E. A. Dupont, appear on the first bus, while Bennett appears alongside the cinematographer and art director on the second bus, subordinate to the corporate body and the eye of its director. The relative position of the screenwriter in the production hierarchy was something Bennett had complained about in a December 1927 article for *Close Up*. While many correspondents to the avant-garde film magazine discussed the potential of the silent film image, Bennett wanted to re-centre the story, and therefore the screenwriter, as the keystone of film production: 'All other parts of the enterprise are merely parts of an effort to tell the story.' The 'star-producer[s]' and 'master-brain[s]' of cinema 'lose sight of what it is they *are* producing,' Bennett writes. 'The act of creation interests them far less than the act of "putting over" that which has been created. In the judgment of the master-brain of the affair, the author is subordinate to the interpreter.' For this reason, 'The screen has laid hands on some of the greatest stories in the world, and has cheapened, soiled, ravaged, and poisoned them by the crudest fatuities.' Cinema must be a transparent medium for the unadulterated projection of an author's vision, Bennett argues. The medium's status as art ('I am thinking of art and not of dividends') depends on this vision; without it, films cannot transcend the cheapening, soiling, commercial realities that produced it.[94]

Bennett's conception of film authorship shows his difficulty adjusting to the 'interdependent, socially embedded, and institutionally circumscribed' praxis of screenwriting, as Alix Beeston describes F. Scott Fitzgerald's Hollywood work. 'The collaborative or corporate author – the author in composite – is a repressed figure in all literary production,' Beeston writes, though 'the composite author is less completely hidden in studio-era Hollywood, and so less easily ignored.'[95] Stefan Solomon, examining William Faulkner's Hollywood experience, argues that studio-era screenwriting was marked by 'managerial oversight and multiple authorship, [. . .] governed by industrial textual models, and [. . .] subject to technological restrictions', effecting the transfer of power away from the author and the 'sublimation' of the author's 'idiosyncrasy into the larger design of the respective studios'.[96] Bennett's insistence on his centrality was a response to this fragmentation and sublimation of authorial subjectivity within the film corporation. *Imperial Palace*, too, as a portrait of absolute authorial agency, can be read as a response to the vertiginous dread of the corporation.

Bennett was not alone in this dread: Hitchcock, too, was trying to define himself as a singular artist within the nascent British studio system. Fresh from his success with *The Lodger* (1927) and having moved to BIP with a lucrative contract, Hitchcock was given the autonomy to write and direct the film project of his choice. The film, *The Ring* (1927), was a box-office failure and resulted in BIP abruptly withdrawing Hitchcock's autonomy. Subsequently, Hitchcock was assigned projects by BIP management, most likely including the *Punch and Judy* project advocated by Bennett and supported by J. A. Thorpe.[97] In their meeting, therefore, both Hitchcock and Bennett had reason to feel artistically diminished by the manoeuvrings of the studio that brought them together. It is in this context of diminishment, about six weeks after *The Ring* was released, that Hitchcock wrote an article for the *London Evening News* asserting that for films to be art, they needed to be 'One-Man Pictures':

> Film directors live with their pictures while they are being made. They are their babies just as much as an author's novel is the offspring of his imagination. And that seems to make it all the more certain that when moving pictures are really artistic they will be created entirely by one man. It often happens today that the author's story is made into screen form on paper by one man, who may have been overseen by some important executive, filmed by another, cut by another, and edited by another. Suppose novels were produced in this way![98]

In a magazine article a few months later, Hitchcock again uses the language of paternity (a director is 'a kind of film father providing for his family') while following through with the logic of the one-man picture (he is the 'omnipotent autocrat of the studio'). Hitchcock reflects on his own power as artist by describing his manner of sculpting the bodies and the emotions of his female stars, who are subsumed 'under the influence of the combined attack of the director, the artistes and the camera'. It is he, not they, who 'manufacture[s]' their affective performances (who 'make[s] her smile'), while the actors' own 'emotional nature lay dormant'. Though Hitchcock denies he is 'a bully at heart', he admits to subjecting his stars to 'some pretty rough handling at times', using 'a raging, tearing temper' to 'bring them into his line'.[99] It is striking that these violent statements of directorial dominion come in response to the dispersal and sublimation of his authorial voice. Film theory, argues Kaja Silverman, has long been preoccupied with precisely this subject: with masculine fears of lack and loss, and the elements of the cinematic apparatus that threaten the stability of male subjectivity.[100] Brooke Rollins uses Silverman's work to argue that auteurist theories of film authorship – which position a single individual like the director, screenwriter or producer as a film's sole shaping and controlling power – are expressions of these masculine anxieties. The auteur figure, Rollins argues, restores a vision of wholeness to the compartmentalised business of corporate storytelling:

> Auteurism's valorization of independence and unity – and its love for those male directors like Welles, Howard Hawks, and John Ford whose strong personalities were said to transcend filmmaking's industrial nature – already suggests that the theory itself was as interested in the values of the classical male subject as it was in those of the romantic author. The very thing that made auteurs auteurs was their ability to maintain their authority, independence, and autonomy despite the industrial and commercial constraints inherent in film production. In the face of this collaborative milieu the auteur was the man who endowed the film with meaning.[101]

Asserting the sovereignty of the omnipotent autocrat of the studio was a means of salvaging a liberal humanist model of artistic production as it collided with the realities of corporate capital. Zooming out, we can see the auteur figure as a more broadly emblematic response to the rise of the corporation. Film scholar Jeff Menne makes this connection in relation to post-war auteur theory, reading the auteur as representative of a counter-cultural generation of baby-boomer professionals trying to reconcile their own creative individualism within a corporatised and technocratic economy. '[B]ecause directors were figures of creative labour entirely dependent on capital,' Menne writes:

> They became emblems for a segment of the workforce that rose to dominance in a postindustrial economy – the college graduates; the knowledge workers, as management theorist Peter Drucker would call them; what, down the road, would be called the 'creative class.' The lot of this class would be to depend on capital, as directors do, but to insist all the while on their own authority by way of their claims to expertise.[102]

We can trace this structure of feeling back to the interwar period, to the emergence of a technical-scientific-commercial-managerial class that both Lewis and Bennett took to be their natural constituency. *Imperial Palace* speaks to the anxieties of this class by proposing a prototypically auteurist solution to the problem of individual agency in the corporation. The Imperial's managing director, unlike Weagle, does not personally master all of the hotel's tasks. He is surrounded by thirty departments and thirty sub-managers, along with a day-to-day hotel manager, Emile Cousin, who himself has an assistant manager, Monsieur Pozzi. Nonetheless, Orcham imagines that all of these technicians are instruments of his singular authorial vision. Through the free indirect discourse that imprints Orcham's voice on the narration, the text tells us that Orcham 'created' the hotel's monumental industrial laundry, even though Orcham 'had not designed the buildings nor the machinery, nor laid brick on brick nor welded pipe to pipe, nor dug the Artesian wells nor paved the yards.' Orcham, unlike Weagle, doesn't have time for pipes or wells. Instead, Orcham had 'thought the whole place and its efficiency and its spirit into being'.[103] His vision unifies the compartmentalised organisation and endows it with meaning.

Orcham's power of vision underlines the resemblance of the managing director to a film auteur. He maintains his sovereign subjecthood by standing apart from or above the scene and framing his staff with a directorial eye. If James's hotels were telegraphic, the Imperial Palace (like Bowen's hotel) is immanently cinematic. The suites are filled with film-kings and film-stars, and leaders of 'cinematographic [. . .] society' fill its grill-room.[104] The blazing ballroom on New Year's Eve, decorated with Chinese lanterns and featuring a performance involving 'glittering Indian clubs', recalls the coruscating Orientalist stage-show in BIP's *Piccadilly*.[105] As part of these celebrations in the adjacent hall, a dense crowd watches a Punch and Judy show, a visitation from the opening scene of Bennett's abandoned screenplay derided by Hitchcock, here transplanted as a hotel attraction. Orcham appoints himself the auteur of this spectacle by interpellating his staff as actors performing his script. As Emma Short notes, while *Imperial Palace* surveys many of the hotel's various departments, the voices we hear with very few exceptions belong to those in positions of authority, from departmental managers upwards. The bulk of the hotel's 1,300 employees 'are typically unknown and unheard.'[106] But they are *seen*. The directorial eye of *Imperial Palace* distances and frames hotel labour as a spectacle. When 'the creator' sits back with 'a benevolent expression on his face' and watches his departmental heads 'fiercely disputing, some in the correctness of morning-coats, others (who had no contacts with the clientèle), in undandiacal lounge-suits, smoking, gesticulating', he transforms his staff into a pageant of vivid gestures and costumes, like a silent film. Their argument is inaudible; he simply 'enjoy[s] the grand spectacle of their passion'. This scene, too, has been 'created' by the director. He is watching actors that he has trained, directed and authored: he is 'their god'.[107]

Appropriately, Orcham (whose name etymologically links him with the horticultural and the testicular) stages his own Genesis scene when he stands in the hotel's great hall in the early morning to witness 'the spectacle of the tremendous monster stirring out of its uneasy slumber':

> Evelyn [. . .] was the creative artist surveying and displaying his creation – the hotel. He was like a youth.
>
> A procession of girls and women followed Miss Maclaren through the vista of the restaurant and the foyer into the great hall. They wore a

blue uniform with brown apron, and carried pails, brooms, brushes and dusters. Some of them swerved off into the corridor leading towards the grill-room. Others began to dust the Enquiries and Reception counters. Others were soon on their knees, in formation, cleaning the immense floor of the hall.[108]

These women perform aesthetic labour. Their job is not only to clean and maintain, but also to wear uniforms and work in 'procession' and 'formation' – to perform the predictability and uniformity of the bureaucratic apparatus, if only for the benefit of the director himself. (Later they appear as a 'troop of blue and brown charwomen', passing 'in a file through the foyer.')[109] As aesthetic labourers, their work is corporeal, a matter of costume and posture, their comportment subject to close monitoring and discipline ('Miss Maclaren spoke sharply, curtly, now and then to one or other of them' while mummering 'apologetically to Evelyn').[110] Moving in what Orcham perceives as formation, their work is aligned with the chorus girls who enter this space in a later scene, during the New Year's Eve procession that Orcham also stands to witness. Through Orcham's eyes, the scene of uniformed bodies moving with precision through immense, gleaming spaces anticipates the Busby Berkeley musical (Figures 5.1 and 5.2).

Unglamorous service work undertaken by women is directly linked to show business in the Imperial's laundry. The laundry not only employs, feeds and tends to the health of its two hundred mostly young female employees but also, unexpectedly, teaches them 'to sing and to act and to dance and to sew and to make frocks'.[111] The skills of home economics and show business are brought together in the same breath. The nightclub manager in the Bennett-scripted *Piccadilly* falls for Shosho, a dishwasher in the club kitchens who is also a talented dancer; in a similar manner, Orcham is immediately attracted

Figure 5.1 Dancing bellhops. Still from *The Cocoanuts*, directed by Robert Florey and Joseph Santley, Paramount, 1929

Figure 5.2 Dancing bellhops. Still from *The Cocoanuts*, directed by Robert Florey and Joseph Santley, Paramount, 1929

to Violet Powler, the staff manageress in the hotel laundry who is also a triple threat (or more: she can 'dance, act, sing, direct a stage').[112] A member of the Imperial Palace Hotel Laundry Amateur Dramatic (and Operatic) Society, Violet in one scene knowingly mimics the stage and screen archetype of the 'vamp' in order to extract a favour from a male headwaiter.[113] She will eventually win the director's heart, too, at which point her identity will be merged with his own ('"You are all I have in the world now! I haven't even myself now!"' she thinks as she embraces him).[114] Their relationship is coded as the relationship of an ingénue plucked out of obscurity by a director who trains and produces her as a star: 'he had discovered her as a candidate for floor-housekeepership', Orcham muses; 'as such she was his creation.' He manages her appearance: 'As a housekeeper at the Imperial Palace she would have to wear black, and high heels', Orcham insists, covertly inspecting her ankles, feet, figure and face; furthermore, 'Those pale pink lips would never do on the Floors of the Palace.'[115] He advises her to wear powder and rouge – an art, she replies, that she's already familiar with as an amateur dramatist. In *Piccadilly*, the nightclub manager assesses the body of Shosho in the same way, with the same mix of sexual and professional interest, as the camera traces a path from Shosho's legs up to her face. As well as her body, Orcham also manages Violet's affect. The affective calibration that he most values in Violet, both as worker and as potential romantic partner, is that of the chorus girl: a form of cheerfulness that signals a flexible and passive accommodation to the demands of the routine. The model for this affective state is the dancer Volivia, a raging success in the Imperial Palace's cabaret, who begins her routine with a 'performer's smile' that was not 'better than good-natured', and ends in extremis, still smiling: she 'suddenly dropped on to the hard floor in a violent *entrechat*. And kept the pose, smiling, her bosom heaving in rapid respirations, her tremendous legs stretched out at right-angles to her torso'.[116] The chorus girl, argues Mark Franko, 'exemplified the emotional equilibrium that Taylorist management sought in workers. [. . .] Cheerfulness becomes a figure of pacification. The chorine's demeanour [. . .] fostered a positive and entertaining image of unskilled labour under the regime of machine culture.'[117] Violet lives up to this ideal. She attracts Orcham because she is 'sedate, cheerful, kindly, tactful, equable'; later, these qualities are underlined as economically valuable, when unnamed guests commend her to management in nearly identical terms for her 'cheerfulness, obligingness, tactfulness, helpfulness, efficiency'.[118] But this equability is a performance that we see her practising ('She prepared a discreet smile for Sir Henry') and planning ('She divined that the key to the handling of Beatrice was a resolute and unfluctuating cheerfulness').[119] Violet internalises the desirability of this affective state and disciplines herself to reign in her emotions. Her position is representative of the precarious service worker, who as Sianne Ngai writes is required to invest her affect and subjectivity into her role in a way that breaks down distinctions between public and private, work and leisure, service and performance. This kind of work makes visible the similarities between 'cultural performance and job performance'.[120] Fittingly, Violet's rise will take her out of the anonymity of the laundry chorus line, becoming not only the hotel's head housekeeper but its 'star housekeeper'.[121] Orcham's power over his staff expresses itself, therefore, as the libidinised power of a director over a feminised cast of extras and stars. Standing aloof, Orcham observes and directs the female body in performance as a means of imbuing the hotel's aesthetic and affective atmospheres with his authority. But the coding of Orcham and Violet's relationship as a director-actor relationship not only fulfils Orcham's fantasy of authorial control; it also touches on something fundamental about the predicament of hotel labour.

Corporate Art

The arrival of Sir Henry Savott, the hotel and film baron, who is also described as a 'poet' of business, represents a hinge point and the central conflict of the novel.[122] Orcham initially resists Savott's proposal to buy and merge their hotel systems. He reads it as a threat not only to his power but to his authorship: '"I can't quite understand this mania for mergers,"' he tells Sir Henry. '"It seems to me to mean the destroying of individuality."'[123] As the 'author of the great hotel-merger',[124] Sir Henry must assure Orcham that the future conglomerate would still value his auteurist vision: 'It would mean the extension of *your* individuality,' Sir Henry argues. 'It would give your individuality a scope [. . .]. A merger means the spread of your efficiency; it means the spread of the Imperial Palace standard.'[125] Sir Henry works to re-inflate and re-enchant Orcham's conception of himself as poet, even as the merger threatens to subsume him within ever-more complex corporate structures, by proposing to name the new organisation the 'Orcham Company'.[126] Believing that Orcham's name has value, Sir Henry intends to franchise Orcham as a Ritz-like brand. This is an unlikely new role for 'the great invisible Mr. Orcham', the aloof and faceless administrator, who is conscious of his crooked teeth and who has never been photographed, and who has neither the personality nor the celebrity of a Ritz or a Boomer.[127] Nonetheless, the gambit works. Orcham is feted by the press ('Mr. Orcham's name had suddenly become familiar to citizens, astonished by the abrupt revelation of the importance of someone whom they had never heard of')[128] and he begins to see himself in Hitchcockian terms as 'the autocrat and the godfather' of the vast new conglomerate.[129] Autocracy, repeatedly invoked in this text ('he would be autocrat or he would be nothing'), appears to be the price that must be paid for the preservation of the liberal humanist subject.[130] But Orcham, transformed into the Orcham Company, is no longer the autonomous individual he believes he is. He has handed his personality over to the business. Through the sale, 'Orcham' is traded as intangible property; the name represents, as the company chairman notes, 'our prestige', without which the merger 'is worth exactly elevenpence three farthings.' While the chairman insists that 'we're selling something that can't *be* valued', he does indeed put a value on it: £2 15s per share.[131] Reified and commodified, Orcham (like Ritz before him) has become a personification of the values and goodwill that adheres within the brand; he's become an incarnation of that most lucrative of twentieth-century fictions, the corporate person. These financial manoeuvrings effect a critique of romantic authorship that the text itself, too invested in Orcham as the narrative's focaliser and structuring principle, cannot articulate. The manoeuvrings show the personification of the corporation in the body of Orcham to be a mere business strategy, one that was common in the interwar years. Corporations increasingly represented themselves to governments and the general public in a personified form, argues Jerome Christensen, exploiting the 'apparently ineradicable tendency of people to personify groups of men and women working together as one gigantic human being'.[132] Personification, as Roland Marchand writes, manufactured the romantic illusion of a corporate 'personality', 'voice' and 'soul'.[133] It allowed large-scale firms to 'take on the traits and capacities of persons and attract public support by the strategic profession of "ideals"'.[134] Orcham's construction of himself as poet and auteur began as a means to imaginatively claim the hotel as his intellectual property, but the merger agreement reveals his language of authorship to be indistinguishable from the corporation's public relations strategy. It's a cover story. The genius of the auteur is merely a way of figuring the hotel's services in human terms, in terms consumers will identify with and pay for.

The real and unheralded artist of *Imperial Palace* is the corporation itself. Christensen proposes just such a model of corporate art in his study of the

American corporate film studio. Studios themselves should be considered the authors of their films, Christensen argues, not merely in the sense that the films exhibit a house style or ideology, but more crucially because the films are tools of corporate strategy. It is an idea Christensen finds expressed in a 1932 *Fortune* magazine profile of Hollywood studio Metro-Goldwyn-Mayer, which located agency for the studio's productions not in its directors, nor even its head of production, Irving Thalberg, whom the article lionises, but in the supra-personal body that contains them all:

> MGM is neither one man nor a collection of men. It is a corporation. Whenever a motion picture becomes a work of art it is unquestionably due to men. But the moving pictures have been born and bred not of men but of corporations. Corporations have set up the easels, bought the pigments, arranged the views, and hired the potential artists. Until the artists emerge, at least, the corporation is bigger than the sum of its parts. Somehow, although our poets have not yet defined it for us, a corporation lives a life and finds a fate outside the lives and fates of its human constituents.[135]

The one shot that epitomises MGM's corporate art, Christensen argues, is the bird's-eye view of the hotel lobby in the star-studded blockbuster *Grand Hotel* (1932) (Figure 5.3), a film that invites comparisons between the corporate hotel and the corporate film studio. This moment in the opening minutes of the film takes us from a perspective down among the busy and disorganised streams of arriving guests to a perspective floating six floors above, peering at the distant movements of the lobby through concentric balconies encircling each floor. As Mark Goble describes it, 'the sudden remov[al] of our visual perspective from a crowded space, practically clogged with narrative, suggests a kind of surveillance

Figure 5.3 Hovering above the lobby. Still from *Grand Hotel*, directed by Edmund Goulding, Metro-Goldwyn-Mayer, 1932

and power over the microscopic scene below.'[136] The shot, Christensen writes, composes 'in its ambit all the workers and guests, masters and servants, rooms and corridors, into a reassuring pattern of concentric circles.'[137] It orders the promiscuous crowd. The central point that structures its movement is the circular registration desk in the middle of the lobby hall – the pupil of the hotel eye – which gives the hotel's administrative function a geometric form. This geometric patterning is then imprinted on the point of view and the movements of the ground-level shots that follow. The camera is placed in the middle of the circle of the registration desk, just above the heads of the registry staff, for most of the subsequent scene, with the camera pivoting on its axis to track the circular movements processing around it (Figure 5.4). No longer impassively recording a disorganised crowd, the camera movement starts to follow and individuate key characters and valuable studio properties, beginning with the Baron, played by top-billed star John Barrymore. The desk functions as an expository and publicity device that registers identities and brings them to the attention of the audience. Registered identities sometimes precede flesh and blood characters. The name of Greta Garbo's character, Madam Grusinskaya, is in the air, on the lips of multiple extras, before her arrival, through discussions between her staff and the registration clerks who themselves remain nameless. The scene is still clogged with narrative, movement and talk, but its hierarchy of stars and extras begins to take shape through the desk's administration of the narrative.

The film lacks a charismatic manager figure and the administrative function is mostly faceless. Its influence is abstract; we see the hotel's prodigious organisational powers less through the efficiency of its clerks and more through the invisible management of the lobby's rhythms and geometries. The supra-human qualities of the hotel's management are signalled by the overhead shot that centres the administrative function, which assumes an impossible perspective beyond the architectural bounds of the set. The art deco hotel space designed

Figure 5.4 Guests at the registration desk. Still from *Grand Hotel*, directed by Edmund Goulding, Metro-Goldwyn-Mayer, 1932

by Cedric Gibbons comprised a series of unconnected sets on separate sound stages that were edited together to create the illusion of continuous space. The lobby was constructed on a single-level sound stage, so the bird's-eye view, and its ziggurat of balconies, was a contrivance created through compositing. The impossible vantage of the shot 'not only represents the design that comprehends all the action that will ensue', Christensen writes, 'but unlike any other shot from the Thalberg era, it reflexively refers to the camera that, transcending the action, makes it possible for that design to be recorded and projected.'[138] It is Orcham's distancing and abstracting gaze rendered as a supra-human organising intelligence, working as an advertisement for the corporate apparatus of MGM and the grand hotel itself.

Terminus

The supremacy of the manager-author's abstract vision falls apart in Henry Green's *Party Going* (1939). Set at the terminus point of the grand hotel era, Green's novel is a narrative of misprision and inertia, mired in a London fog. It reveals the manager-author as a class fantasy, willed into being by the privileged party goers as a way of transcending the anonymous, miasmic relations of the crowd. As Jonathan Foltz writes in his illuminating reading of *Party Going*, Green shows how 'literary authority and social privilege share common conditions and equally common fallibilities.'[139] The novel confounds all claims to complete omniscience and authority.

Party Going collects together a group of young travellers and their servants, preparing to take the boat train from London's Victoria Station to Calais. Max Adey, a wealthy young playboy, has organised the trip, but his complicated relationship with Julia Wray (who is invited) and Amabel (who isn't), means he is wavering on whether to come along. There are Robert and Claire Hignam and their aunt, May Fellowes, who is seeing them off, along with Evelyn, Alex and the insecurely coupled Angela and Robin. When the train is cancelled because of the fog, a restless crowd of thwarted commuters begins to swell. The stationmaster, Mr Roberts, has been sent to 'look out for' Julia by her uncle, Mr Wray, who is a director of the railway company.[140] Locating the party, he ushers them into the railway hotel ('It belongs to the Company and I am sure you will be very comfortable there'), which is promptly shuttered and barricaded against the crowd.[141] The narrative and the city are snarled. Despite its ground-level confusions, however, Green's novel keeps insisting (as Clive Hart describes it) on a 'godlike, omniscient, aloof point of view', as when Max guides Julia to the window of their hotel suite:

> Looking down she saw the whole of that station below them, lit now by electricity, and covered from end to end by one mass of people [. . .] like those illustrations you saw in weekly papers, of corpuscles in blood,

for here and there a narrow stream of people shoved and moved in lines three deep and where they did this they were like veins. She wondered if this were what you saw when you stood on your wedding day, a Queen, on your balcony looking at subjects massed below.[142]

On the one hand, this privileged position of coherence and sovereign power is 'a structural substitute for the Archimedean point of narrative omniscience'.[143] The point of view literalises the distance and oversight of a third-person narrator. Less grandly, the point of view is also coterminous with Mr Roberts, the manager. While the party goers are still lost downstairs among the crowd, it is Mr Roberts who first activates this godlike point of view: 'At this moment Mr. Roberts, ensconced in his office where he could see hundreds below, for his windows overlooked the station, was telephoning for police reinforcements'.[144] We return to Mr Roberts looking out of his office window a few pages later, when Angela stands in the crowd on the railway concourse and imagines what she might look like:

> If that swarm of people could be likened to a pond for her lily then you could not see her like, and certainly not her kind, anywhere about her, nor was her likeness mirrored in their faces. Electric lights had been lit by now, fog still came in by the open end of this station, below that vast green vault of glass roof with every third person smoking it might all have looked to Mr. Roberts, ensconced in his office away above, like November sun striking through mist rising off water.[145]

Here the narrative voice playfully hovers between an omniscient perspective and Angela's perspective (showing us how she views herself as exceptional, as a lily unlike any other), before invoking a third point of view – Mr Roberts. The passage imagines a Mr Roberts figure (someone Angela is not yet aware of) looking down and picking out Angela as unique among the crowd. In some sense, Angela wills this Mr Roberts into being. Her exceptionality in the crowd is an insecure whimsy, resting delicately on that opening conditional 'If'. Her individuality depends, in other words, on a Mr Roberts: on a way of seeing that makes such similes possible. Looking down from the gods always elicits comically excessive similes in *Party Going*; in later chapters, the crowd seen from above is said to resemble not just corpuscles of blood, but also 'office carpet' and 'the holy Kaaba soon to set out for Mecca'.[146] By likewise seeing the crowd as a pond, this passage is seeing the crowd as if from above, abstracting and aestheticising it, and transforming it into an undifferentiated mass, out of which Angela blooms in her supposed individuality. The simile allows Angela to see herself above herself. But this paragraph is also about *not* seeing ('you could not see her like'). The passage not only demonstrates the power of the high vantage to aestheticise and abstract, but its failure to see. The view from the gods has turned the crowd into a pond, but the gods can't see the pond because another simile bedazzles the pond's surface ('like November sun striking through mist rising off water'). The excessive similes cancel each other out. The imagined vantage does not provide clarity, but confusion and misprision.

The recognisable hotel anxiety that pulses through this novel is the anxiety of becoming indistinct in the crowd and the fog, of losing a sense of one's own clear outline. The novel's second chapter shows Julia stepping out of a bubble of identity and agency seemingly guaranteed by her connection with the manager (she 'stepped out into the darkness of fog above and left warm rooms with bells and servants and her uncle who was one of Mr. Roberts' directors – a rich important man –') before finding her selfhood evaporated in the darkness of fog ('she lost her name and was all at once anonymous; if it had not been for her rich coat she might have been any typist making her way home').[147] Without her coat, and without her bells and servants and uncle, Julia would be one of the 'thousands of Smiths, thousands of Alberts, hundreds of Marys' crowding the concourse, or one of the revellers' misremembered servants ('her maid whatever her name is').[148] It is this anxiety that makes the party-goers gravitate toward Mr Roberts as a means not only of securing their safety, their comfort and their luggage, but also their social and narratorial distinctiveness. The party-goers' connection with Mr Roberts provides them with access to a privileged space high in the hotel, and equally importantly, a privileged way of seeing that mimics the manager's own. The point of view of the managerial eye allows them to figuratively differentiate themselves from the 'thousands of Smiths' on the concourse. It enables them to feel, as different members of the party keep insisting, 'infinitely remote' from the mass of humanity.[149] But managerial powers are hardly panoptic as the fog descends. Mr Roberts himself is quickly dislodged from his secure vantage point above the chaos. At the very moment that Angela summons a Mr Roberts figure to witness the panorama from above, Mr Roberts is in fact down on the railway concourse, himself lost among the crowd on a mission to find Julia Wray; two paragraphs after Angela's reverie about her unmistakable uniqueness, Mr Roberts bumps into Angela herself, asking if she is in fact Julia. Later, the stationmaster rejects Robert's request over the telephone to locate a porter still out on the concourse with the party's luggage. Locating a single individual on the concourse is not possible, the stationmaster insists; rather than a lily in a pond, it would be like looking for '"A needle in a – a needle in a –" and he was searching for some better word, "a haystack," he said at last, at a loss.'[150] Overworked and flustered, the manager can't see his way out of the fog. His figurative powers escape him. If the manager is established as a structural alternative to an omniscient narrator in the novel's opening chapters, a few chapters later he is already admitting defeat. *Party Going* thematisises this crumbling of narratorial and managerial authority.

Robert, Robin, Mr Roberts

Julia Wray's power, she believes, resides in her venerable name: a name that opens doors. She is flummoxed, then, when her name fails to motivate Mr Roberts, during his telephone call with Robert, to send out a search party for her porter and her luggage: '"Are you sure you gave my name?" she said to Robert.'[151] But names, like the 'Amabel' that Amabel writes in steam on a befogged hotel bathroom mirror, are vaporous in this novel. Mr Roberts, for instance, doesn't catch Robert's name during their phone call; he uses his (incorrect) surname instead ('My dear Mr. Hinham') and then gives up altogether ('My dear sir').[152] The manager himself can't differentiate one name from another. What goes unremarked is that the name Mr Roberts doesn't catch is virtually his own, while another character in the novel, Robin, has a diminutive version of the same. The similarity of their names does not signal a hidden figurative fraternity between the trio, but rather points to the indistinctiveness of all identities in *Party Going*.

Nick Shepley argues that the hollowing out or annihilation of names as signifiers is a thread running through all of Green's work. Names in Green's fiction become 'multi-use, polyphonic, shifting, and often dysfunctional containers'; they are often 'misheard, misremembered, used out of context, deliberately misused, shortened, confused'.[153] Even Henry Vincent Yorke's own choice of nom de plume, 'Green', is a dysfunctional container, Shepley argues: a noun that is both richly, excessively connotative (signifying too much) while being one of the most common names in the British telephone directory (signifying too little). His nom de plume is 'easily repeatable or "iterable". Such iterability allows the one to be broken down into many others; a nebulous multitude of others that lack specificity'.[154] The nebulous cluster of Robert, Robin and Mr Roberts is symptomatic of Green's prismatic construction of *Party Going*. This is not a novel of distinct, monadic individuals, of singular and exceptional lilies – which are, in any case, rhizomatic and anything but singular. It's a novel of nebulous multitudes of others, in which figures are sketchily characterised; a novel 'unwillin[g] to provide concrete particulars' – in which, as Naomi Milthorpe writes, 'human subjects and material objects are both designated under the rubric "things," suggestive of his characters' inadequate engagement with these things in their specificity'.[155] *Party Going* is also a novel where different characters express a fantasy of their own uniqueness using the same generic words and sentiments. Foltz points to four different characters who talk about social remoteness in the same way: including Angela, who claims that she and her partner Robin are distinct from the crowd in these terms ('Like two lilies in a pond, romantically part of it but infinitely remote'), and Julia and Max, who 'could not but feel infinitely remote' from the crowd as they look down from their hotel window.[156] 'The phrases that circulate throughout the book (the figure of the remote is simply one remarkable index) find themselves, like this foggy and diaphanous medium, in the mouths of many characters,' Foltz writes. 'These phrases show, in their indiscriminate circulation, the avid promiscuity of a language that will ultimately betray the fictions of identity it is taken to support.'[157]

While the party-goers yearn for a managerial eye overlooking events, for vertical relations of difference and hierarchy, the novel instead offers a cluster of forms – the rhizome, miasma and the hotel suite – which confound the vertical and instead encourage horizontal relations of contiguity and connection. *Party Going* does not just represent the hotel's verticality, but explores its depth and dimensionality. Every space has its mirror image, or multiple images. When Julia and Alex climb from the lobby to their rooms ('up short flights from landing to landing on deep plush carpets with sofas covered in tartan on each landing') a parallel procession is taking place 'up the back stairs' ('For every step Alex and Julia took Miss Fellowes was taken up one too, slumped on one of those chromium-plated seats, her parcel on her lap').[158] The repeated sequence of flights, landings and landing furniture branches off and forms a variation – 'one' becomes 'too' – while the pairing of Julia and Alex becomes two hotel porters, two nannies and an untidy remainder – 'that same man who had sat next her, he who winked'.[159] On the vertical plane, Max has booked rooms on multiple floors; on the horizontal plane, those rooms have internal doors and compartments, each of which leads out in turn onto corridors. Rod Mengham points to the 'Regressive movement, similar to that in *The Castle*, *The Trial*, and *The Burrow* of Kafka' at work in this 'arterial labyrinth',[160] and indeed there are depths we may never plumb: '"They said they would take us along this floor through the hotel and then the office till we can get down by a lift on to the place they keep for visiting big noises, where they receive them you see"'.[161] Yet as well as a peripheral blur, a localised hardness and exactitude are crucial to Green's spatial constructions. So while Max has another room booked – a secret bower, a 'special room' – we also know that much of the action takes place contiguously in rooms 95, 96 and 196.[162] There is a numbered grid, but there are also remainders – fractures, mistakes and hidden dimensions that unsettle the grid.

The thin walls (through which a jealous lover might hear, or think he hears, a slap), the doors (Alex talks to Amabel in her bath through her door) and the multiple blocks and tiers of hotel space allow Green to imagine his characters connected in a cellular but permeable system, in which the thresholds and markers of difference are subtle and porous (some characters slip in and out of even the most shuttered thresholds as if by osmosis), but are no less significant for being subtle and porous. The rationalisation of hotel space into individual cells and grids paradoxically provides the conditions for these new forms of identity to emerge. *Party Going*, opening out laterally, is an exploration of this organism.

Like Bowen, Green populates his hotel with too many characters, arranged in complex geometric relations. There is a level of redundancy and interchangeability in this system, a level of replication among its parts. Though the novel is full of mirrors, doubles and understudies (nearly all the rich characters have a servant), *Party Going* is not about the intimacy of pairs. Green is always bursting apart stable pairings and inserting an untidy remainder. Green writes of so-called 'Embassy Richard' (who appears untidily at the novel's conclusion) that 'when he spoke it was never to less than three people'; in the same way, *Party Going* is about triples and quadruples, about networks of relations within a system.[163] In one scene, Claire and Evelyn are in a bedroom with two telephones, speaking simultaneously. Not only does this open up two exterior and unseen spaces, but their conversation also penetrates the unconscious dreams of Miss Fellowes in the next bedroom. Characteristically, the scene slides without a break into another bedroom, where another drama (a fake love triangle) is in the process of playing out, staged between a sitting-room, a bedroom and the corridor. Sliding sideways into a contiguous situation is part of this novel's restless art:

> 'But what about my claustrophobia?' Alex asked. They all heard the man near them say to his companion, a woman, no, he would certainly do nothing of the kind.[164]

Party Going proceeds by moving sideways through the network, repeating situations with different personnel and making connections. In this way, the porous spaces of the hotel become, like the fog, a way of imagining the 'physiological intersubjectivity' of its inhabitants.[165]

Hotel Purgatory

The unnamed railway station in *Party Going* must be Victoria Station, as this is where the boat train to Calais departed from; logically, then, the unnamed railway hotel must be the Grosvenor, one of the joint-stock palaces built by railway corporations in the 1850s and 1860s that answered the clamour for a new standard of English hospitality (Figure 5.5). In 1863, the writer and physician Andrew Wynter imagined a provincial rube apprehending the Grosvenor as it looms

> in the distance, far over the head of the royal palace; as he gets nearer it seems to grow into the air; and as he *debouches* full upon it from some side-street, it towers up like a mountain before him – a mountain chiselled from basement to garret with clustered fruit and flowers, all wrought in enduring stone.[166]

Figure 5.5 Interior view looking along a corridor at the Grosvenor Hotel, 1900 (Source: Historic England Archive)

With an elaborate Second Empire mansard roof, busts of Victoria, Albert and Lord Palmerston, one of the first steam-powered lifts in the capital, and private water closets in two-thirds of the rooms, the hotel was a monument to Victorian industrialism. The hotel was remodelled in the 1890s, and its capacity was nearly doubled in 1907.[167] Green's *Party Going* represents a culmination and a terminus for this model of industrial luxury hotel whose cultural influence was beginning to wane.

Green worked on *Party Going*, drafting and revising, from 1931 to 1938, while hotels like the Grosvenor were slowly dying. The Grosvenor was owned by the British firm Gordon Hotels Limited, which had been the largest hotel business in the world during the 1890s, with fifteen Brobdingnagian properties in England and Europe.[168] Its share price peaked at £24.60 in 1896, but in the interwar period it never exceeded £6.[169] Its business model was already shaky before the Depression hit, and large losses and stoic annual reports were to follow: 'With regard to prospects, I can only say, as I said last year, that we are largely dependent on a revival of international trade and of international, and especially trans-Atlantic, travel.'[170] There were larger underlying problems, however. Fewer people wanted a rail holiday – a long stay in a single city, with half or full board at a hotel – and more people wanted short and impromptu travel – overnight and weekend breaks, with bed and breakfast.[171] The rival British chain Trust Houses Limited fared far better during the slump, and pointed the way to the future. Lightweight and flexible, it aggressively bought new properties, and grew strongly through most of the 1930s. The Trust Houses chain emerged out of a group of public trusts that aimed to rescue from dereliction Britain's pre-railway-era lodging houses – now once again accessible and viable thanks to the automobile.[172] A decentralised collection of small, individual operating units, situated almost entirely in small provincial towns, Trust Houses thrived by providing basic accommodation for the mobile middle and lower-middle classes.[173] Looking backward toward lodging-houses and forward toward the motorways, the enterprise was an idiosyncratically British expression of the emergent motel era.[174]

The infrastructural failure in *Party Going* reinforces the old-fashionedness of the novel's technologies: the railway and the grand hotel, whose breakdowns radiate outwards across the city. With its dirty centrepiece chandelier, Green's hotel has seen better days. The party-goers retreat into a space surrounded by 'porters like mourners', blanketed in a 'pall', and filled with blank and twitchy figures biding their time in its corridors.[175] One of Green's guests compares the hotel to 'an enormous doctor's waiting room': '[I]t would be like that', she thinks, 'when they were all dead and waiting at the gates.'[176] But while these descriptions mirror the real Grosvenor's waning fortunes and are indicative of a broader, historical decline in the institutional prestige of grand hotels, the hotel as a haunted space, or as a purgatorial space for 'waiting at the gates',

Figure 5.6 A seated ghost in a long exposure photograph, in the lobby of the Hotel Richmond, Virginia, c.1900–20 (Source: Library of Congress)

are recurring tropes in hotel texts past and present (Figure 5.6). Writing on hotels in contemporary cinema, Katherine Lawrie Van de Ven notes that the hotel is commonly represented in purgatorial terms as a space of stopping and transience, and an 'elsewhere' reserved for the 'working through of crises of identity, morality, and memory'.[177]

We can trace this trope back to Wilkie Collins's *The Haunted Hotel* (1878), in which a conspiracy and murder unfolds in an old Venetian palace. Countess Narona arranges for the murder of her husband and the substitution of his body for another in order to claim her husband's lavish life insurance. Her husband's severed head remains locked away in the palace, even as the site is bought up by a joint-stock company, hollowed out and turned into a luxury hotel. The Countess, haunted by guilt, comes to stay at the remodelled hotel, where she sets to work on a play that will act as her confession. She describes the corporate hotel as 'The old hell, transformed into the new purgatory.'[178] A later echo of the trope can be found in May Sinclair's 'Where Their Fire Is Not Quenched', published in *Uncanny Stories* (1923), which describes the life and afterlife of Harriott Leigh. In life, Harriott struggles to escape from an affair with a married man, which reaches its nadir during a two-week tryst in the 'hideously ugly' Hotel Saint Pierre in Paris.[179] Miserable in the extended company of the coarse and dull Oscar Wade, and enervated by the hotel itself, Harriott desperately hopes that the pair never find themselves married. Marriage would be purgatory: it would be 'the Hotel Saint Pierre all over again, without any possibility of escape'.[180] The story jumps forward: Harriott dies and passes over into what might either be purgatory or hell, finding herself in an eternal present, a realm which simultaneously contains 'All space and time' and also 'no time'.[181] It is composed of corridors, streets, stairs and portentous gates and doorways drawn from different stages of Harriott's life, which all keep leading her back, eternally, to the looming face of Oscar and to her bedroom in the Hotel Saint Pierre. The aesthetics of the early-twentieth-century hotel – its muted colours, mechanical interpolations, and vertical and horizontal elongations – are easily translated into the eternal 'no time' of the spirit world: 'she made straight for the great grey carpeted staircase; she climbed the endless flights that turned round and round the caged-in shaft of the well, past the latticed doors of the lift, and came up on to a landing that she knew, and into the long, ash-grey, foreign corridor lit by a dull window at one end.'[182]

The hotel is easily imagined as purgatorial because of those spatial and temporal qualities I discussed in Chapter 2: its bare, stain-resistant surfaces that suppressed the accretions of time and attenuated any connection to history. Ideally, the hotel maintained the illusion of an eternal present, wiping away any trace of prior occupation or any sense of settled dwelling. This was an effect that rubbed off on the hotel guests in James's fiction, whose actions (like the consumption of out-of-order Tauchnitz editions, or Mr Dosson's endless waiting in *The Reverberator*) appear directionless and amnesic. The hotel's spaces therefore conspired to derange one's lived experience of time. The culmination of this stain-resistant aesthetic, discussed in Chapter 3, was the racialised, hospital-like whiteness of the Ritz and the Plaza. For Fitzgerald, these spaces offered an escape, safe from the noise and multiplicity of the city; a negation of the social world that felt like a form of death. *The Beautiful and Damned*, 'The Diamond as Big as the Ritz' and 'May Day' all rendered hotel space as purgatorial, especially the space of the hotel roof garden which stood exposed to the heavens. As one of the first hotel chains, spreading across the globe through assimilation and metamorphosis, installing its aesthetic and ambience in golf clubs, apartment blocks and ocean liners, the Ritz not only hovered in 'no time', but was starting to become a non-place – an anywhere and a nowhere.

Representing the hotel as haunted was also a means of grappling with the decentring of individual agency in hotel space, which has been the central focus of this book. From the unruly objects (boots, cigars, chairs, toothpicks, spittoons) connected to the bodies of the lobby loungers (bodies replete with self-stretching legs and self-twirling moustaches) discussed in Chapter 1, to the scornful objects in Proust's hotel bedroom and the menacing rows of Bowen's empty armchairs discussed in Chapter 4, to Chomón and Mathieu's impassive subservience to hotel objects discussed in the present chapter, hotel texts have long represented the *mise-en-scène* as being 'queerly important', as Bowen writes in *The Hotel*.[183] The uncannily animate objects in these texts have the power to determine the movement and behaviour of hotel guests, who in the case of Chomón and Mathieu are reduced to being mere puppets. In James's oversized American hotel lobbies and piazzas, lively objects confound the boundary between self and stuff, while cigar smoke and spittle create forms of involuntary connectedness or 'physiological intersubjectivity' among the mass of loungers.[184] In Bowen's hotel, objects observe and collude, chatter and screech. Parlour furniture appears like a studio set awaiting the camera – a set which itself seems to structure hotel sociability and script encounters. These texts warp and decentre the idea of the fictional 'character', suggesting instead that the individual hotel guest exists within larger corporate, architectural, informatic and technological networks.

The haunted hotel was also, finally, a means of coming to terms with the non-human or supra-human agency that adhered within the corporate person – a legal and economic construction described by Victorian jurist Frederic Maitland as 'the ghost of a fiction'.[185] From James's telegraphic vibrations and voices to the extraction of 'Orcham' from the body of Bennett's hotel manager and the hovering watchfulness of MGM's machinery described in the present chapter, hotel texts explored ways to represent the power of the corporation over social space – whether as a mystified and heroic personification, or as an ambient vapour or hovering spectre. To live inside a hotel corporation was to live with this non-human presence, to sense its 'awful intelligence'.[186]

Notes

1. Matthew Solomon, 'Up-to-Date Magic: Theatrical Conjuring and the Trick Film', 58 (4) *Theatre Journal* (2006), p. 612.
2. 'Comparison of a Hotel Manager with Other Modern Mercantile Magnates', *Hotel World* (July 1897), p. 13.
3. Google Ngram Viewer, '([hotelkeeping] + [hotel – keeping] + [hotel keeping]), [hotel management]', 1850–1950 in English (2019).
4. John F. Wilson and Andrew Thomson, *The Making of Modern Management: British Management in Historical Perspective* (Oxford: Oxford University Press, 2006), pp. 57–9.
5. Ross McKibbin, *Classes and Cultures: England 1918–1951* (Oxford and New York: Oxford University Press, 2008), p. 49.
6. Lucius M. Boomer, *Hotel Management: Principles and Practice* (New York: Harper, 1925), pp. 246 and 243.
7. Quoted in John A. Jakle and Keith A. Sculle, *America's Main Street Hotels: Transiency and Community in the Early Auto Age* (Knoxville, TN: University of Tennessee Press, 2009), p. 81.
8. Boomer, *Hotel Management*, p. 258.

9. George W. Sweeney, 'Geo. W. Sweeney, Representing the A.H.A. at the Monaco International Hotel Congress, Cites the Commodore as an Example of the Modern Large Hotel', 92 (17) *Hotel World* (April 1921), p. 10.
10. Boomer, *Hotel Management*, p. 258.
11. Henry James, *The American Scene*, in *Collected Travel Writings: Great Britain and America*, ed. Richard Howard (New York: Library of America, 1993), p. 440.
12. Ibid., pp. 443–4.
13. Henry James, *The Reverberator*, in *Novels: 1886–1890*, ed. Daniel Mark Fogel (New York: Library of America, 1989), p. 568.
14. Henry James, *The Ambassadors* (London: Methuen, 190), p. 230.
15. James, *The Reverberator*, p. 574.
16. 'Telephone Men Justify Rates', *New York Times*, 5 February 1910, p. 8.
17. Albin Pasteur Dearing, *The Elegant Inn* (Secaucus, NJ: Lyle Stuart, 1986), p. 81.
18. 'The Western Union Withdraws', *New-York Tribune*, 6 November 1897, p. 12.
19. 'Crowds Watch Bulletins', *New-York Tribune*, 14 September 1901, p. 9.
20. 'Wireless Stations About New York: No. 2 – Station at the Waldorf-Astoria', *Modern Electrics* (September 1909), pp. 253–4.
21. James, *The American Scene*, pp. 440–3.
22. Ibid., p. 444.
23. Henry James, 'The Art of Fiction', in *Literary Criticism: Essays on Literature, American Writers, English Writers*, eds Leon Edel and Mark Wilson (New York: Library of America, 1984), p. 52.
24. Ellen Wayland-Smith, '"Conductors and Revealers": Henry James's Electric Messengers in *The Ambassadors*', 32 (2) *Henry James Review* (Summer 2011), p. 121.
25. James, *The American Scene*, p. 444.
26. Ross Posnock, *The Trial of Curiosity: Henry James, William James, and the Challenge of Modernity* (Oxford: Oxford University Press, 1991), p. 265.
27. Ibid., p. 266.
28. Kevin R. McNamara, *Urban Verbs: Arts and Discourses of American Cities* (Stanford, CA: Stanford University Press, 1996), p. 38.
29. Anna Despotopoulou, 'Monuments of an Artless Age: Hotels and Women's Mobility in the Work of Henry James', 50 (4) *Studies in the Novel* (Winter 2018), p. 503.
30. James, *The American Scene*, pp. 617–18.
31. James R. Beniger, *The Control Revolution: Technological and Economic Origins of the Information Society* (Cambridge, MA and London: Harvard University Press, 1986), pp. 15–16.
32. Ibid., p. 15.
33. James, *The American Scene*, p. 689.
34. Henry James, *The Bostonians*, in *Novels: 1881–1886*, ed. William T. Stafford (New York: Library of America, 1985), p. 916.
35. Ibid., p. 916.
36. Ibid., p. 1193.
37. Ibid., p. 916.
38. James, *The American Scene*, pp. 689–90.

39. 'Prominent Arrivals at the Hotels', *New York Tribune*, 3 January 1905, p. 11.
40. Mark Goble, *Beautiful Circuits: Modernism and the Mediated Life* (New York: Columbia University Press, 2010), p. 119.
41. Ibid., p. 97.
42. James, *The American Scene*, p. 441.
43. Ibid., p. 440. Hotel baron John McEntee Bowman articulated this interest in educating desire:

> One of the business man's most important jobs is always to be aware that the great masses of people are becoming educated more and more each year to new desires. When a sufficient number of people consciously recognize these desires which have formerly been somewhat vague or uncrystallized, and when large numbers also recognize the possibility of having these desires satisfied by some business institution, then the desires change into economic demand. ('How We Find What Will Sell Best', *System: The Magazine of Business* (April 1923), p. 461.)

44. James, *The American Scene*, pp. 725–6.
45. Ibid., p. 3441.
46. Ibid., p. 726.
47. Henry James, *Prefaces to the New York Edition*, in *Literary Criticism: French Writers, Other European Writers, The Prefaces to the New York Edition*, eds Leon Edel and Mark Wilson (New York: Library of America, 1984), p. 1041.
48. James Purdon, *Modernist Informatics: Literature, Information, and the State* (Oxford: Oxford University Press, 2016), p. 30.
49. Mark Seltzer, *Henry James and the Art of Power* (Ithaca, NY and London: Cornell University Press, 1984), p. 114.
50. Ibid., p. 115.
51. McNamara, *Urban Verbs*, pp. 18–19.
52. Gert Buelens, 'Henry James's Oblique Possession: Plottings of Desire and Mastery in *The American Scene*', 116 (2) *PMLA* (March 2001), p. 305.
53. Arnold Bennett, *The Grand Babylon Hotel* (Peterborough: Broadview, 2016), pp. 56–7.
54. Randi Saloman, 'Arnold Bennett's Hotels', 58 (1) *Twentieth Century Literature* (Spring 2012), p. 8.
55. Emma Short, *Mobility and the Hotel in Modern Literature: Passing Through* (Cham: Palgrave, 2019), p. 51.
56. Bennett, *The Grand Babylon*, p. 64.
57. Ibid., p. 84.
58. Ibid., pp. 63 and 143.
59. Ibid., p. 128.
60. Kevin J. James, 'Aliens, Subjects and the State: Surveillance in British Hotels during World War I', 36 (3) *Immigrants and Minorities* (2018), p. 200.
61. Arnold Bennett, *Imperial Palace* (London: Cassell, 1930), p. 93.
62. Ibid., p. 124.
63. Ibid., p. 239.

64. Ibid., p. 277.
65. Ibid., p. 32.
66. Ibid., p 59.
67. Georges Lafourcade, *Arnold Bennett: A Study* (London: Frederick Muller, 1939), p. 209.
68. Margaret Drabble, *Arnold Bennett: A Biography* (New York: Alfred A. Knopf, 1974), p. 342.
69. Bennett, *Imperial Palace*, p. 109.
70. Ibid., p. 210.
71. Ibid., p. 111.
72. Ibid., p. 379.
73. Ibid., p. 459.
74. Arnold Bennett, *The Old Wives' Tale* (Toronto: McLeod & Allen, 1908), p. 388.
75. Arnold Bennett, *Clayhanger* (London: Metheun, 1910), p. 98.
76. Arnold Bennett, *Those United States* (London: Martin Secker, 1912), pp. 149–50.
77. John Nash, 'Arnold Bennett and Home Management: Domestic Efficiency', 59 (2) *English Literature in Transition, 1880–1920* (2016), p. 222.
78. Bennett, *Imperial Palace*, pp. 129–30.
79. Michael Augspurger, 'Sinclair Lewis' Primers for the Professional Managerial Class: *Babbitt, Arrowsmith*, and *Dodsworth*', 34 (2) *Journal of the Midwest Modern Language Association* (2001), pp. 74–5.
80. Ibid., p. 81.
81. Sinclair Lewis, *Work of Art* (New York: P. F. Collier, 1934), pp. 183–4.
82. Ibid., p. 23.
83. Ibid., pp. 100–1.
84. Ibid., p. 97.
85. Ibid., p. 256.
86. Douglas Tallack, '"Waiting, Waiting": The Hotel Lobby in the Modern City', in *The Hieroglyphics of Space*, ed. Neil Leach (London: Routledge, 2002), p. 140; Daniel Defoe, *Robinson Crusoe*, eds Thomas Keymer and James Kelly (Oxford and New York: Oxford University Press, 2007), p. 59.
87. Lewis, *Work of Art*, p. 178.
88. Ibid., p. 373.
89. Arnold Bennett, *The Savour of Life: Essays in Gusto* (London: Cassell, 1928), p. 227.
90. Ibid., p. 228.
91. Jesse L. Lasky, 'What Kind of a "Menace" Are the Movies?', 212 (776) *North American Review* (1920), p. 91.
92. Bennett, *The Savour of Life*, p. 226.
93. Arnold Bennett, *Journal 1929* (London: Cassell, 1930), p. 45; Arnold Bennett, *Letters of Arnold Bennett: Volume I. Letters to J. B. Pinker*, ed. James Hepburn (London: Oxford University Press, 1966), pp. 388–91.
94. Arnold Bennett, 'The Film "Story"', 1 (6) *Close Up* (December 1927), pp. 29–30.
95. Alix Beeston, *In and Out of Sight: Modernist Writing and the Photographic Unseen* (Oxford: Oxford University Press, 2018), p. 151.

96. Stefan Solomon, *William Faulkner in Hollywood: Screenwriting for the Studios* (Athens, GA: University of Georgia Press, 2017), p. 10.
97. Leslie H. Abramson, *Hitchcock and the Anxiety of Authorship* (New York: Palgrave, 2015), pp. 36–7.
98. Alfred Hitchcock, 'Films We Could Make', in *Hitchcock on Hitchcock, Volume 1: Selected Writings and Interviews*, ed. Sidney Gottlieb (Berkley, CA: University of California Press, 1995), p. 167.
99. Alfred Hitchcock, 'An Autocrat of the Film Studio', in *Hitchcock on Hitchcock, Volume 2: Selected Writings and Interviews*, ed. Sidney Gottlieb (Berkeley, CA: University of California Press, 2015), pp. 116–23.
100. Kaija Silverman, *The Acoustic Mirror: The Female Voice in Psychoanalysis and Cinema* (Bloomington, IN: Indiana University Press, 1988), p. 2.
101. Brooke Rollins, '"Some Kind of a Man": Orson Welles as *Touch of Evil's* Masculine Auteur', 57 Velvet Light Trap (2006), p. 35.
102. Jeff Menne, *Post-Fordist Cinema: Hollywood Auteurs and the Corporate Counterculture* (New York: Columbia University Press, 2019), pp. 2–3.
103. Bennett, *Imperial Palace*, p. 50.
104. Ibid., p. 300.
105. Ibid., p. 365.
106. Short, *Mobility and the Hotel*, pp. 196–7.
107. Bennett, *Imperial Palace*, pp. 44–5.
108. Ibid., p. 30.
109. Ibid., p. 597.
110. Ibid., p. 30.
111. Ibid., p. 50.
112. Ibid., p. 61.
113. Ibid., pp. 313–16.
114. Ibid., p. 630.
115. Ibid., p. 117.
116. Ibid., pp. 84–5.
117. Mark Franko, *The Work of Dance: Labor, Movement, and Identity in the 1930s* (Middletown, CT: Wesleyan University Press, 2002), pp. 31–2.
118. Bennett, *Imperial Palace*, pp. 121 and 294.
119. Ibid., pp. 240 and 218.
120. Sianne Ngai, *Our Aesthetic Categories: Zany, Cute, Interesting* (Cambridge, MA: Harvard University Press, 2012), p. 181.
121. Bennett, *Imperial Palace*, p. 600.
122. Ibid., p. 282.
123. Ibid., p. 154.
124. Ibid., p. 344.
125. Ibid., p. 154.
126. Ibid., p. 278.
127. Ibid., p. 198.
128. Ibid., p. 293.
129. Ibid., p. 350.

130. Ibid., p. 139.
131. Ibid., p. 281.
132. Jerome Christensen, *America's Corporate Art: The Studio Authorship of Hollywood Motion Pictures* (Stanford, CA: Stanford University Press, 2012), p. 29.
133. Roland Marchand, *Creating the Corporate Soul: The Rise of Public Relations and Corporate Imagery in American Big Business* (Berkeley, CA: University of California Press, 2001), p. 28.
134. Christensen, *America's Corporate Art*, p. 72.
135. 'Metro-Goldwyn-Mayer [1932]' in *The American Film Industry*, ed. Tino Balio (Madison, WI: University of Wisconsin Press, 1979), p. 318.
136. Goble, *Beautiful Circuits*, p. 117.
137. Christensen, *America's Corporate Art*, p. 28.
138. Ibid.
139. Jonathan Foltz, *The Novel after Film: Modernism and the Decline of Autonomy* (Oxford: Oxford University Press, 2018), p. 162.
140. Ibid., p. 10.
141. Ibid., p. 54.
142. Clive Hart, 'The Structure and Technique of *Party Going*', 1 Yearbook of English Studies (1971), p. 188; Henry Green, Party Going (London: Hogarth Press, 1962), pp. 86–7.
143. Foltz, *The Novel after Film*, p. 161.
144. Green, *Party Going*, p. 15.
145. Ibid., p. 28.
146. Ibid., p. 150.
147. Ibid., pp. 15–16.
148. Ibid., pp. 150 and 211.
149. Ibid., p. 150.
150. Ibid., p. 76.
151. Ibid., p. 83.
152. Ibid., p. 76.
153. Nick Shepley, *Henry Green: Class, Style, and the Everyday* (Oxford: Oxford University Press, 2016), p. 45.
154. Ibid., p. 30.
155. Naomi Milthorpe, 'Things and Nothings: Henry Green and the Late Modernist Banal', 50 (1) *Novel: A Forum on Fiction* (2017), p. 104.
156. Green, *Party Going*, pp. 27 and 150.
157. Foltz, *The Novel after Film*, p. 163.
158. Green, *Party Going*, p. 63.
159. Ibid., p. 63.
160. Rod Mengham, *The Idiom of Time: The Writings of Henry Green* (Cambridge and New York: Cambridge University Press, 1982), p. 37.
161. Green, *Party Going*, p. 250.
162. Ibid., p. 91.
163. Ibid., p. 254.
164. Ibid., pp. 62–3.

165. Tina Young Choi, *Anonymous Connections: The Body and Narratives of the Social in Victorian Britain* (Ann Arbor, MI: University of Michigan Press, 2015), p. 37.
166. Andrew Wynter, *Subtle Brains and Lissom Fingers. Being Some of the Chisel-Marks of Our Industrial and Scientific Progress. And Other Papers* (London: Robert Hardwicke, 1863), p. 83.
167. Oliver Carter, *An Illustrated History of British Railway Hotels: 1838–1983* (St Michael's: Silver Link, 1990), p. 11.
168. Elaine Denby, *Grand Hotels: Reality and Illusion* (London: Reaktion Books, 1998), p. 241.
169. Derek Taylor, *Fortune, Fame and Folly: British Hotels and Catering from 1878 to 1978* (Andover: Chapel River Press, 1977), pp. 4, 6 and 33.
170. 'Gordon Hotels, Limited', 4733 *The Economist* (12 May 1934), p. 1054.
171. Rex Pope, 'A Consumer Service in Interwar Britain: The Hotel Trade, 1924–1938', 74 (4) *Business History Review* (Winter, 2000), p. 670.
172. Taylor, *Fortune, Fame and Folly*, p. 5.
173. Pope, 'A Consumer Service in Interwar Britain', p. 681.
174. Trust Houses in the 1960s, by then the biggest accommodation company in Britain, bought a stake in America's Travelodge Corporation; in the 1970s they merged with the Forte Group of roadside restaurants and service stations, forming a multi-billion pound conglomerate.
175. Green, *Party Going*, p. 40 and p. 14.
176. Ibid., p. 59.
177. Katherine Lawrie Van de Ven, '"Just an Anonymous Room:" Cinematic Hotels and Motels as Mnemonic Purgatories', in *Moving Pictures/Stopping Places: Hotels and Motels on Film*, eds David B. Clarke, Valerie Crawford Pfannhauser and Marcus A. Doel (Lanham, MD: Lexington Books, 2009), p. 235.
178. Wilkie Collins, *The Haunted Hotel*, in *Miss or Mrs? – The Haunted Hotel – The Guilty River*, eds Norman Page and Toru Sasaki (Oxford: Oxford University Press, 2008), p. 181.
179. May Sinclair, 'Where Their Fire is Not Quenched', in *Uncanny Stories* (London: Hutchinson, 1923), p. 18.
180. Ibid., p. 19.
181. Ibid., pp. 28–9.
182. Ibid., pp. 27–8.
183. Elizabeth Bowen, *The Hotel* (London: Vintage, 2003), p. 105.
184. Tina Young Choi, *Anonymous Connections: The Body and Narratives of the Social in Victorian Britain* (Ann Arbor, MI: University of Michigan Press, 2015), p. 37.
185. Quoted in Gail Turley Houston, *From Dickens to Dracula: Gothic, Economics and Victorian Fiction* (Cambridge: Cambridge University Press, 2005), p. 115.
186. Bowen, *The Hotel*, p. 106.

BIBLIOGRAPHY

'1939 – Your Hotel in Twenty Years', 88 (14) *Hotel World* (April 1919), pp. 32–3.
Abramson, Daniel M. *Obsolescence: An Architectural History* (Chicago and London: Chicago University Press, 2016).
Abramson, Leslie H., *Hitchcock and the Anxiety of Authorship* (New York: Palgrave, 2015).
Allen, Irving Lewis, *The City in Slang: New York Life and Popular Speech* (Oxford and New York: Oxford University Press, 1993).
Anesko, Michael, *'Friction with the Market': Henry James and the Profession of Authorship* (Oxford and New York: Oxford University Press, 1986).
'Anglo-German Film Agreement. Mutual Distribution', *The Times*, 12 December 1927, p. 19.
'Another Fine Hotel Now On the City's List', *New York Times*, 29 September 1907, p. 3.
Armstead, Myra Beth Young, *Lord, Please Don't Take Me in August: African Americans in Newport and Saratoga, 1870–1930* (Champaign, IL: University of Illinois Press, 1999).
Arvidsson, Adam, *Brands: Meaning and Value in Media Culture* (New York: Routledge, 2006).
Augé, Marc, *Non-Places: Introduction to an Anthropology of Supermodernity*, trans. John Howe (London and New York: Verso, 1995).

Augspurger, Michael, 'Sinclair Lewis' Primers for the Professional Managerial Class: *Babbitt, Arrowsmith*, and *Dodsworth*', 34 (2) *Journal of the Midwest Modern Language Association* (2001), pp. 73–97.
Badowska, Eva, 'On the Track of Things: Sensation and Modernity in Mary Elizabeth Braddon's *Lady Audley's Secret*', 37 (1) *Victorian Literature and Culture* (2009), pp. 157–75.
Barry, Iris, *Let's Go to the Pictures* (London: Chatto & Windus, 1926).
Bauman, Zygmunt, *Liquid Modernity* (Cambridge: Polity Press, 2000).
Beeston, Alix, *In and Out of Sight: Modernist Writing and the Photographic Unseen* (Oxford: Oxford University Press, 2018).
Beniger, James R., *The Control Revolution: Technological and Economic Origins of the Information Society* (Cambridge, MA and London: Harvard University Press, 1986).
Benjamin, Walter. *The Arcades Project*, trans. Howard Eiland and Kevin McLaughlin (Cambridge, MA and London: Belknap Press of Harvard University Press, 1999).
Benjamin, Walter, 'Experience and Poverty', in *Walter Benjamin: Selected Writings: Volume 2, Part 2, 1931–1934*, eds Michael W. Jennings et al. (Cambridge, MA and London: Belknap Press of Harvard University Press, 1999), pp. 731–6.
Benjamin, Walter, 'Little History of Photography', in *Walter Benjamin: Selected Writings: 1927–1934*, eds Michael W. Jennings, Howard Eiland and Gary Smith (Cambridge, MA and London: Harvard University Press, 1999), pp. 507–30.
Bennett, Andrew and Nicholas Royle, *Elizabeth Bowen and the Dissolution of the Novel: Still Lives* (Basingstoke: Macmillan, 1995).
Bennett, Arnold, *Clayhanger* (London: Metheun, 1910).
Bennett, Arnold, 'The Film "Story"', 1 (6) *Close Up* (December 1927), pp. 29–30.
Bennett, Arnold, *The Grand Babylon Hotel*, ed. Randi Saloman (Peterborough: Broadview, 2016).
Bennett, Arnold, *Imperial Palace* (London: Cassell, 1930).
Bennett, Arnold, *Journal 1929* (London: Cassell, 1930).
Bennett, Arnold, *Letters of Arnold Bennett: Volume I. Letters to J. B. Pinker*, ed. James Hepburn (London: Oxford University Press, 1966).
Bennett, Arnold, *The Old Wives' Tale* (Toronto: McLeod & Allen, 1908).
Bennett, Arnold, *The Savour of Life: Essays in Gusto* (London: Cassell, 1928).
Bennett, Arnold, *Those United States* (London: Martin Secker, 1912).
Berger, Molly W., 'A House Divided: The Culture of the American Luxury Hotel, 1825–1860', in *His and Hers: Gender, Consumption, and Technology*, ed. Roger Horowitz (Charlottesville, VA: University Press of Virginia, 1998), pp. 39–65.

Berger, Molly W., *Hotel Dreams: Luxury, Technology, and Urban Ambition in America, 1829–1929* (Baltimore, MD: Johns Hopkins University Press, 2011).

Berman, Marshall, *All That Is Solid Melts into Air: The Experience of Modernity* (London: Verso, 1983).

Bertarelli, L. V., *Northern Italy: From the Alps to Rome*, ed. Findlay Muirhead (London: Macmillan, 1924).

'Bigelow-Harford', *New-York Tribune*, 12 June 1921, p. 90.

Bishop, Isabella Bird, *The Englishwoman in America* (London: John Murray, 1856).

Black, Iain S., 'Spaces of Capital: Bank Office Building in the City of London, 1830–1870', 26 (3) *Journal of Historical Geography* (2000), pp. 351–75.

Blake, Peter, 'Charles Dickens, George Augustus Sala and *Household Words*', 26 *Dickens Quarterly* (March 2009), pp. 24–41.

Boomer, Lucius M., *Hotel Management: Principles and Practice* (New York and London: Harper, 1925).

Bowen, Elizabeth, *Afterthought: Pieces About Writing* (London: Longmans, 1962).

Bowen, Elizabeth, *Bowen's Court* (London: Longmans, 1964).

Bowen, Elizabeth, 'Dead Mabelle', in *Collected Stories* (London: Vintage, 1999).

Bowen, Elizabeth, 'Frankly Speaking: Interview, 1959', in *Listening In: Broadcasts, Speeches, and Interviews by Elizabeth Bowen*, ed. Allan Hepburn (Edinburgh: Edinburgh University Press, 2010), pp. 323–43.

Bowen, Elizabeth, *The Hotel* (London: Vintage, 2003).

Bowen, Elizabeth, *Love's Civil War: Elizabeth Bowen and Charles Ritchie: Letters and Diaries 1941–1973*, ed. Victoria Glendinning (Toronto: Emblem, 2009).

Bowen, Elizabeth, 'Modern Lighting', in *People, Places, Things: Essays by Elizabeth Bowen*, ed. Allan Hepburn (Edinburgh: Edinburgh University Press, 2008), pp. 26–7.

Bowen, Elizabeth, 'Notes on Writing a Novel', in *Pictures and Conversations* (London: Allen Lane, 1975), pp. 169–93.

Bowen, Elizabeth, 'Why I Go to the Cinema', in *Listening In: Broadcasts, Speeches, and Interviews by Elizabeth Bowen*, ed. Allan Hepburn (Edinburgh: Edinburgh University Press, 2010), pp. 192–202.

Bowman, John McEntee, 'How We Find What Will Sell Best', *System: The Magazine of Business* (April 1923), pp. 460–63 and 520–3.

Braddon, Mary Elizabeth, 'From Paddington to the Land's End', 27 *Belgravia* (August 1875), pp. 199–212.

Braddon, Mary Elizabeth, *Lady Audley's Secret*, ed. Lyn Pykett (Oxford: Oxford University Press, 2012).

Breitwieser, Mitchell, 'Jazz Fractures: F. Scott Fitzgerald and Epochal Representation', 12 (3) *American Literary History* (Autumn 2000), pp. 359–81.
British American Guide-Book: Being a Condensed Gazetteer, Directory and Guide, to Canada, the Western States, and Principal Cities on the Seaboard (New York: Bailliere, 1859).
Brown, Adrienne, *The Black Skyscraper: Architecture and the Perception of Race* (Baltimore, MD: Johns Hopkins University Press, 2017).
Browne, Junius Henri, *The Great Metropolis: A Mirror of New York* (Hartford, CT: American Publishing, 1869).
Brucken, Carolyn, 'In the Public Eye: Women and the American Luxury Hotel', 31 (4) *Winterthur Portfolio* (Winter 1996), pp. 203–20.
Buckingham Hotel, Fifth Avenue, New York (New York: Buckingham Hotel, 1877).
Buelens, Gert, 'Henry James's Oblique Possession: Plottings of Desire and Mastery in *The American Scene*', 16 (2) *PMLA* (March 2001), pp. 300–13.
Caddy, Florence, *Lares and Penates: or, The Background of Life* (London: Chatto & Windus, 1881).
'Call Out 500 from Two More Hotels', *New York Times*, 10 November 1918, p. 12.
Campbell, C. Lawton., 'The Fitzgeralds Were My Friends', 10 *Fitzgerald/ Hemmingway Annual* (1978), pp. 37–54.
'Carlton Hotel, Limited', 3298 *The Economist*, 10 November 1906, p. 1837.
'Carlton Hotel, Limited', 3350 *The Economist*, 9 November 1907, p. 1934.
'Carlton Hotel (Limited): A Record Year', *The Times*, 27 November 1919, p. 25.
Carter, Oliver, *An Illustrated History of British Railway Hotels: 1838–1983* (St Michael's: Silver Link, 1990).
Cather, Willa, 'The Novel Démeublé', 30 *New Republic* (12 April 1922), pp. 5–6.
Chase, Karen and Michael Levenson, *The Spectacle of Intimacy: A Public Life for the Victorian Family* (Princeton, NJ and Oxford: Princeton University Press, 2000).
Cheng, Anne Anlin, *Second Skin: Josephine Baker and the Modern Surface* (Oxford and New York: Oxford University Press, 2011).
Choi, Tina Young, *Anonymous Connections: The Body and Narratives of the Social in Victorian Britain* (Ann Arbor, MI: University of Michigan Press, 2015).
Christensen, Jerome, *America's Corporate Art: The Studio Authorship of Hollywood Motion Pictures* (Stanford, CA: Stanford University Press, 2012).
Clark, Peter, *The English Alehouse: A Social History, 1200–1830* (London: Longman, 1983).

Cleere, Eileen, 'Victorian Dust Traps', in *Filth: Dirt, Disgust and Modern Life*, eds William Cohen and Ryan Johnson (Minneapolis, MN: University of Minnesota Press, 2005), pp. 133–54.
'Club Life in New York', *New York Times*, 8 November 1885, p. 6.
Clymer, Jeffory A., 'The Market in Male Bodies: Henry James's *The American* and Late-Nineteenth-Century Boxing', 25 (2) *Henry James Review* (Spring 2004), pp. 127–45.
Collini, Stefan, *Public Moralists: Political Thought and Intellectual Life in Britain, 1850–1930* (Oxford: Clarendon Press, 1991).
Collins' Guide to London and Neighbourhood (London: William Collins, 1880).
Collins, Wilkie. *Basil* (Oxford: Oxford University Press, 2008).
Collins, Wilkie, *The Haunted Hotel*, in *Miss or Mrs? – The Haunted Hotel – The Guilty River*, eds Norman Page and Toru Sasaki (Oxford: Oxford University Press, 2008), pp. 85–240.
'Comparison of a Hotel Manager with Other Modern Mercantile Magnates', *Hotel World* (July 1897), p. 13.
Conan Doyle, Arthur, *The Hound of the Baskervilles* (London: George Newnes, 1902).
Conrad, Peter, *The Art of the City: Views and Versions of New York* (New York and Oxford: Oxford University Press, 1984).
Cook, Clarence, *The House Beautiful: Essays on Beds and Tables, Stools and Candlesticks* (New York: Scribner, Armstrong and Company, 1878).
Corcoran, Neil, *Elizabeth Bowen: The Enforced Return* (Oxford and New York: Oxford University Press, 2004).
'Cork Street and Savile Row Area: Introduction', in *Survey of London: Volumes 31 and 32, St James Westminster, Part 2*, ed. F. H. W. Sheppard (London: London County Council, 1963), pp. 442–55.
Coulson, Victoria, *Henry James, Women and Realism* (Cambridge: Cambridge University Press, 2007).
Coulson, Victoria, 'Prisons, Palaces, and the Architecture of the Imagination', in *Palgrave Advances in Henry James Studies*, ed. Peter Rawlings (London: Palgrave Macmillan, 2007), pp. 169–91.
Coulson, Victoria, 'Sticky Realism: Armchair Hermeneutics in Late James', 25 (2) *Henry James Review* (Spring 2004), pp. 115–26.
Cox, Jim, *American Radio Networks: A History* (Jefferson, NC: McFarland, 2009).
'Crowds Watch Bulletins', *New-York Tribune*, 14 September 1901, p. 9.
'Crystal Room of the Ritz-Carlton', *New-York Tribune*, 27 November 1921, p. 4.
Curtiss, Philip. 'When Is a Ford Not a Ford?' 145 (867) *Harper's* (August 1922), pp. 407–10.
Daly, Nicholas, 'Railway Novels: Sensation Fiction and the Modernization of the Senses', 66 (2) *ELH* (Summer 1999), pp. 461–87.

Davidson, Lisa Pfueller, 'Early Twentieth-Century Hotel Architects and the Origins of Standardization', 25 *Journal of Decorative and Propaganda Arts* (2005), pp. 9–37.

Davidson, Robert A., *The Hotel: Occupied Space* (Toronto: University of Toronto Press, 2018).

Dearing, Albin Pasteur, *The Elegant Inn* (Secaucus, NJ: Lyle Stuart, 1986).

Defoe, Daniel, *Robinson Crusoe*, eds Thomas Keymer and James Kelly (Oxford and New York: Oxford University Press, 2007).

Denby, Elaine, *Grand Hotels: Reality and Illusion* (London: Reaktion Books, 1998).

A Description of Tremont House (Boston: Gray & Bowen, 1830).

Despotopoulou, Anna, 'Monuments of an Artless Age: Hotels and Women's Mobility in the Work of Henry James', 59 (4) *Studies in the Novel* (Winter 2018), pp. 501–22.

Dickens, Charles, *American Notes for General Circulation*, eds John S. Whitley and Arnold Goldman (Penguin: Harmondsworth, 1972).

Dickens, Charles, *Martin Chuzzlewit*, ed. Margaret Cardwell (Oxford: Clarendon Press, 1982).

Dickens, Charles, 'An Unsettled Neighbourhood', *Selected Journalism: 1850–1870* (London: Penguin, 1997).

Domosh, Mona, *Invented Cities: The Creation of Landscape in Nineteenth-Century New York and Boston* (New Haven, CT: Yale University Press, 1996).

Doyle, Mary, *Life Was Like That* (Boston and New York: Houghton Mifflin, 1936), p. 49.

Drabble, Margaret, *Arnold Bennett: A Biography* (New York: Alfred A. Knopf, 1974).

Eberlein, H. Donaldson and Abbot McClure, 'The Modern Hotel and Its Furniture', *Good Furniture* (May 1916), pp. 273–94.

Eisner, Lotte H., *Murnau* (London: Secker & Warburg, 1973).

Eisner, Lotte H., *The Haunted Screen: Expressionism in the German Cinema and the Influence of Max Reinhardt*, trans. Roger Greaves (Berkeley, CA and Los Angeles: University of California Press, 2008).

Eliot, George. *Adam Bede* (Oxford: Oxford University Press, 1996).

Ellison, David A., 'Mobile Homes, Fallen Furniture, and the Dickens Cure', 108 (1) *South Atlantic Quarterly* (2009), pp. 87–114.

Ellmann, Maud, *Elizabeth Bowen: The Shadow across the Page* (Edinburgh: Edinburgh University Press, 2004).

Ellmann, Maud, *The Nets of Modernism: Henry James, Virginia Woolf, James Joyce, and Sigmund Freud* (Cambridge: Cambridge University Press, 2010).

'Enamolin', 29 (4) *House and Garden* (April 1916), p. 81.

'Encaustic Tiles', *New-York Tribune Illustrated Supplement*, 7 November 1897, p. 13.
'English Hotels', *The Standard*, 24 August 1878, p. 2.
'Farmyard on a Hotel Roof', *New York Times*, 31 August 1913, p. 9.
'Fashion in Review Exhibits Eyelashes: Aside From This Artificiality, There Is a Display of Chinese Bathing Suits', *New York Times*, 27 February 1921, p. 15.
'Fatima', *New-York Tribune*, 20 February 1920, p. 10.
Feigel, Lara, *Literature, Cinema and Politics, 1930–1945: Reading Between the Frames* (Edinburgh: Edinburgh University Press, 2010).
Fern, Fanny, 'City Scenes and City Life: Number Three', in *Fern Leaves from Fanny's Portfolio: Second Series* (Auburn and Buffalo, NY: Miller, Orton & Mulligan, 1854), pp. 322–5.
Fern, Fanny, *Ginger-Snaps* (New York: Carleton, 1870).
Fitzgerald, F. Scott, *The Beautiful and Damned*, ed. James L. W. West (Cambridge: Cambridge University Press, 2008).
Fitzgerald, F. Scott, 'The Diamond as Big as the Ritz', in *Tales of the Jazz Age*, ed. James L. W. West (Cambridge: Cambridge University Press, 2002), pp. 127–68.
Fitzgerald, F. Scott, *F. Scott Fitzgerald on Authorship*, eds Matthew J. Bruccoli and Judith Baughman (Columbia, SC: University of South Carolina, 1996).
Fitzgerald, F. Scott, 'The Freshest Boy', in *The Basil, Josephine, and Gwen Stories*, ed. James L. W. West (Cambridge: Cambridge University Press, 2009), pp. 55–77.
Fitzgerald, F. Scott, *The Great Gatsby*, ed. Matthew J. Bruccoli (Cambridge: Cambridge University Press, 1991).
Fitzgerald, F. Scott, 'May Day', in *Tales of the Jazz Age*, ed. James L. W. West (Cambridge: Cambridge University Press, 2002), pp. 61–114.
Fitzgerald, F. Scott, 'My Lost City', in *My Lost City: Personal Essays, 1920–1940*, ed. James L. W. West (Cambridge: Cambridge University Press, 2005), pp. 106–15.
Fitzgerald, F. Scott, 'Ten Years in the Advertising Business', in *Last Kiss*, ed. James L. W. West (Cambridge: Cambridge University Press, 2017), pp. 414–15.
Fitzgerald, F. Scott, *This Side of Paradise*, ed. James L. W. West (Cambridge: Cambridge University Press, 1995).
'Floor-Cloth', *Chambers's Encyclopaedia: Volume IV* (London: Chambers, 1874), p. 379.
Foltz, Jonathan, *The Novel after Film: Modernism and the Decline of Autonomy* (Oxford: Oxford University Press, 2018).
Forster, E. M., *A Room with a View*, ed. Malcolm Bradbury (New York and London: Penguin, 2000).

Frank, Lawrence, *Charles Dickens and the Romantic Self* (Lincoln, NB: Nebraska University Press, 1984).
Franko, Mark, *The Work of Dance: Labor, Movement, and Identity in the 1930s* (Middletown, CT: Wesleyan University Press, 2002).
Freedgood, Elaine, *The Ideas in Things: Fugitive Meaning in the Victorian Novel* (Chicago and London: University of Chicago Press, 2006).
'Future Unfolds as Radio Show Opens on Roof', *New York Tribune*, 8 March 1922, p. 22.
Gatewood, William B., *Aristocrats of Color: The Black Elite 1880–1920* (Fayetteville, AR: University of Arkansas Press, 2000).
Gilmore, Garrett Bridger, 'Refracting Blackness: Slavery and Fitzgerald's Historical Consciousness', 70/71 (2) *Mississippi Quarterly* (Spring 2017), pp. 181–203.
'Gimbels', *New York Times*, 26 July 1915, p. 5.
Glendinning, Victoria, *Elizabeth Bowen: Portrait of a Writer* (London: Weidenfeld & Nicolson, 1977).
Goble, Mark, *Beautiful Circuits: Modernism and the Mediated Life* (New York: Columbia University Press, 2010).
Goble, Mark, 'Delirious Henry James: A Small Boy and New York', 50 (2) *MFS Modern Fiction Studies* (2004), pp. 351–84.
Godden, Richard, 'A Diamond Bigger Than the Ritz: F Scott Fitzgerald and the Gold Standard', 77 *ELH* (2010), pp. 589–613.
Google Ngram Viewer, '([hotelkeeping] + [hotel – keeping] + [hotel keeping]), [hotel management]', 1850–1950 in English (2019).
Green, Henry, *Party Going* (London: Hogarth Press, 1962).
Greene, Lorenzo J. and Carter G. Woodson, *The Negro Wage Earner* (Washington, DC: Association for the Study of Negro Life and History, 1930).
Greene, Lorenzo J. and Myra Colson Callis, *The Employment of Negroes in the District of Columbia* (Washington, DC: Association for the Study of Negro Life and History, 1936).
'The Grosvenor Hotel', *The Builder*, 1 June 1861, p. 375.
'Growth of Hotel Luxury', *The Evening World*, 27 July 1904, p. 10.
Gumbrecht, Hans Ulrich, *In 1926: Living at the Edge of Time* (Cambridge, MA and London: Harvard University Press, 1997).
Gunning, Tom, *The Films of Fritz Lang: Allegories of Vision and Modernity* (London: British Film Institute, 2000).
Gunning, Tom, 'Landscape and the Fantasy of Moving Pictures: Early Cinema's Phantom Rides', in *Cinema and Landscape*, eds Graeme Harper and Jonathan Rayner (Bristol and Chicago: Intellect, 2010), pp. 31–70.
Hall, N. John, *Max Beerbohm Caricatures* (New Haven, CT: Yale University Press, 1997).

Halttunen, Karen, *Confidence Men and Painted Women: A Study of Middle-class Culture in America, 1830–1870* (New Haven, CT: Yale University Press, 1982).

Hamilton, Gail, 'The Hotel of the Future', 11 (1) *Scribner's Monthly* (November 1875), pp. 108–12.

Hanlon, Bernadette, John R. Short and Thomas J. Vicino, *Cities and Suburbs: New Metropolitan Realities in the US* (Oxford and New York: Routledge, 2010).

Hannah, Daniel, '"Massed Ambiguity": Fatness in Henry James's *The Ivory Tower*', 53 (4) *Twentieth Century Literature* (Winter 2007), pp. 460–87.

Haralson, Eric, 'James's *The American*: A (New)man is Being Beaten', 64 (3) *American Literature* (September 1992), pp. 475–95.

Hart, Clive, 'The Structure and Technique of *Party Going*', 1 *Yearbook of English Studies* (1971), pp. 185–99.

Hawthorne, Nathaniel, *The Blithedale Romance* (Boston: Ticknor, Reed, & Fields, 1852).

Hay, James. 'Revisiting the Grand Hotel (and Its Place within the Cultural Economy of Fascist Italy)', in David B. Clarke and Marcus A. Doel, *Moving Pictures/Stopping Places: Hotels and Motels on Film*, eds David B. Clarke, Valerie Crawford Pfannhauser and Marcus A. Doel (Lanham, MD: Lexington Books, 2009), pp. 13–48.

Hayner, Norman S., 'Hotel Life and Personality', 33 (5) *American Journal of Sociology* (March, 1928), pp. 784–95.

Heynickx, Rajesh, 'Tracing Tracks: Illusion and Reality at Work in the Lobby', in *Hotel Lobbies and Lounges: The Architecture of Professional Hospitality*, eds Anne Massey and Tom Avermaete (Abingdon and New York: Routledge, 2013), pp. 103–18.

Hilton, Timothy, *John Ruskin* (New Haven, CT and London: Yale University Press, 2002).

Hirsch, Jeff, *Manhatten Hotels: 1880–1920* (Charleston, SC: Arcadia Publishing, 1997).

Hitchcock, Alfred, 'An Autocrat of the Film Studio', in *Hitchcock on Hitchcock, Volume 2: Selected Writings and Interviews*, ed. Sidney Gottlieb (Berkeley, CA: University of California Press, 2015), pp. 116–23.

Hitchcock, Alfred, 'Films We Could Make', in *Hitchcock on Hitchcock, Volume 1: Selected Writings and Interviews*, ed. Sidney Gottlieb (Berkeley, CA: University of California Press, 1995), pp. 165–7.

Hochschild, Arlie Russell, *The Managed Heart: Commercialization of Human Feeling* (Berkeley, CA: University of California Press, 2012).

hoogland, renée c, *Elizabeth Bowen: A Reputation in Writing* (New York and London: New York University Press, 1994).

Hornby, Louise, 'Downwrong: The Pose of Tiredness', 65 (1) *Modern Fiction Studies* (2019), pp. 207–27.

'Hotel Hygiene', *Scientific American Supplement*, 963, 16 June 1894, p. 15393.

'Hotel Syndicate Plans Big Merger', 8 (19) *New York Hotel Record*, 14 June 1910, p. 4.

'Hotels', *Chambers's Journal of Popular Literature, Science and Art*, 30 May 1863, p. 345–8.

House of Commons Select Committee on Joint Stock Companies, *First Report of the Select Committee on Joint Stock Companies, Together with the Minutes of Evidence (taken in 1841 and 1843), Appendix, and Index* (1844).

Houston, Gail Turley, *From Dickens to Dracula: Gothic, Economics, and Victorian Fiction* (Cambridge: Cambridge University Press, 2005).

Howard, Blanche Willis, *Tony, The Maid: A Novelette* (New York: Harper, 1887).

Howard, Vicki, *From Main Street to Mall: The Rise and Fall of the American Department Store* (Philadelphia, PA: University of Pennsylvania Press, 2015).

'Hull and Holderness Railway', *Herapath's Journal*, 12 January 1856, p. 48.

Iarocci, Louisa, *The Urban Department Store in America, 1850–1930* (Farnham: Ashgate, 2014).

Illustrated Guide to London and Neighbourhood (London: William Collins, 1875).

Ingram, Paul and Joel A. C. Baum, 'Chain Affiliation and the Failure of Manhattan Hotels, 1898–1980', 42 (1) *Administrative Science Quarterly* (March 1997), pp. 68–102.

Ireland, Paddy, 'Capitalism without the Capitalist: The Joint Stock Company Share and the Emergence of the Modern Doctrine of Separate Corporate Personality', 17 (1) *Journal of Legal History* (1996), pp. 41–73.

Jakle John A. and Keith A. Sculle, *America's Main Street Hotels: Transiency and Community in the Early Auto Age* (Knoxville, TN: University of Tennessee Press, 2009).

Jakle, John A. and Keith A. Sculle, *The Gas Station in America* (Baltimore, MD: Johns Hopkins University Press, 1994).

Jakle, John A., Keith A. Schulle and Jefferson S. Rogers, *The Motel in America* (Baltimore, MD: Johns Hopkins University Press, 1996).

James, Henry, *The Ambassadors* (London: Methuen, 1903).

James, Henry, *The American*, in *Novels: 1871–1880*, ed. William T. Stafford (New York: Library of America, 1983).

James, Henry, *The American Scene*, in *Collected Travel Writings: Great Britain and America*, ed. Richard Howard (New York: Library of America, 1993).

James, Henry, *The Bostonians*, in *Novels: 1881–1886*, ed. William T. Stafford (New York: Library of America, 1985).

James, Henry, *The Complete Notebooks of Henry James*, eds Leon Edel and Lyall H. Powers (Oxford and New York: Oxford University Press, 1987).

James, Henry 'Daisy Miller: A Study', in *Complete Stories: 1874–1884*, ed. by William L. Vance (New York: Library of America, 1999), pp. 238–95.

James, Henry, 'Daisy Miller', in *Daisy Miller, Pandora, Patagonia, and Other Tales* (New York: Charles Scribner's Sons, 1909), pp. 1–94.

James, Henry, 'An English Winter Watering-place', in *Collected Travel Writings: Great Britain and America*, ed. Richard Howard (New York: Library of America, 1993).

James, Henry, 'The Future of the Novel', in *Literary Criticism: Essays on Literature, American Writers, English Writers*, eds Leon Edel and Mark Wilson (New York: Library of America, 1984).

James, Henry, 'Gabriele D'Annunzio', in *Literary Criticism: French Writers, Other European Writers, The Prefaces to the New York Edition*, eds Leon Edel and Mark Wilson (New York: Library of America, 1984).

James, Henry, 'Guest's Confession', in *Complete Stories: 1864–1874*, ed. Jean Strouse (New York: Library of America, 1999).

James, Henry, *Henry James: A Life in Letters*, ed. Philip Horne (London: Allen Lane, 1999).

James, Henry, 'An International Episode', in *Complete Stories: 1874–1884*, ed. William L. Vance (New York: Library of America, 1999), pp. 326–400.

James, Henry, *Italian Hours*, in *Collected Travel Writings: The Continent*, ed. Richard Howard (New York: Library of America, 1993).

James, Henry, *Letters: Volume 1, 1843–1875*, ed. Leon Edel (Cambridge, MA: Harvard University Press, 1984).

James, Henry, *Letters: Volume 4, 1895–1916*, ed. Leon Edel (Cambridge, MA: Harvard University Press, 1984).

James, Henry, 'London', in *Collected Travel Writings: Great Britain and America*, ed. Richard Howard (New York: Library of America, 1993).

James, Henry, 'Newport', in *Collected Travel Writings: Great Britain and America*, ed. Richard Howard (New York: Library of America, 1993).

James, Henry, 'Pandora', in *Complete Stories: 1874–1884*, ed. William L. Vance (New York: Library of America, 1999), pp. 816–64.

James, Henry, *Parisian Sketches: Letters to the New York Tribune, 1875–1876*, eds Leon Edel and Ilse Dusoir Lind (London: Rupert Hart-Davis, 1958).

James, Henry, 'A Passionate Pilgrim', in *Complete Stories: 1864–1874*, ed. Jean Strouse (New York: Library of America, 1999).

James, Henry, *The Portrait of a Lady*, vol. 1 (New York: Charles Scribner's Sons, 1908).

James, Henry, *The Portrait of a Lady*, in *Novels: 1881–1886*, ed. William T. Stafford (New York: Library of America, 1985).

James, Henry, *Prefaces*, in *Literary Criticism: French Writers; Other European Writers; The Prefaces to the New York Edition*, eds Leon Edel and Mark Wilson (New York: Library of America, 1984).

James, Henry, *The Reverberator*, in *Novels: 1886–1890*, ed. Daniel Mark Fogel (New York: Library of America, 1989).

James, Henry, *The Reverberator*, in *The Reverberator, Madame de Mauves, A Passionate Pilgrim, and Other Tales* (New York: Charles Scribner's Sons, 1908), pp. 1–212.

James, Henry, *Roderick Hudson*, in *Novels: 1871–1880*, ed. William T. Stafford (New York: Library of America, 1983).

James, Henry, 'A Round of Visits', in *Complete Stories: 1898–1910*, ed. Denis Donoghue (New York: Library of America, 1996), pp. 896–924.

James, Henry, 'Saratoga', in *Collected Travel Writings: Great Britain and America*, ed. Richard Howard (New York: Library of America, 1993).

James, Henry, *A Small Boy and Others* (New York: Charles Scribner's Sons, 1913).

James, Henry, *The Tragic Muse*, in *Novels: 1886–1890*, ed. Daniel Mark Fogel. New York: Library of America, 1989).

James, Henry, *Watch and Ward* in *Novels: 1871–1880*, ed. William T. Stafford (New York: Library of America, 1983).

James, Henry, *What Maisie Knew*, in *Novels: 1896–1899*, ed. Myra Jehlen (New York: Library of America, 2003).

James, Henry, *The Wings of the Dove*, in *Novels: 1901–1902*, ed. Leo Bersani (New York: Library of America, 2006).

James, Kevin J., 'Afterword', in *Anglo-American Travelers and the Hotel Experience in Nineteenth-Century Literature*, eds Monika M. Elbert and Susanne Schmid (New York and London: Routledge, 2018), pp. 269–82.

James, Kevin J., 'Aliens, Subjects and the State: Surveillance in British Hotels during World War I', 36 (3) *Immigrants and Minorities* (2018), pp. 199–231.

James, Kevin J., A. K. Sandoval-Strausz, Daniel Maudlin, Maurizio Peleggi, Cédric Humair and Molly W. Berger, 'The Hotel in History: Evolving Perspectives', 9 (1) *Journal of Tourism History* (2017), pp. 92–111.

James, M. E., *How to Decorate Our Ceilings, Walls and Floors* (London: George Bell, 1883).

James, William and Henry James, *William and Henry James: Selected Letters*, eds Ignas K. Skrupskelis and Elizabeth M. Berkeley (Charlottesville, VA: University of Virginia Press, 1997).

'Japanese Garden Atop Hotel Astor', *New York Times*, 4 March 1923, p. 14.

Jarzombek, Mark, 'Corridor Spaces', 36 (4) *Critical Inquiry* (Summer 2010), pp. 728–70.

Johnson, Marilyn, 'Art Furniture: Wedding the Beautiful to the Useful', in *Pursuit of Beauty: Americans and the Aesthetic Movement*, ed. Doreen Bolger Burke (New York: Metropolitan Museum of Art, 1986), pp. 143–75.

'Joint-Stock Speculations: Their Value and Prospects. No. VII. – Hotel Companies', *The London Review of Politics, Society, Literature, Art, and Science*, 11, 12 August 1865, pp. 169–70.

Kaszynski, William, *The American Highway: The History and Culture of Roads in the United States*, (Jefferson, NC: McFarland, 2000).

Katz, Marc, 'The Hotel Kracauer', 11 (2) *Differences* (1999), pp. 134–52.

Kellett, John R., *The Impact of Railways on Victorian Cities* (London: Routledge & Kegan Paul, 1969).

Klimasmith, Betsy, *At Home in the City: Urban Domesticity in American Literature and Culture 1850–1930* (Hanover, NH: University of New Hampshire Press, 2005).

Knight, Peter, *Reading the Market: Genres of Financial Capitalism in Gilded Age America* (Baltimore, MD: Johns Hopkins University Press, 2016).

Koolhaas, Rem, *Delirious New York: A Retroactive Manifesto for Manhattan* (New York: Monacelli Press, 1994).

Kornbluh, Anna, *Realizing Capital: Financial and Psychic Economies in Victorian Form* (New York: Fordham University Press, 2014).

Kracauer, Siegfried, 'The Hotel Lobby', in *The Mass Ornament: Weimar Essays*, ed. and trans. by Thomas Y. Levin (Cambridge, MA: Harvard University Press, 1995), pp. 173–85.

Kreimeier, Klaus, *The Ufa Story: A History of Germany's Greatest Film Company, 1918–1945* (Berkeley, CA and London: University of California Press, 1999).

Lafourcade, Georges, *Arnold Bennett: A Study* (London: Frederick Muller, 1939).

Lamonaca, Marianne and Jonathan Mogul (eds) *Grand Hotels of the Jazz Age: The Architecture of Schultze & Weaver* (New York: Princeton Architectural Press, 2005).

Lapointe, Julie, 'Les Sociétés Anonymes à Vocation Hôtelière de l'Arc Lémanique (1826–1914)', in *Le Dlient de l'Architecte. Du Notable à la Société Immobilière: Les Mutations du Maître de l'Ouvrage en Suisse au XIXe Siècle*, ed. Dave Lüthi (Lausanne: Études de Lettres, 2010), pp. 211–40.

Lasky, Jesse L., 'What Kind of a "Menace" Are the Movies?', 212 (776) *North American Review* (July 1920), pp. 88–92.

Lassner, Phyllis, 'Out of the Shadows: The Newly Collected Elizabeth Bowen', 17 (3) *Modernism/Modernity* (2010), pp. 669–76.

Lee, Hermione, *Elizabeth Bowen* (London: Vintage, 1999).

Lee, Vernon, *Hortus Vitae: Essays on the Gardening of Life* (London and New York: John Lane, 1904).

Leigh, R., 'Securing Apartment House Tenants through National Advertising', 27 *Advertising and Selling* (December 1917), p. 13.
Levine, Caroline, *Forms: Whole, Rhythm, Hierarchy, Network* (Princeton, NJ: Princeton University Press, 2015).
Lewes, G. H., 'Recent Novels, French and English', 36 *Fraser's Magazine* (1846), pp. 686–95.
Lewis, R. W. B., *The Jameses: A Family Narrative* (New York: Farrar, Straus, Giroux, 1991).
Lewis, Sinclair, *Work of Art* (New York: P. F. Collier, 1934).
Ling, Sally J. *A History of Boca Raton* (Charleston, SC: History Press, 2007).
Logan, Thad, *The Victorian Parlour: A Cultural Study* (Cambridge: Cambridge University Press, 2001).
London and Its Environs: A Practical Guide to the Metropolis and Its Vicinity (Edinburgh: Adam & Charles Black, 1862).
Loos, Adolf, 'Ornament and Crime', in *Ornament and Crime: Selected Essays*, trans. Michael Mitchell (Riverside, CA: Ariadne Press, 1998), pp. 167–76.
Luckhurst, Roger, *Corridors: Passages of Modernity* (London: Reaktion Books, 2019).
Lustig, T. J., *Henry James and the Ghostly* (Cambridge: Cambridge University Press, 1994).
Luria, Sarah, 'The Architecture of Manners: Henry James, Edith Wharton and The Mount', in *Domestic Space: Reading the Nineteenth-Century Interior*, eds Igna Bryden and Janet Floyd (Manchester: Manchester University Press, 1999), pp. 186–210.
McCleery, Alistair. 'The Paperback Evolution: Tauchnitz, Albatross and Penguin', in *Judging a Book by Its Cover: Fans, Publishers, Designers, and the Marketing of Fiction*, eds Nicole Matthews and Nickianne Moody (Aldershot: Ashgate, 2007), pp. 3–18.
MacGregor, William Laird, 'Hotel Life in San Francisco', 27 *Victoria Magazine* (May–October 1876), pp. 525–6.
McGurl, Mark, 'Making It Big: Picturing the Radio Age in *King Kong*', 22 (3) *Critical Inquiry* (Spring, 1996), pp. 415–55.
McKibbin, Ross, *Classes and Cultures: England 1918–1951* (Oxford and New York: Oxford University Press, 2008).
McNamara, Kevin R., *Urban Verbs: Arts and Discourses of American Cities* (Stanford, CA: Stanford University Press, 1996).
McWeeny, Gage, *The Comfort of Strangers: Social Life and Literary Form* (Oxford: Oxford University Press, 2016).
Marchand, Roland, *Advertising the American Dream: Making Way for Modernity, 1920–1940* (Berkeley, CA: University of California Press, 1985).

Marchand, Roland, *Creating the Corporate Soul: The Rise of Public Relations and Corporate Imagery in American Big Business* (Berkeley, CA: University of California Press, 2001).

Markus, Thomas A., *Buildings and Power: Freedom and Control in the Origin of Modern Building Types* (London: Routledge, 1993).

Marshall, Kate, *Corridor: Media Architectures in American Fiction* (Minneapolis, MN and London: University of Minnesota Press, 2013).

Meehan, Adam, 'Repetition, Race, and Desire in *The Great Gatsby*', 37 (2) *Journal of Modern Literature* (Winter 2014), pp. 76–91.

Mellor, Leo, *Reading the Ruins: Modernism, Bombsites and British Culture* (Cambridge: Cambridge University Press, 2011).

Mengham, Rod, *The Idiom of Time: The Writings of Henry Green* (Cambridge and New York: Cambridge University Press, 1982).

Menne, Jeff, *Post-Fordist Cinema: Hollywood Auteurs and the Corporate Counterculture* (New York: Columbia University Press, 2019).

Mennell, Stephen, *All Manners of Food: Eating and Taste in England and France from the Middle Ages to the Present* (Champaign, IL: Illini Books, 1996).

'Metro-Goldwyn-Mayer [1932]' in *The American Film Industry*, ed. Tino Balio (Madison, WI: University of Wisconsin Press, 1979), pp. 311–33.

Miller, Andrew H., 'The Discourse of Liability in the Joint Stock Companies Act of 1856 and Gaskell's *Cranford*', 61 (1) *ELH* (1994), pp. 139–57.

Milthorpe, Naomi, 'Things and Nothings: Henry Green and the Late Modernist Banal', 50 (1) *Novel: A Forum on Fiction* (2017), pp. 97–111.

M. N. S., 'How to Keep an Inn', *The Nation*, 16 June 1887, p. 508.

Monfried, Walter, 'Swank, by Ritz: Swiss Peasant Lad Introduced World to Luxury in Hotels', *Decatur Herald*, 16 October 1939, p. 4.

Montgomery, Maureen E., 'Henry James and "The Testimony of the Hotel" to Transatlantic Encounters', in *Anglo-American Travelers and the Hotel Experience in Nineteenth-Century Literature*, eds Monika M. Elbert and Susanne Schmid (New York and London: Routledge, 2018), pp. 140–65.

Montgomery-Massingberd, Hugh and David Watkin, *The London Ritz: A Social and Architectural History* (London: Aurum, 1980).

Moore, Robbie, 'Corporate Space', in *The Routledge Companion to Literature and Economics*, eds Matt Seybold and Michelle Chihara (New York: Routledge, 2019), pp. 210–18.

'Mr. Wilde on Decorative Art: An Outline of his Observations in Wallack's Theatre Yesterday', *New York Times*, 12 May 1882, p. 8.

Nash, John, 'Arnold Bennett and Home Management: Domestic Efficiency', 59 (2) *English Literature in Transition, 1880–1920* (2016), pp. 210–33.

Nearing, Scott, *Black America* (New York: Vanguard Press, 1929).

'Negro Help for Hotels', *Boston Globe*, 31 May 1912, p. 9.

'Negro Waiters in Best Hotels', *New York Age*, 6 June 1912, p. 1.

Neocleous, Mark, *Imagining the State* (Maidenhead: Open University Press, 2003).

'A New Hotel on 5th Avenue', *The Sun* (New York), 3 September 1908, p. 1.

'New Ritz-Carlton Formally Opened', *New York Times*, 15 December 1910, p. 9.

'A New Toilet Companion', *New-York Tribune*, 7 July 1918, p. 12.

'New York's Amateur Show', *Wireless Age* (April 1922), p. 17.

Ngai, Sianne, *Our Aesthetic Categories: Zany, Cute, Interesting* (Cambridge, MA: Harvard University Press, 2012).

Nies, Betsy, *Eugenic Fantasies: Racial Ideology in the Literature and Popular Culture of the 1920s* (New York: Routledge, 2002).

'No Paintings in New Plaza Hotel. Manager Says Patrons These Days Have a Preference for Simplicity', *New-York Daily Tribune*, 1 August 1907, p. 7.

'No Ritz Hotel Here: European Restaurateur Will Not Permit His Name to be Used', *New York Times*, 9 July 1908, p. 1.

Nye, David E., 'The Sublime and the Skyline: The New York Skyscraper', in *The American Skyscraper: Cultural Histories*, ed. Roberta Moudry (Cambridge: Cambridge University Press, 2005), pp. 255–70.

O'Brien, John, *Literature Incorporated: The Cultural Unconscious of the Business Corporation, 1650–1850* (Chicago: University of Chicago Press, 2016).

O'Farrell, Mary Ann, 'Manners', in *Henry James in Context*, ed. David McWhirter (Cambridge: Cambridge University Press, 2010), pp. 192–202.

Oldbuck, Jonathan, 'Attendance Included in the Bill', *Morning Post*, 2 July 1863, p. 3.

Osmundson, Theodore, *Roof Gardens: History, Design, and Construction* (New York: Norton, 1999).

Otten, Thomas, *A Superficial Reading of Henry James: Preoccupations with the Material World* (Columbus, OH: Ohio State University Press, 2006).

Pascoe, Charles Eyre, *London of To-day: An Illustrated Handbook for the Season* (Boston: Roberts Brothers, 1888).

Penner, Barbara, '"Colleges for the Teaching of Extravagance": New York Palace Hotels', 44 (2/3) *Winterthur Portfolio* (Summer/Autumn 2010), pp. 159–92.

'Plans Chain of Hotels', *New-York Tribune*, 3 June 1910, p. 5.

Poe, Edgar Allan, 'The Business Man', in *Poetry and Tales*, ed. Patrick Quinn (New York: Library of America, 1984), pp. 373–81.

'Police', *The Times*, 18 March 1880, p. 2.

Poore, George Vivian, *The Dwelling House* (New York and Bombay: Longmans, 1897).

Poovey, Mary, *Genres of the Credit Economy: Mediating Value in Eighteenth- and Nineteenth-Century Britain* (Chicago: University of Chicago Press, 2008).

Pope, Rex, 'A Consumer Service in Interwar Britain: The Hotel Trade, 1924–1938', 74 (4) *Business History Review* (Winter, 2000), pp. 657–82.
Posnock, Ross, *The Trial of Curiosity: Henry James, William James, and the Challenge of Modernity* (New York and Oxford: Oxford University Press, 1991).
Price, Matlack, 'Great Modern Hotels of America: Architectural Distinction in the Ritz Hotels', 20 (3) *Arts and Decoration* (July 1924), pp. 39–41.
'Prominent Arrivals at the Hotels', *New York Tribune*, 3 January 1905, p. 11.
Proust, Marcel, *Within a Budding Grove*, trans. C. K. Scott Moncrieff (New York: Modern Library, 1951).
Purdon, James, *Modernist Informatics: Literature, Information, and the State* (Oxford: Oxford University Press, 2016).
'Quiet London Style for New Hotel Here', *New York Times*, 12 April 1908, p. 1.
Reichard, Ruth D. 'A "National Distemper": The National Hotel Sickness of 1857, Public Health and Sanitation, and the Limits of Rationality', 15 (3) *Journal of Planning History* (2016), pp. 175–90.
Richardson, Dorothy, 'Continuous Performance: Narcissus', in *Red Velvet Seat: Women's Writings on the First Fifty Years of Cinema*, eds Antonia Lant and Ingrid Periz (London and New York: Verso, 2006), pp. 237–9.
'Ritz-Carlton', *Evening Public Ledger* (Philadelphia), 3 June 1918, p. 3.
'The Ritz-Carlton Hotel', 5 (1) *New York Architect* (January 1911), pp. 8–11.
'The Ritz-Carlton Hotel, New York', 99 (1832) *American Architect* (February 1911), pp. 45–48.
'Ritz-Carlton Plans: Hotel to Cost "2,000,000"', *New-York Daily Tribune*, 11 July 1908, p. 13.
Ritz, Marie-Louise, *César Ritz: Host to the World* (London: George G. Harrap, 1938).
Robinson, John Beverley, *Architectural Composition: An Attempt to Order and Phrase Ideas which Hitherto Have Been Only Felt by the Instinctive Taste of Designers* (New York: Van Nostrand, 1908).
Rollins, Brooke, '"Some Kind of a Man": Orson Welles as *Touch of Evil*'s Masculine Auteur', 57 *Velvet Light Trap* (2006), pp. 32–41.
Ross, Shawna. 'The Two Hotels of Elizabeth Bowen: Utopian Leisure in the Age of Mechanized Hospitality', in *Utopianism, Modernism, and Literature in the Twentieth Century*, eds Alice Reeve-Tucker and Nathan Waddell (Basingstoke: Palgrave Macmillan, 2013), pp. 148–67.
Roth, Joseph, *Hotel Savoy*, trans. by John Hoare (London: Picador, 1988).
Rousseau, René, 'René Rousseau on Proust's Psychology and Art: *Le Mercure de France*, January 1922', in *Marcel Proust: The Critical Heritage*, ed. Leighton Hodson (London: Routledge, 1989), pp. 164–7.

Row, Jess, *White Flights: Race, Fiction, and the American Imagination* (Minneapolis, MN: Graywolf Press, 2019).
Rowe, John Carlos, 'Henry James in a New Century', in *A Companion to American Fiction, 1865–1914*, eds Robert Paul Lamb and G. R. Thompson (Malden, MA: Blackwell, 2005), pp. 518–35.
Rubery, Matthew, 'Wishing to Be Interviewed in Henry James's *The Reverberator*', 28 (1) *Henry James Review* (Winter 2007), pp. 57–72.
Sala, George Augustus, *London Up to Date* (London: Adam & Charles Black, 1895).
Sala, George Augustus, *My Diary in America in the Midst of War: Volume II* (London: Tinsley Brothers, 1865).
Salmon, Richard, *Henry James and the Culture of Publicity* (Cambridge: Cambridge University Press, 1997).
Saloman, Randi, 'Arnold Bennett's Hotels', 58 (1) *Twentieth Century Literature* (Spring 2012), pp. 1–25.
Sandoval-Strausz, A. K., *Hotel: An American History* (New Haven, CT and London: Yale University Press, 2007).
Sandoval-Strausz, A. K. and Daniel Levinson Wilk, 'Princes and Maids of the City Hotel: The Cultural Politics of Commercial Hospitality in America', in *Journal of Decorative and Propaganda Arts 25: The American Hotel*, ed. Molly W. Berger (June 2005), pp. 160–85.
'Sawtay', *Evening Public Ledger* (Philadelphia), 15 January 1918, p. 6.
Sayeau, Michael, 'Waiting', in *Restless Cities*, eds Matthew Beaumont and Gregory Dart (London: Verso, 2010), pp. 279–98.
Sayeau, Michael, 'Work, Unemployment, and the Exhaustion of Fiction in Heart of Darkness', 39 (3) *Novel* (2006), pp. 337–60.
Seaside Watering Places: Being a Guide to Strangers in Search of a Suitable Place in Which to Spend Their Holidays (London: The Bazaar, 1876).
Schlichting, Kurt, *Grand Central Terminal: Railroads, Engineering, and Architecture in New York City* (Baltimore, MD: Johns Hopkins University Press, 2001).
Seltzer, Mark, *Henry James and the Art of Power* (Ithaca, NY and London: Cornell University Press, 1984).
Sexton, Jamie, 'The Film Society and the Creation of an Alternative British Film Culture in the 1920s', in *Young and Innocent? Cinema and Britain 1896–1930*, ed. Andrew Higson (Exeter: Exeter University Press, 2002), pp. 291–305.
Shepley, Nick, *Henry Green: Class, Style, and the Everyday* (Oxford: Oxford University Press, 2016).
Sherwood, M. E. W., *The American Code of Manners: A Study of the Usages, Laws and Observances which Govern Intercourse in the Best Social Circles* (New York: W. R. Andrews, 1880).

Short, Emma, *Mobility and the Hotel in Modern Literature: Passing Through* (Cham: Palgrave, 2019).
Silver, Nathan, *Lost New York* (New York: Houghton Mifflin, 2000).
Silverman, Kaija, *The Acoustic Mirror: The Female Voice in Psychoanalysis and Cinema* (Bloomington, IN: Indiana University Press, 1988).
Simmons, Jack, *The Railway in Town and Country 1830–1914* (London: David & Charles, 1986).
Sinclair, May, *The Immortal Moment: The Story of Kitty Tailleur* (New York: Doubleday Page, 1908).
Sinclair, May, 'Where Their Fire Is Not Quenched', in *Uncanny Stories* (London: Hutchinson, 1923), pp. 9–38.
Smethurst, James, *The African American Roots of Modernism: From Reconstruction to the Harlem Renaissance* (Chapel Hill, NC: University of North Carolina Press, 2011).
Smith, Albert, *The English Hotel Nuisance* (London: David Bryce, 1855).
Solomon, Matthew, 'Up-to-Date Magic: Theatrical Conjuring and the Trick Film', 58 (4) *Theatre Journal* (2006), pp. 595–615.
Solomon, Stefan, *William Faulkner in Hollywood: Screenwriting for the Studios* (Athens, GA: University of Georgia Press, 2017).
Sterngass, Jon, *First Resorts: Pursuing Pleasure at Saratoga Springs, Newport, and Coney Island* (Baltimore, MD: Johns Hopkins University Press, 2001).
Standard Italian Travel Association, *The Standard Guide to Italy* (New York: Standard Italian Travel Association, 1912).
Strychacz, Thomas F., *Modernism, Mass Culture, and Professionalism* (Cambridge: Cambridge University Press, 1993).
Sweeney, George W., 'Geo. W. Sweeney, Representing the A.H.A. at the Monaco International Hotel Congress, Cites the Commodore as an Example of the Modern Large Hotel', 92 (17) *Hotel World* (April 1921), pp. 10–11.
Talairach-Vielmas, Laurence. 'Modern Phantasmagorias and Visual Culture in Wilkie Collins's *Basil*', in *Monstrous Media/Spectral Subjects: Imaging Gothic Fictions from the Nineteenth Century to the Present*, eds Fred Botting and Catherine Spooner (Manchester: Manchester University Press, 2015), pp. 56–72.
Tallack, Douglas, '"Waiting, Waiting": The Hotel Lobby in the Modern City', in *The Hieroglyphics of Space*, ed. Neil Leach (London: Routledge, 2002), pp. 139–51.
Taussig, Michael, 'Tactility and Distraction', in *Beyond the Body Proper: Reading the Anthropology of Material Life*, eds Margaret Lock and Judith Farquhar (Durham, NC: Duke University Press, 2007), pp. 259–65.
Taylor, Derek, *Fortune, Fame and Folly: British Hotels and Catering from 1878 to 1978* (Andover: Chapel River Press, 1977).

Taylor, James, *Creating Capitalism: Joint-Stock Enterprise in British Politics and Culture, 1800–1870* (London: Royal Historical Society, 2006).
'Telephone Men Justify Rates', *New York Times*, 5 February 1910, p. 8.
Thomas, Kate, *Postal Pleasures: Sex, Scandal, and Victorian Letters* (Oxford: Oxford University Press, 2012).
'To Inaugurate Roof Garden Tennis at the Ritz-Carlton', *New York Times*, 17 December 1921, p. 21.
Tomes, Nancy, *The Gospel of Germs: Men, Women, and the Microbe in American Life* (Cambridge, MA: Harvard University Press, 1998).
Trachtenberg, Alan, *The Incorporation of America: Culture and Society in the Gilded Age*, 2nd ed (New York: Hill & Wang, 2007).
Trollope, Anthony, *North America: Volume II* (Philadelphia: J. B. Lippincott, 1863).
Trotter, David, *Cinema and Modernism* (Malden, MA: Blackwell, 2007).
Trotter, David, *Cooking with Mud: The Idea of Mess in Nineteenth-Century Art and Fiction* (Oxford: Oxford University Press, 2000).
Trotter, David, 'Techno-Primitivism: Á Propos of *Lady Chatterley's Lover*', 18 (1) *Modernism/modernity* (January 2011), pp. 149–66.
'The Troubles of Tourists', 3 (881) *Saturday Review*, 14 September 1872, p. 339.
Turvey, Gerry, 'Towards a Critical Practice: Ivor Montagu and British Film Culture in the 1920s', in *Young and Innocent? Cinema and Britain 1896–1930*, ed. Andrew Higson (Exeter: Exeter University Press, 2002), pp. 306–20.
Upton, Dell, 'Architecture in Everyday Life', 33 (4) *New Literary History* (Autumn 2002), pp. 707–23.
Van de Ven, Katherine Lawrie, '"Just an Anonymous Room:" Cinematic Hotels and Motels as Mnemonic Purgatories', in *Moving Pictures/Stopping Places: Hotels and Motels on Film*, eds David B. Clarke, Valerie Crawford Pfannhauser and Marcus A. Doel (Lanham, MD: Lexington Books, 2009), pp. 235–54.
Veeder, William, 'Henry James and the Uses of the Feminine', in *Out of Bounds: Male Writers and Gender(ed) Criticism*, eds Laura Claridge and Elizabeth Langland (Amherst, MA: University of Massachusetts Press, 1990), pp. 219–51.
'The Visitors'-Book at Our Swiss Inn', 15 (381) *London Review*, 19 October 1867, p. 428.
'Vitreous Hotel China', in *Montgomery Ward & Co. Catalogue and Buyers' Guide, 1895: Unabridged Facsimile* (New York: Skyhorse, 2008), p. 530.
Wagner, W. Sydney, 'The Statler Idea in Hotel Planning and Equipment', 27 (5) *Architectural Forum* (November 1917), pp. 115–18.
Walford, Edward, *Old and New London: Volume 4* (London: Cassell, Petter & Galpin, 1878).

Walker, Ian, *So Exotic, So Homemade: Surrealism, Englishness and Documentary Photography* (Manchester: Manchester University Press, 2007).
Walsh, Keri, 'Elizabeth Bowen, Surrealist', 42 (3/4) *Éire-Ireland* (2007), pp. 126–47.
Wayland-Smith, Ellen, '"Conductors and Revealers": Henry James's Electric Messengers in *The Ambassadors*', 32 (2) *Henry James Review* (Summer 2011), pp. 118–39.
'The Western Union Withdraws', *New-York Tribune*, 6 November 1897, p. 12.
Wharton, Annabel Jane, *Building the Cold War: Hilton International Hotels and Modern Architecture* (Chicago: Chicago University Press, 2001).
Wharton, Annabel Jane, 'Two Waldorf-Astorias: Spatial Economies as Totem and Fetish', 85 (3) *Art Bulletin* (September 2003), pp. 523–43.
Wharton, Edith, *The Custom of the Country*, in *Novels*, ed. R. W. B. Lewis (New York: Library of America, 1985), pp. 621–1014.
Wharton, Edith, *The Writing of Fiction* (London: Scribner's Sons, 1925).
Wharton, Edith and Ogden Codman Jr, *The Decoration of Houses* (London: Batsford, 1898).
Whiting, James, *The New York Shippers' and Consignees' Guide* (New York: Butler, 1861).
Wigoder, Meir, 'The "Solar Eye" of Vision: Emergence of the Skyscraper-Viewer in the Discourse on Heights in New York City, 1890–1920', 61 (2) *Journal of the Society of Architectural Historians* (June 2002), pp. 152–69.
Wilson, John F. and Andrew Thomson, *The Making of Modern Management: British Management in Historical Perspective* (Oxford: Oxford University Press, 2006).
'Wireless Stations about New York: No. 2 – Station at the Waldorf-Astoria', *Modern Electrics* (September 1909), pp. 253–4.
Woloch, Alex, *The One vs. the Many: Minor Characters and the Space of the Protagonist in the Novel* (Princeton, NJ and Oxford: Princeton University Press, 2003).
Woolf, Virginia, 'Mr Bennett and Mrs Brown', in *Selected Essays*, ed. David Bradshaw (Oxford and New York: Oxford University Press, 2008), pp. 32–6.
Wynter, Andrew, *Subtle Brains and Lissom Fingers. Being Some of the Chisel-Marks of Our Industrial and Scientific Progress. And Other Papers* (London: Robert Hardwicke, 1863).
Yablon, Nick, *Untimely Ruins: An Archaeology of American Urban Modernity: 1819–1919* (Chicago: University of Chicago Press, 2009).
'Yuban', *The Sun Pictorial Magazine* (New York), 29 August 1915, p. 40.
Zanini, Andrea, 'La promozione turistica durante la Belle Époque: il caso della Riviera ligure', in *Pensar con la historia desde el siglo XXI: actas del XII Congreso de la Asociación de Historia Contemporánea*, eds Pilar Folguera and Juan Carlos Pereira (Madrid: UAM Ediciones, 2015), pp. 365–81.

INDEX

Allen, Irving Lewis, 99
Ambassador Hotel (New York), 94, 112
American Encaustic Tiling Company, 68
Anesko, Michael, 91n
Arbuckle, Fatty, 143
Astaire, Fred, 100
Astor House (New York), 27, 115
Atget, Eugène, 130
Augé, Marc, 61
Augspurger, Michael, 164
Auteur theory, 167–8; *see also* corporations

Badowska, Eva, 71
banks, 10–11, 35, 68, 79
Barry, Iris, 128, 129
Barrymore, John, 175
Barthes, Roland, 64
Bauman, Zygmunt, 93–4
Beerbohm, Max, 30
Beeston, Alix, 166
Belmont Hotel (New York), 94
Beniger, James, 9, 157
Benjamin, Walter, 62, 65, 76, 130

Bennett, Arnold, 3, 19, 154, 162, 168
 and Alfred Hitchcock, 165–6, 169
 The Grand Babylon Hotel, 160–1
 Imperial Palace, 160, 161–4, 167, 168–73, 186
 management ethic, 163–4
 Piccadilly, 166, 169, 170, 171
 Punch and Judy, 165–6, 167, 169
 These United States, 163
 writing for film, 165–7
Berger, Molly, 11, 17, 36
Berman, Marshall, 115
Biltmore Hotel (New York), 94, 100–11
Bird, Isabella, 36–7
Black Americans, 40
 elision of, 108–9
 see also hotel workers
Black, Iain S., 10–11
bodies, 18, 31–4, 38, 40–5, 47–9, 50–3
 intermingling, 33, 36, 40–2
 long legs, 18, 31–4, 42, 43, 44, 55n, 185
 melding with objects, 33, 36, 40–5, 185
Boomer, Jørgine, 153

Boomer, Lucius M., 80–1, 153–4, 173
  Hotel Management: Principles and Practice, 153–4
Borden, Mary, 111
Bordighera, 125
Boston Exchange Coffee House, 80
Bowen, Elizabeth, 3, 19, 127–30
  'Ann Lee's', 127–8
  and cinema, 19, 123, 125, 128–30, 131, 132, 133, 136–8, 139, 146, 148n
  and comedy, 144–6
  compared to Virginia Woolf, 123, 124
  'Dead Mabelle', 128, 136–7
  The Hotel, 19, 122–3, 124, 125, 127, 131–6, 137–8, 139–40, 144–6
  influence of Marcel Proust, 125–7
  'Modern Lighting', 127
  'Mysterious Kôr', 130
  'Notes on Writing a Novel', 131, 133
  objects, 123–4, 128, 129–30, 131, 185, 186
  'The Secession', 124
  'Why I Go to the Cinema', 128
Bowman, John McEntee, 188n
Braddon, Mary Elizabeth, 64, 73
  Lady Audley's Secret, 14–15, 59, 62, 71
brands, 100–1; *see also* hotels
Brandt, Bill, 130
British International Pictures (BIP), 165–6, 167
British Select Committee on Joint-Stock Companies, 72
Brontë, Charlotte, 64
Brown, Adrienne, 107, 111–12
Buckingham Hotel (New York), 67, 115
Buelens, Gert, 160
Burkeley, Busby, 170

Caddy, Florence, 64–5
Cameron, Alan, 128
Cather, Willa
  'The Novel Démeublé', 123
Chaplin, Charlie, 19, 143
character (element of literary form), 3, 33, 133–4
  and class, 132, 134–6, 140, 144
  indistinctness of, 179–80
  minor characters, 49–52, 131, 133, 134–6, 145–6, 175, 178, 181
  and space, 134–5, 144
character (personal qualities)
  as basis of business decisions, 9
  connected to living spaces, 64–5, 70–2
  difficulty of ascertaining, 69–73
Chase, Karen, 75
Choi, Tina Young, 53
chorus girls, 170, 171–2
Christensen, Jerome, 173–4, 175, 176
cinema, 19, 123, 125, 128–30, 131, 132, 133, 136–8, 151–2
  German, 128–9, 131, 139, 142–3, 148n
  mobile spatiality, 136–9
  see also auteur theory; Bennett, Arnold; Bowen, Elizabeth; Chaplin, Charlie; Chomón, Segundo; Murnau, F. W.
Cheng, Anne Anlin, 106
Chomón, Segundo
  Hôtel Électrique, 151–2, 185, 186
  Le Roi des Dollars, 151–2
City Hotel (Baltimore), 11
class, 19, 34, 70, 124–5
  anxiety about *déclassement*, 123, 132–3, 135, 144–5, 146, 178
  Black upper class, 40
  creative class, 168
  hotel management, sympathy for, 19, 176, 178–80
  hotel women, 46–8
  inns, appeal of, 15
  motels, appeal of, 183
  and neoclassical aesthetics, 136, 140
  nouveau riche, 70
  private hotels, appeal of, 7
  rise of the technical-scientific-commercial-managerial class, 132, 153, 164, 168
  see also character (element of literary form)

Cleere, Eileen, 67
Close Up, 136, 166
Colley, Edie, 125
Colley, George, 125
Collini, Stefan, 9
Collins, Wilkie, 73
   Basil, 70–2
   The Haunted Hotel, 184
Commodore Hotel (New York), 94, 153
Cook, Clarence, 62–3
Corbusier, Le, 106, 111
Corcoran, Neil, 144
corporate space
   defined, 2–3, 11–12
corporations, 8–12, 65
   auteur theory as response to, 168–9, 172–3
   as authors, 173–6
   conflict with individualist ethic, 164, 165, 168, 172–3
   growth of, 8–9, 72
   management, 9, 11
   personification, 173, 186
   see also railways
Coulson, Victoria, 31, 40–1
Crawford, Joan, 47
Crusoe, Robinson, 165
Curtiss, Philip, 100

Daly, Nicholas, 14
Davidson, Robert A., 61
department stores, 10, 11–12
Despotopoulou, Anna, 156
Dickens, Charles, 12–13, 71
   American Notes, 12–13
   Great Expectations, 71
   Martin Chuzzlewit, 12, 41–2
   Our Mutual Friend, 70
domestic architecture, 89n
   Victorian, 4, 17, 33, 34, 43–4, 75
domestic objects 33, 77–8, 129–30, 131
   eighteenth century, 41
   Victorian, 63–5
Doyle, Arthur Conan
   The Hound of the Baskervilles, 81

Doyle, Mary, 107
Dreiser, Theodore
   Sister Carrie, 85
Du Bois, W. E. B., 109
Dupont, Ewald Andre
   Piccadilly, 166, 169, 170, 171
   Variety, 142

eclecticism (architecture), 106–7
Eisner, Lotte, 138, 142
Eliot, George, 64
Ellison, David, 63
Ellmann, Maud, 3, 124, 133,
encaustic tiles, 18, 68
Escoffier, Auguste, 98
everyday life, 31, 47–8

family businesses, 1–2, 3–4, 8, 9, 11, 124
Faulkner, William, 166
Federal Aid Highway Act (1956), 20
Fern, Fanny, 37–8
Fitzgerald, F. Scott, 3, 18–19, 92, 94, 95
   The Beautiful and Damned, 113–14
   'The Diamond as Big as the Ritz', 19, 95–6, 101–5, 108, 114–15, 185
   'The Freshest Boy', 92
   The Great Gatsby, 95, 99, 107–8, 109, 113
   marketing, 95, 100
   'May Day', 110–11
   'My Lost City', 111
   This Side of Paradise, 92
   writing for film, 166
Fitzgerald, Zelda, 92, 94
Foltz, Jonathan, 176, 179, 180
Forster, E. M.
   A Room With a View, 123, 124–5
Franko, Mark, 172
Freund, Karl, 138–9
furniture, 7, 17, 33, 38, 41–2, 63, 64, 65, 67, 98, 123, 127, 131–2, 186

Garbo, Greta, 175
general store, 10

Gibbons, Cedric, 176
Gilmore, Garrett Bridger, 108
Glendinning, Victoria, 144
Goble, Mark, 158, 174
Goelet, Robert Walton, 97
Grand Hotel, 19, 47, 154, 158, 174–6, 186
Grand Union Hotel (Saratoga), 35, 40, 59
Great Western Royal Hotel (London), 13
Green, Henry, 3
   and names, 178, 179
   Party Going, 19, 154, 176–81, 183
Greene, Lorenzo J., 109
Grosvenor Hotel (London), 13, 19, 181–3
Gumbrecht, Hans Ulrich, 111
Gunning, Tom, 136, 143

Halttunen, Karen, 70
Hamilton, Gail, 67
Harris, William, 96, 97, 117n
Hart, Clive, 176
Hartley, L. P., 127
Hawthorne, Nathaniel
   The Blithedale Romance, 12
Hay, James, 105–6
Hilton Hotels, 21
Hitchcock, Alfred, 129, 165–6, 167, 169, 173
   The Lodger, 167
   The Ring, 167
Hochschild, Arlie Russell, 2
Holiday Inn, 20
Hornby, Louise, 77
Hotel Angst (Bordighera), 125, 144
Hotel Astor, 94, 112
hotel management, 17, 19, 92, 93–4, 95, 96, 97, 124
   as author, 163, 155–6, 157, 158–9, 160, 161, 162–4, 165, 168–72, 177, 178–9
   compared to the term 'hotelkeeping', 152–4
   deflating the authority of, 176, 178–9
   and gender, 153
   professionalisation, 152–4, 164
   and science, 153
   and social preprocessing, 156, 157, 158–60
Hotel Pennsylvania (New York), 94, 96, 113
hotels
   American, 12–13, 20–21, 35–40, 41–2, 43, 45, 59, 46–7, 61, 62–3, 67, 68, 96
   anonymity, 3, 45, 48–50, 52, 79–80, 134, 143, 176
   architecture, 6–7, 11, 34, 94, 103, 106, 181–3
   bathrooms, 67, 144–5
   bedrooms, 4, 6, 7, 63, 98, 105, 106, 126, 140, 145
   books sold in, 82–3
   brands, 17, 93–5, 96, 115, 173
   British, 7, 13–16, 68, 71, 161, 181–3
   chains, 17, 21, 93–5, 117n, 161, 185
   cleanliness, 66–8, 80–1, 90–1n, 105, 106
   compared to factories, 63
   compared to film sets, 131, 132, 169, 170–2, 174, 186
   compared to homes, 4, 6–7, 8, 16–17, 62–6
   compared to hospitals, 68, 105, 185
   compared to inns, 1–2, 11, 12–13, 14, 15–17, 34, 62, 183
   compared to motels, 20, 183
   compared to motor hotels, 20–21
   compared to *pensioni*, 2, 34, 124–5
   corridors, 4, 49–50, 68, 123, 138, 140–5, 180, 185
   decline, 20–1, 183
   depreciation, 92, 115
   dining rooms, 40, 67, 135, 158
   duplicable spaces, 73–4, 95, 143
   elevators, 109, 110, 111, 123, 139, 145–6
   etiquette, 37–40, 79
   financing, 3, 11, 34

hotels (*Cont.*)
  information systems, 3, 142, 158, 161–2
  Italian, 76, 125
  and Jim Crow, 108–9
  and journalism, 5, 77, 80, 82, 154, 157–8, 159, 160
  lobbies, 34–5, 42, 43–4, 45, 47–9, 50, 52, 61, 106, 154–5, 157, 174–6, 185, 186
  lounging in, 17, 18, 34–43, 45–52, 185, 186
  men in, 35, 36–8, 40–2, 46–7, 48, 79
  modernity, 17–18
  morality of, 4
  non-place, 61–2
  objects, 18, 63–4, 65–6, 67, 126–7, 151–2, 185
  obsolescence, 11, 92, 115
  parlours and sitting rooms, 7, 18, 59–62, 63–6, 73–7
  permeable spaces, 4–7, 73–5, 79, 106, 180
  piazzas, 27–8, 34, 35–40, 41–2, 46, 73–4, 186
  private hotels, 3–4, 6–8
  publicity, 4–8, 17, 30, 34–5, 38, 47, 79–80, 157–9
  purgatorial, 183–6
  radio broadcasting, 113, 120n, 155
  reading in, 37, 76, 78, 81–5
  reading rooms, 18, 78–80, 81, 83, 84, 86
  roof gardens, 103, 111–16, 185
  scale, 2, 11, 34, 94, 96
  sex, 5–6, 29–30, 53–4n
  slipperiness, 78
  spitting, 38, 42, 83
  surfaces, 18, 66–9, 78, 82, 88n, 105–7, 185
  Swiss, 47
  telegraphy, 154–5, 169, 186
  telephones, 154–5
  terminology, 11, 16
  and time, 82, 185

vitreous hotel china, 66
waste, 80–2, 83, 84, 85
women in, 4–8, 17, 30, 37–8, 46–7, 57n, 62, 79
see also furniture; hotel management; hotel workers; railways; white space
hotel workers, 1–2, 11, 14, 40, 46, 122–23, 124
  aesthetic labour, 170–2
  affect of, 2, 171–2
  Black American, 40, 108–9
  chambermaids and housekeepers, 1–2, 169–72
  clerks, 1–2, 175
  negative reactions to, 1–2
  precarity, 109, 172
  strike, 108–9
  waiters, 4, 40, 46, 108–9, 122
Howard, Blanche Willis
  Tony, The Maid, 61, 76
Howard, Vicki, 10
Hyatt Hotels, 21

impersonal intimacy, 28–9, 52–3
InterContinental Hotels, 21
interiority, 30, 43, 73, 76, 142

Jakle, John, 94–5
James, Henry, 1–2, 3–8, 15–16, 18, 19, 66, 76, 92, 123, 159
  The Ambassadors, 78, 154
  The American, 31, 33, 34, 43–5, 46, 84
  The American Scene, 68, 154–6, 157, 158–60
  'The Art of Fiction', 155
  bodies, 18, 31–4, 40–5, 47–9, 50–3, 54n, 186
  The Bostonians, 30, 33, 42, 45, 82–3, 157–8
  childhood, 27
  development as writer, 8, 27–9, 83–4, 85
  'Daisy Miller', 18, 30, 45, 47–53, 84
  department stores, 10

doorways, 5–6
elastic imagery, 44–5, 156–7
'The Future of the Novel', 84
'Guest's Confession', 73–5, 79
'An International Episode', 45, 53n
'In the Cage', 1
London, 7, 8, 28
'London', 28
'Pandora', 84
'A Passionate Pilgrim', 15–16
'The Pension Beaurepas', 33
The Portrait of a Lady, 3–8, 29, 33, 66
publishing industry, 83–4, 91n
The Reverberator, 18, 30, 76–80, 82, 84–6, 154, 157, 185
Roderick Hudson, 33, 46
'A Round of Visits', 106–7
'Saratoga', 35–6, 40, 41, 46–7, 59
A Small Boy and Others, 10, 27, 29
The Spoils of Poynton, 70
Tauchnitz editions, 83–4, 91n
travel, 8, 16, 35, 92, 154
travel writing, 1–2, 18, 30, 35, 66
Watch and Ward, 30, 32–3, 34
What Maisie Knew, 29
The Wings of the Dove, 42
James, Kevin J., 15, 16, 63, 161
James, M. E., 65
James, William, 27, 91n
Jannings, Emil, 139
Jarzombek, Mark, 49
joint-stock companies *see* corporations

Kafka, Franz, 180
Katz, Marc, 62
Keaton, Buster, 143
Keller, Albert, 98
Klimasmith, Betsy, 30
Koolhaas, Rem, 115
Kornbluh, Anna, 66
Kracauer, Siegfried, 62

Lang, Fritz, 143, 148n
Langlois, Henri, 131

Lasky, Jesse, 165
Lee, Vernon, 76, 86
Leni, Paul
  Waxworks, 129
Levenson, Michael, 75
Levine, Caroline, 4
Lewes, George Henry, 64
Lewis, Sinclair, 19, 154, 164, 168
  Work of Art, 164–5
Limited Liability Act (1855), 9
Lloyd, Harold, 143
Logan, Thad, 64
London, 7, 8, 10, 13, 15, 128, 130, 139, 176
London Film Society, 128–9, 147–8n
  interest in German cinema, 128–9
Loos, Adolf, 106
Luckhurst, Roger, 140, 142
Lustig, T. J., 16

MacGregor, William Laird, 63–4
McGurl, Mark, 9
McKibbin, Ross, 132–3, 153
McNamara, Kevin R., 156
McWeeny, Gage, 28–9
Maitland, Frederic, 186
Marchand, Roland, 173
Marshall, Kate, 50, 142
Marx Brothers, 143
Mathieu, Julienne
  Hôtel Électrique, 151–2, 185, 186
Maudlin, Daniel, 16
Mellor, Leo, 130
Melville, Herman
  The Confidence Man, 69
Mengham, Rod, 180
Menne, Jeff, 168
Metro-Goldwyn-Mayer (MGM), 174, 176, 186
miasma, 52–3, 67, 180
Miller, Andrew H., 72
Milthorpe, Naomi, 179
money, 99–100, 159
Montagu, Ivor, 129

Murnau, F. W., 138
  Der Letze Mann, 19, 123, 131, 138–9, 140

Nash, John, 163
National Hotel disease, 66–7
Nearing, Scott, 109
Newport (New York), 35–6, 47
New York City, 10, 20, 27, 92–4, 108–9, 115, 155
Ngai, Sianne, 172
Nye, David E., 111

O'Brien, John, 9
Otten, Thomas, 31, 52

Paris, 43–4, 76, 77
Penner, Barbara, 62
place-product-packaging, 94–5
Plaza Hotel (New York), 94, 100, 111, 113, 185
  aesthetic, 105, 107–8, 185
  labour practices, 108–9
  see also white space
Poe, Edgar Allan, 9
Poore, George Vivian, 68
Poovey, Mary, 72
Posnock, Ross, 77, 156
Pratt's Hotel (*The Portrait of a Lady*), 3–8, 22n
preprocessing, 19, 157, 158, 159
  and the novel, 159–60
  prominent arrivals lists, 158
Proust, Marcel
  À l'Ombre des Jeunes Filles en Fleur, 125–7, 185
  and light, 127, 147n
Purdon, James, 159

railway
  bookselling, 83, 84–5
  corporations, 8–9, 13, 15
  hotels, 13–15, 17, 71, 176, 181–3
  novels, 14
  stations, 13, 14, 15, 19, 68, 71, 83, 94, 176, 181

Resor, Stanley, 98
Richardson, Dorothy, 136
Ritchie, Charles, 125
Ritz
  aesthetic, 105, 107, 112, 185
  and capitalist desire, 99, 101–2
  -Carlton Hotel (New York), 96, 97–8, 103, 113
  corporate structure, 95, 96–7, 117n
  Hotel (London), 97, 105
  Hôtel (Paris), 96, 105
  hotels, 18–19, 94–100, 116n, 185
  interior replicas, 97, 98
  marketing, 95, 98–9
  name, 95, 96–9, 100–1, 115, 117n, 173
  see also white space
Ritz, César, 96–8, 105, 173
Ritz, Marie-Louise, 97
Robinson, John Beverley, 107
Rogers, Jefferson, 94
Rollins, Brooke, 167–8
Roosevelt Hotel (New York), 94, 95
Ross, Shawna, 133
Roth, Joseph
  Hotel Savoy, 134
Rowe, John Carlos, 48
Royal Poinciana Hotel (Palm Beach), 68, 158–9
rubber, 44–5
Rubery, Matthew, 80
Ruskin, John, 2, 14

St Nicholas Hotel (New York), 62, 115
Sala, George Augustus, 13, 61
Salmon, Richard, 30
Saloman, Randi, 171
Sandoval-Strausz, A. K., 1–2, 11, 16, 17, 62
sanitary reform, 53, 67–8, 105
Saratoga, 35–6, 38, 40, 43, 46–7, 48, 59, 108
Sarmiento, Domingo Faustino, 35
Savoy Hotel (London), 96
Sayeau, Michael, 76–7
Schulle, Keith, 94

Seltzer, Mark, 160
sentimental typology of behaviour, 70, 72
Shepley, Nick, 179
Sheraton Hotels, 21
Sherwood, M. E. W., 38
Short, Emma, 169
Silverman, Kaja, 167–8
Simmel, Georg, 76
Sinclair, May
  The Immortal Moment, 68–9
  'Where Their Fire Is Not Quenched', 184–5
Smith, Alfred, 13
Solomon, Stefan, 166
The Spectator, 127–8, 129
Statler Hotels, 93, 95
Sterngass, Jon, 36
Sterry, Frederick, 105, 108–9
Stewart, A. T., 10
stickiness, 41, 42, 51, 52–3, 59, 70, 71
Strachey, John, 128
subjectivity
  in hotel space, 2–3, 27–8
  networked, 3
  physiological intersubjectivity, 53, 181, 186
Sullivan, Louis, 107
Sweeney, George, 153

Tallack, Douglas, 35, 165
Tauchnitz, Christian Bernhard (Baron), 83
Tauchnitz editions, 18, 82, 83–4, 185
Taylorism, 95, 156, 172
Taylor, James, 9
Thalberg, Irving, 174, 176
Thomas, Kate, 5
Thorpe, J. A., 165–6, 167
Tomes, Nancy, 67
Travelodge, 20, 192n
Tremont House (Boston), 35
Trollope, Anthony, 37, 59
Trotter, David, 44, 70, 128
Trust Houses Limited, 183, 192n

Upton, Dell, 31–2

Valentino, Rudolph, 112
Van de Ven, Katherine Lawrie, 184
Veeder, William, 42
Venice, 66
Vevey, 47

Wagner, W. Sydney, 95
Walker, Ian, 130
Waldorf-Astoria Hotel (New York), 19, 68, 80, 90–1n, 92–3, 106–7, 115, 154–6, 160
  Peacock Alley, 93, 107, 155
Warren and Wetmore, 94, 97, 103
Wharton, Annabel, 21, 92–3
Wharton, Edith, 89n, 147n
  The Custom of the Country, 81–2
white space
  in *The Beautiful and Damned*, 113–14
  deathliness, 110, 113–14, 115–16
  in 'The Diamond as Big as the Ritz', 103–5, 108, 114
  in *The Great Gatsby*, 107–8, 113, 165
  hotel aesthetic, 18, 105–7, 185
  in 'May Day', 110
  negation of the city, 107
  race, 105–7, 109–10, 111–12
  and white flight, 109–10
Wilde, Oscar, 66
Wigoder, Meir, 112–13
Wilk, Daniel Levinson, 1–2
Withernsea, 15
Woloch, Alex, 134–5
Woodson, Carter G., 109
Woolf, Virginia, 77
  'Mr Bennett and Mrs Brown', 123
  The Voyage Out, 123
Wynter, Andrew, 181

Žižek, Slavoj, 99–100

EU representative:
Easy Access System Europe
Mustamäe tee 50, 10621 Tallinn, Estonia
Gpsr.requests@easproject.com

www.ingramcontent.com/pod-product-compliance
Lightning Source LLC
Chambersburg PA
CBHW070351240426
43671CB00013BA/2467